ART FUNDAMENTALS

Theory and Practice

TWELFTH EDITION

ART FUNDAMENTALS

Theory and Practice

TWELFTH EDITION

Otto G. Ocvirk

Robert E. Stinson

Philip R. Wigg

Robert O. Bone

David L. Cayton

School of Art
Bowling Green State University

Connect
Learn
Succeed™

The McGraw·Hill Companies

McGraw Hill

Connect
Learn
Succeed™

Published by McGraw-Hill, an imprint of The McGraw-Hill Companies, Inc., 1221 Avenue of the Americas, New York, NY 10020. Copyright © 2013, 2009, 2006, 2002, 1998, 1994, 1990, 1985, 1981, 1975, 1968. All rights reserved. Printed in the United States of America. No part of this publication may be reproduced or distributed in any form or by any means, or stored in a database or retrieval system, without the prior written consent of The McGraw-Hill Companies, Inc., including, but not limited to, in any network or other electronic storage or transmission, or broadcast for distance learning.

This book is printed on acid-free paper.

1 2 3 4 5 6 7 8 9 0 DOW/DOW 1 0 9 8 7 6 5 4 3 2

ISBN: 978-0-07-337927-2
MHID: 0-07-337927-1

Sponsoring Editor: *Laura Wilk*
Marketing Manager: *Tara Culliney*
Developmental Editor: *Janice Wiggins-Clarke*
Production Editor: *Holly Paulsen*
Manuscript Editor: *Barbara Hacha*
Design Manager: *Cassandra Chu*
Text Designer: *Glenda King*
Cover Designer: *Adrian Morgan/Cassandra Chu*
Photo Research Coordinator: *Alexandra Ambrose*
Photo Researcher: *Deborah Anderson*
Buyer: *Tandra Jorgensen*
Media Project Manager: *Jennifer Barrick*
Composition: *10/13 Palatino by Laserwords Private Limited*
Printing: *60# Orion Satin, R. R. Donnelley & Sons*

Vice President Editorial: *Michael Ryan*
Publisher: *Christopher Freitag*
Editorial Director: *William Glass*
Director of Development: *Rhona Robbin*

Cover: Gabriel Dawe, *Plexus no. 3*, 2010. Gütermann thread, wood, and nails, 12 × 6 × 16 ft. Site-specific installation at Guerillaarts. © Gabriel Dawe, Dallas, TX.

Library of Congress Cataloging-in-Publication Data

Art fundamentals : theory and practice / Otto G. Ocvirk . . . [et al.].—12th ed.
  p. cm.
  Includes bibliographical references and index.
  ISBN-13: 978-0-07-337927-2 (alk. paper)
  ISBN-10: 0-07-337927-1 (alk. paper)
  1. Art—Technique. 2. Art. I. Ocvirk, Otto G.
  N7430.A697 2012
  701'.8—dc23

                    2011045559

The Internet addresses listed in the text were accurate at the time of publication. The inclusion of a website does not indicate an endorsement by the authors or McGraw-Hill, and McGraw-Hill does not guarantee the accuracy of the information presented at these sites.

www.mhhe.com

CONTENTS

The original textbook that set the standard for introduction to art courses across the country, *Art Fundamentals* has guided generations of students through both the essential elements of art and the rich and varied history of their uses. We have organized *Art Fundamentals* to assist with "knowing" and "feeling" the fundamental concepts of refined creation. Numerous visual examples elevate the lessons beyond mere discussion to demonstrating instead of telling. As always, our intent is to stimulate without locking students into a restricted mind-set or mechanical copying of ideas.

The study of art foundation is as vital as ever, and this edition aims to meet that need with comprehensive coverage of the art elements, clarity, plentiful illustrated examples, carefully chosen color images, and well-defined concepts. The elements and the principles that aid in their application, as in the past, are still employed by all artists, with the evolution of technologies having expanded and modified the way in which the elements can be put to use. *Art Fundamentals* looks at aspects of the components individually and in context. Although no individual component can be developed in isolation, for all must work in unison, our intent is for the student to become so familiar with each element that it may be used subconsciously and integrated with the others without struggle.

HALLMARK FEATURES

To help students understand the concepts and apply them, these proven features have been revised and updated:

- A list of keywords, arranged alphabetically, appears at the beginning of each chapter. This placement allows students to preview the keywords before beginning the chapter and reference them while reading the words in context; the keywords are also boldfaced within the text.
- Numerous color illustrations representing a broad array of media and diverse artists, such as Käthe Kollwitz, Amir Nour, Yasuo Ohba, and Ismael Rodriguez Rueda, demonstrate the various concepts and show how other artists have applied them to their work. The twelfth edition of *Art Fundamentals* contains more than 400 images that include Pablo Picasso's *The Bull,* states I–XI; Alexander Calder's *Myxomatose;* Robert Rauschenberg's *Canyon;* David Hockney's *Mother I, York-shire Moors, August, 1985, #1;* and Katherine D. Crone's *Tokyo Sunday.* Allow these images to spark curiosity, and have students try to understand what the artists have done in each piece to make it work.

NEW TO THE TWELFTH EDITION

The twelfth edition includes the following revisions:

- Greater emphasis on graphic design, product design, animation, and computer-aided art throughout. Students today are increasingly interested in these more commercial forms of art, and they are now explored with greater emphasis in the prose of the text as well as in the visual examples.
- More contemporary art with the inclusion of several artworks produced within the past several years. These new works represent various mediums—from installation art, to street art, to computer art.
- Throughout the book, many references to contemporary culture and society, such as movies and video games, have been included so that students can easily relate to the artistic content presented.

PREFACE

- For enhanced clarity and cohesiveness, various explanations and other prose have been revised.

SUPPLEMENTS

Additional resources to supplement *Art Fundamentals,* twelfth edition, can be found online at **www.mhhe.com/ ocvirk12e.** The student section of the Online Learning Center (OLC) contains study materials such as quizzes, key terms, and flash cards. *MyArtStudio* is an interactive site that allows students to study and experiment with various elements and principles of art and to view videos of techniques and artists at work. Exercises on the OLC guide students to *MyArtStudio* at appropriate points in the text.

The instructor section includes sample student projects and a link to **Connect Image Bank.** Instructors can incorporate images from *Connect Image Bank* in presentations that can be used in the classroom.

ACKNOWLEDGMENTS

We would like to express our gratitude to Evan Wilson for the countless hours spent editing and helping to bring this edition to life, to Barbara Hacha for her keen and exacting eye, and to Deborah Anderson for her resourcefulness in searching for new images. And, as ever, we send immeasurable thanks to our reviewers, whose thorough commentary helped us evaluate our delivery of information. The diversity of our reviewers—from longtime fans to instructors who had never before used the book—provided us a broad perspective and great insight into the interests of current students. Like any artwork, revision and critique must be utilized until the text effectively conveys what the author wants to communicate. Our deep appreciation also goes out to the artists, museums, galleries, and art owners for providing us with permissions and materials for the numerous visual reproductions of their artwork. In addition, we are grateful for the hard work done by our publisher, McGraw-Hill, and its Higher Education staff, who have finalized all the details necessary for publication to go forward. Finally, we must thank our many readers and instructors—we hope this edition serves you well.

REVIEWERS

Paris Almond, Truckee Meadows
    Community College
James Baken, Rocky Mountain College
Laurence J. Bradshaw, University of
    Nebraska–Omaha
Michael J. Buono, Drury University
Derrick Burbul, University of
    Nebraska–Kearney
Carolyn Castano, Long Beach City
    College
Ron Clark, El Paso Community
    College
Jennifer Costa, Illinois Central College
Dwayne Crigger, Missouri State
    University
Kathleen Driscoll, Mount Ida College
Alison Gates, University of
    Wisconsin–Green Bay
Kay A. Klotzbach, Camden County
    College
Robert McCann, Michigan State
    University
Christine McCullough, Youngstown
    State University
Michael Miller, Texas A & M, Commerce
Isaac Powell, Northwestern State
    University
Liz Roth, Oklahoma State University
Erik Sandgren, Grays Harbor College
Sherry M. Stephens, Palm Beach
    Community College
Terrell Taylor, Meridian Community
    College
Anne Toner, Northwest College
Jason Travers, Lehigh University
Fred Vodvarka, Loyola University of
    Chicago
Cathy Wilkin, Northern Virginia
    Community College

Introduction

CHAPTER ONE

Olafur Eliasson, *I only see things when they move*, 2004. Wood, color-effect filter glass, stainless steel, aluminum, HMI lamp, tripod, glass cylinder, motors, control unit, variable sizes.

Installation view at Tanya Bonakdar Gallery. Photograph by Fabian Birgfeld, PhotoTECTONICS. Gift of Marie-Josée and Henry Kravis in Honor of Mimi Haas. Courtesy of The Museum of Modern Art, New York. © 2004 Olafur Eliasson.

THE VOCABULARY OF
INTRODUCTORY TERMS

Art —"The formal expression of a conceived image or imagined conception in terms of a given medium."—Sheldon Cheney

abstraction
A process or visual effect characterized by the simplification and/or rearrangement of the image.

addition
A sculptural term that means building up, assembling, or putting on material.

aesthetic, aesthetics
1. Sensitive to art or beauty. "Aesthetically pleasing" implies intellectual or visual beauty (i.e., creative, eloquent, or expressive qualities of form, as opposed to the mere recording of facts in visual, descriptive, or objective ways). 2. The study or theory of beauty—traditionally a branch of philosophy but now a compound of the philosophy, psychology, and sociology of art—dealing with the definition, inspiration, intent, forms, and psychological effects of art and beauty.

art
"The formal expression of a conceived image or imagined conception in terms of a given medium." (Sheldon Cheney)

assemblage
A technique that involves grouping found or created three-dimensional objects, which are often displayed *in situ*—that is, in a natural position or in the middle of the room rather than on a wall.

Bauhaus
Originally a German school of architecture that flourished between World War I and World War II. The Bauhaus attracted many leading experimental artists of both two- and three-dimensional fields.

casting
A sculptural technique in which liquid materials are shaped by being poured into a mold. This technique is also known as **substitution.**

concept
1. A comprehensive idea or generalization.
2. An idea that brings diverse elements into a basic relationship.

Conceptual artists
Artists who focus on the idea, or "concept," of the work and are much more concerned with conveying a message or analyzing an idea than with the final product.

conceptual perception
Creative vision derived from the imagination; the opposite of **optical perception.**

content
The expression, essential meaning, significance, or aesthetic value of a work of art. Content refers to the sensory, subjective, psychological, or emotional properties we feel in a work of art, as opposed to our perception of its descriptive aspects alone.

craftsmanship
Aptitude, skill, or quality workmanship in the use of tools and materials.

Cubism
The name given to the painting style invented by Pablo Picasso and Georges Braque between 1907 and 1912, which uses multiple views of objects to create the effect of three-dimensionality while acknowledging the two-dimensional surface of the picture plane. Signaling the beginning of abstract art, Cubism is a semiabstract style that continued the strong trend away from representational art initiated by Cézanne in the late 1800s.

decorative (art)
The two-dimensional nature of an artwork or any of its elements, which emphasizes the essential flatness of a surface; also has generically referred to the ornamentation or enrichment of a surface.

descriptive (art)
A type of art that is based on adherence to actual appearances.

design
The underlying plan on which artists base their total work. In a broader sense, *design* may be considered synonymous with the term **form.**

elements of art
Line, shape, value, texture, and color—the basic ingredients the artist uses separately or in combination to produce artistic imagery. Their use produces the visual language of art.

expression
1. The manifestation through artistic form of thought, emotion, or quality of meaning. 2. In art, expression is synonymous with the term **content.**

form
1. The total appearance, organization, or inventive arrangement of all the visual elements according to the principles that will develop unity in the artwork; composition. 2. In sculpture, can also refer to the three-dimensional shape of the work.

glyptic
1. The quality of an art material like stone, wood, or metal that can be carved or engraved. 2. An art form that retains the color, tensile, and tactile qualities of the material from which it was created. 3. The quality of hardness, solidity, or resistance found in carved or engraved materials.

graphic (art)
Two-dimensional art processes such as drawing, painting, photography, printmaking, and so on that generally exist on a flat surface and can create the illusion of depth. Commercial applications include posters, newspapers, books, and magazines.

installations
Interior or exterior settings of media created by artists to heighten the viewers' awareness of the environmental space.

manipulation
The sculptural technique of shaping pliable materials by hand or with the use of tools—also known as **modeling.**

mass
1. In graphic art, a shape that appears to stand out three-dimensionally from the space surrounding it or that appears to create the illusion of a solid body of material. 2. In the plastic arts, the physical bulk of a solid body of material.

medium, media (pl.)
The material(s) and tool(s) used by the artist to create the visual elements perceived by the viewer.

modeling
A sculptural term for shaping a pliable material.

Naturalism
The approach to art that is essentially a description of things visually experienced. Pure naturalism would contain no personal interpretation introduced by the artist.

negative area
The unoccupied or empty space left after the positive images have been created by the artist. Consideration of the negative areas is just as important to the organization of form as the positive areas.

nonobjective, nonrepresentational art
A type of art that is completely imaginative, in which the elements, their organization, and their treatment are entirely personalized, and the image is not derived from anything visually perceived by the artist.

objective
That which is based on the physical reality of the object and reflects no personal interpretation, bias, or emotion; the opposite of **subjective.**

optical perception
A purely visual experience with no exaggeration or creative interpretation of that which is seen; the opposite of **conceptual perception.**

organic unity
A condition in which the components of art (subject, form, and content) are completely interdependent. Though not a guarantee of "greatness," the resulting wholeness is vital to a successful work.

picture frame
The outermost limits or boundary of the picture plane.

picture plane
The actual flat surface on which the artist executes a pictorial image. In some cases, the picture plane acts merely as a transparent plane of reference to establish the illusion of forms existing in a three-dimensional space.

plane
1. An area that is essentially two-dimensional, having height and width. 2. A two-dimensional pictorial surface that can support the illusion of advancing or receding elements. 3. A flat sculptural surface.

plastic (art)
1. The use of the elements to create the illusion of the third dimension on a two-dimensional surface. 2. Three-dimensional art forms such as architecture, sculpture, ceramics, and so on.

positive area
The subject—whether representational or nonrepresentational—which is produced by the art elements (shape, line, etc.) or their combination. (See **negative area.**)

principles of organization
Concepts that guide the arrangement and integration of the elements in achieving a sense of visual order and overall visual unity. They are harmony, variety, balance, proportion, dominance, movement, and economy.

Process artists
Artists who focus on the execution, or "process," of the work and are much more concerned with the technique they employ in creating the work than with the final product.

realism, Realism (art movement)
A style of art that emphasizes universal characteristics rather than specific information

(e.g., a generalization of all "motherhood" rather than an extremely detailed portrait of a specific woman). As a movement, it relates to painters like Honoré Daumier in nineteenth-century France and Winslow Homer in the United States in the 1850s.

relief sculpture
An artwork, graphic in concept but sculptural in application, utilizing relatively shallow depth to establish images. The space development may range from very limited projection, known as *low relief*, to more exaggerated space development, known as *high relief*. Relief sculpture is meant to be viewed frontally, not in the round.

representational art
A type of art in which the subject is presented through the visual art elements so that the observer is reminded of actual objects (see **naturalism** and **realism**).

sculpture
The art of shaping three-dimensional materials to express an idea.

shape
An area that stands out from its surroundings because of a defined or implied boundary or because of differences of value, color, or texture.

space
The interval, or measurable distance, between points or images; can be actual or illusionary.

style
The specific artistic character and dominant trends of form noted during periods of history and art movements. Style may also refer to artists' expressive use of media to give their works individual character.

subject
1. In a descriptive approach to art, refers to the persons or things represented. 2. In more abstract applications, refers to visual images that may have little to do with anything experienced in the natural environment.

subjective
That which is derived from the mind, instead of physical reality, and reflects a personal bias, emotion, or innovative interpretation; the opposite of **objective.**

substitution

In sculpture, replacing one material or medium with another. (See also **casting.**)

subtraction

A sculptural term meaning the carving or cutting away of material.

technique

The manner and skill with which artists employ their tools and materials to achieve an expressive effect.

three-dimensional

Possesses the dimensions of (or illusions of) height, width, and depth. In the graphic arts, the feeling of depth is an illusion, while in the plastic arts, the work has actual depth.

two-dimensional

Possesses the dimensions of height and width, especially when considering the flat surface, or picture plane.

unity

The result of bringing the elements of art into the appropriate ratio between harmony and variety to give a sense of oneness.

volume

The measurable amount of defined or occupied space in a three-dimensional object.

THE EVOLVING NATURE OF ART

The desire to create is not a new phenomenon. It appears to be a fundamental yearning that can be traced back to the earliest recesses of history. Our prehistoric ancestors crawled through dark cave passages, where, by flickering torchlight, they created amazing images of bison and horses, engraved on antler, and sculpted bulbous figures (figs. 1.1 and 1.2). Why did they work in grottos of protruding rock with such limited access? Were the images meant to be shared with others? Were they part of a shaman's ritual to ensure a successful hunt, worship the spirits of bison and horses, or ensure fertility and the continuation of the tribe? Although we may speculate about their purposes, these early images reveal something as old as humanity itself—the magical urge and need to create.

Even now, as we live in a digital and mechanized world, we seem as driven as the ancients to interpret the workings of the universe and our immediate environment through art (fig. 1.3). In fact, the amount of artwork being created today is unrivaled. Art presents the ordinary in an extraordinary way and gives meaning to the mundane. It provides the subtext that brings vitality to everyday experiences and transports us to somewhere beyond. With art, we

1.1 *Running Horse Attacked by Arrows.* Paleolithic cave painting, c. 15,000–10,000 B.C.E., Lascaux, France. In the context of fine art, one meaning of the word *fundamental* is the essential or basic urge to create art. Bettmann/ Corbis.

1.2 *Venus of Lespugue*, carving from the Aurignacian Period, c. 25,000–18,000 B.C.E., found in Rideaux Cave of Lespugue in the foothills of the Pyrenees, France. 5¾ in. high. Possibly used as a magical fertility fetish, the *Venus of Lespugue* was carved from a mammoth tusk during the Aurignacian Period. SCALA/Art Resource, NY.

1.3 Painting on a ceiling, Vanni Vinayagar Temple, Sattur, Virudhunagar District, Tamil Nadu, India. Located in a temple in India, this ceiling painting offers an artistic glimpse into the unknowable mystery of the universe. Through the medium of art, worshippers are inspired and motivated to contemplate questions of existence. © Melvyn Longhurst/Alamy.

can convey complex emotions, soothe the soul, or provoke thought and action; its language expresses our feelings and communicates our ideas like no other. This may be why the fundamental urge to create art objects can be traced back to the earliest recesses of history, and it is certainly why the urge persists in humans yet today.

But what exactly *is* **art**? Its multiple definitions are complex and nearly elusive. The term is often synonymous with **craftsmanship,** which implies knowledge of materials and their skillful handling. In fact, any creative and variable *skill* can be labeled an art.

During the fourteenth, fifteenth, and sixteenth centuries, the craft guilds (or unions) that upheld the standards and traditions of the artists' trades were designated as "Arti." Today, the term *the arts* refers to branches of learning that study creative skills—such as the musical arts, visual arts, performing arts, and so on. The terms *art* and *works of art*, therefore, also refer to *products* of such skills—products that commonly display intentional structure, unusual perception, and creative intuition. According to some people, a work of art is achieved only when the creation goes beyond simple function or utility

Many philosophers over the years have offered their opinions on the purposes and qualifications of art:

- the formal [structured] expression of a conceived image in terms of a given medium (Cheney)

- the making of a form produced by the cooperation of all the faculties of the mind (Longman)

- significant form (Bell)

- eloquence (Burke)

- unexpected inevitability of formal relations (Fry)

- a unified manifold which is pleasure giving (Mather)

- a diagram or paradigm with a meaning that gives pleasure (Lostowel)

- that which gives pleasure apart from desire (Thomas Aquinas)

- objectified pleasure (Santayana)

- imitation [reflection of life or other ideas]

- propaganda [emphasis on communication rather than expression, implying an effort to influence conduct]

1.4 These philosophical descriptions of "art" exemplify a constant effort to decipher the real nature of art and suggest that it is a different thing for different people. Note that several of these definitions stress "pleasure" as a component of art, although some art seems to have no intention of provoking pleasure. Whatever the definition, art can be a relaxant or stimulant; for the artist, it can also produce frustration—but in most cases, finally, a sense of achievement.

and takes on more than ordinary significance. For others, anything creative counts, regardless of skill level. The purposes and qualifications of art vary with every individual, culture, and time period, so in some sense, the definition of *art* is still developing (fig. 1.4).

Think about your own definition of art . . . and be aware that your opinion may change. Take, for example, the image of a flower. When is it art, and when is it not art? Does it matter if the image is a drawing or a print, a child's finger painting or a paint-by-number picture? What if you can barely recognize the flower?

Certain audiences feel that quality artwork must be "beautiful" (i.e., visu-ally or intellectually pleasing), or else the work is just "craft" instead of "art." Fine craftsmen, however, would surely argue that their crafts are indeed beautiful. In any case, beauty is **subjective** and depends partly on the viewer's expectations. The public often likes and expects images that are familiar, recognizable, sentimental, or pleasant to experience. However, not all people, even of similar backgrounds, would agree on the beauty of a given subject matter, much less its visual treatment. What happens if a work contains an emotional image but is badly executed? Is it still considered beautiful? What if a work lacks a compelling image but is expertly executed?

Aesthetics, the philosophical appreciation of the "beautiful," is a complex study that is still evolving, in part because the **concept** of beauty has changed radically over the course of the last several generations. While searching for new means of self-expression, every generation of artists alters the nature of art. Since the eras of ancient civilizations, techniques and ambitions have changed radically, and today we have an array of different approaches to art. Regardless of the time or place of creation, art has always been produced because an artist has wanted to say something and has chosen a particular way of saying it. For each piece, the artist makes choices

about the structure, media (materials and tools), techniques (methods of using the media), and treatment of subject matter that will best express his or her idea. Over time, an artist's body of work can reveal an expressive character unique to the individual artist, like a signature. This expressive quality is known as an artistic **style.** Some styles, once unique to individual artists, have been adopted by generations of artists and have broader historical application. In many cases, a single artist's style changes as his or her body of work develops and grows. One prime example is the work of Piet Mondrian (figs. 1.5, 1.6, 1.7, and 1.8), whose final style has influenced artists

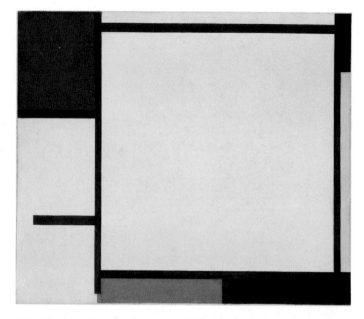

1.8 Piet Mondrian, *Composition with Blue, Black, Yellow and Red,* 1922. **Gouache on paper, 41 × 49 cm.** The primary colors divided by block lines, all in a two-dimensional grid, are typical of Mondrian's later work. This is the style that has generated so much influence through the years. Nationalgalerie, Berlin. Bildarchiv Preussischer Kulturbesitz/Art Resource, NY. © 2011 Mondrian/Holtzman Trust c/o HCR International Washington, DC.

1.7 Piet Mondrian, *Composition,* 1916. Oil on canvas and wood strip, 47¼ × 29½ in. (120 × 74.9 cm). As a follow-up to figs. 1.5 and 1.6, this later work can be seen as even closer to the severity of Mondrian's final style in fig. 1.8. Solomon R. Guggenheim Foundation, New York (FN 4/9.1229). © 2011 Mondrian/Holtzman Trust c/o HCR International Washington, DC.

in other fields (figs. 1.9, 1.10, and 1.11). Young artists are often tempted to prematurely impose a style on their work, instead of allowing it to mature naturally. However, they must remember—just like a signature—one's expressive style truly develops only through time and repeated practice.

Often, the evolution of style and purpose results in artwork that pushes the boundaries of public acceptability. During the nineteenth and twentieth centuries, artists often confounded the public by the increasingly abstract treatment of subject matter. Contemporary artists, too, make expressive choices that the public often doesn't understand or find personally relevant. As a result, many people who want to be actively engaged in art find that much of what they see is not meaningful to them. Before the twentieth century, people often had a better understanding and greater acceptance of what they saw because their exposure was limited; their local art fit into established and familiar aesthetic norms. Unlike those more insular periods, today's sophisticated printing and distribution techniques have made most of the art of both the past and present

1.9 Gerrit Rietveld and Truus Schröder, *Rietveld-Schröder House,* 1920–24. Rietveld (architect and designer) and Schröder (client and codesigner) were members, along with Mondrian, of the de Stijl group in Holland—a fact that probably accounts for the similarities in style. © Nathan Willock/Architectural Association Slide Library, London. © 2011 Gerrit Rietveld/Artists Rights Society (ARS), New York.

1.10 Gerrit Rietveld, *Red/Blue Chair,* designed 1918 (made c. 1950 by G. van de Groenekan). Pine, ebonized and painted, 34⅞ × 23⅝ × 29¾ in. (88.4 × 60 × 75.5 cm). The relationships between horizontals and verticals and the juxtapositions of color within an asymmetrical grid are features shared by this chair and the paintings of Piet Mondrian. Toledo Museum of Art, Toledo, OH. Purchased with funds from the Florence Scott Libbey Bequest, in memory of her father, Maurice A. Scott (1985.48). © 2011 Gerrit Rietveld/Artists Rights Society (ARS), New York.

1.11 Yves Saint Laurent, **Mondrian-inspired dresses.** Models present dresses motivated by painter Piet Mondrian during French legendary fashion designer Yves Saint Laurent's farewell show Tuesday, January 22, 2002, at the Georges Pompidou Center in Paris. © AP Photo/ Remy de la Mauviniere

available to us. In addition, television, the Internet, satellite radio, and air travel have contributed to an emerging global culture.

In order to appreciate the many forms of art to which we have access today, we must understand the foundations from which they have grown. This book seeks to provide such an understanding by examining the many factors involved in producing artwork and the principles that govern those factors.

THE THREE COMPONENTS OF ART

Subject, form, and content have always been the three basic components of a work of art, and they are wed in a way that is inseparable. In general, *subject* may be thought of as the "what" (the topic, focus, or image); *form*, as the "how" (the development of the work, composition, or the substantiation); and *content*, as the "why" (the artist's intention, communication, or meaning behind the work).

Subject

The **subject** of visual art can be a person, an object, a theme, or an idea. Though there are many and varied ways of presenting the subject matter, it is only important to the degree that the artist is motivated by it.

Objective images, which represent people or objects, look as close as possible to their real-world counterparts and can be clearly identified (see figs. 6.1, 6.24, and 8.11). These types of images are also called **representational.**

Artists who explore the process of abstraction (simplification and rearrangement) create images that look less like the object on which they are

1.12 Barbara Chase-Riboud, *Bathers*, 1973. Floor relief, cast aluminum and silk in sixteen pieces, 400 × 400 × 12 cm. Barbara Chase-Riboud does not limit her image to a superficial presentation of subject (bathers). She reveals deeper meanings through the form of the work, with the repetition of cast undulating surface folds and the contrast of metal against flowing silk coils. Courtesy of the artist and Jernigan Wicker Fine Arts, CA.

based, although they may still be recognizable (fig. 1.12; see also figs. 1.5, 4.20, 5.25, 9.9, and 9.13).

In the most extreme type of abstraction, the subject does not refer to any physical object, and this **nonrepresentational** image is thus considered **nonobjective** (see figs. 1.8, 7.25, and T.71). Here, the subject may be difficult for the observer to identify, since it is based solely on the elements of art rather than real-life people or objects. This type of subject often refers to the artist's idea

about energy and movement, which guides the use of raw materials, and it communicates with those who can read the language of form. (Abstraction will be discussed in more detail later in this chapter.)

Music, like visual art, deals with subjects and provides an interesting comparison. Unless there are lyrics, it is often hard to identify a specific subject in a piece of music. Sometimes, the subject is recognizable—the thunderstorms and birdsongs in Beethoven's *Pastoral*

1.13 Charles Sheeler, *Composition around Red (Pennsylvania)*, 1958. Oil on canvas, **26 × 33 in.** The subject—a man-made structure—is clear enough. However, a work of art should be judged not by its subject alone but rather by how that subject is treated. Montgomery Museum of Fine Arts. The Blount Collection of American Art.

Symphony or the taxi horns in Gershwin's *An American in Paris*. Other times, however, the subject is more abstract, and it is an emotion or idea that comes across strongly in the music. Aaron Copland's *Fanfare for the Common Man* is a good example of this: he does not try to describe the subject literally but creates a noble, accessible, and uplifting musical theme that honors the plight of the common man. In a similar way, nonobjective art seeks to present a more general theme or idea as the subject.

Regardless of the type of art, the most important consideration is what is done with the subject. After you recognize the subject in a work (whether it is obvious or not), ask yourself whether the artist has given it **expression** (fig. 1.13).

Form

As a component of art, the word **form** refers to the total overall arrangement or organization of an artwork. It results from using the elements of art, giving them order and meaning through the principles of organization. When studying a work's form, we are analyzing how the piece was created. More specifically, we are examining why the artist made certain choices and how those choices interact to form the artwork's final appearance. In this sense, the word *form* may actually be thought of as a verb rather than a noun.

The **elements of art,** which include *line, texture, color, shape,* and *value,* are the most basic, indispensable, and immediate building blocks for expression. Their characteristics, determined by the artist's choice of media and techniques, can communicate a wide range of complex feelings. All artists must deal with the elements singularly or in combination, and their organization contributes to the aesthetic success or failure of a work.

Based on the intended expression, each artist can arrange the elements in any manner that builds the desired character into the piece. However, the elements are given order and meaningful structure when arranged according to the **principles of organization,** which help integrate and organize the elements. These principles include *harmony, variety, balance, proportion, dominance, movement,* and *economy.* They help create *spatial* relationships and effectively convey the artist's intent. The principles of organization are flexible, not dogmatic, and can be combined and applied in numerous ways. Some artists arrange intuitively, and others are more calculating, but with experience, all of them develop an instinctive feeling for organizing their work. So important are these concepts that a chapter on form will focus on the principles of organization, and separate chapters will cover each of the elements.

Content

The emotional or intellectual message of a work of art is its **content**—a statement, expression, or mood developed by the artist and interpreted by the observer. Of the three components of art, content may be the most difficult to identify, because the audience, without direct communication with the artist, must decipher the artist's thoughts by observing the work's subject and form. For example, in *Young Girl in the Lap of Death* (fig. 1.14), the striking emphasis of the left-to-right diagonals, the sharp contrasts of light and dark values, and the aggressive and powerful drawing strokes give us some insight into Käthe Kollwitz's concern for life, though we may not understand the depth of her passion.

Ideally, the viewer's interpretation is synchronized with the artist's intentions. However, the viewer's diversity of experiences can affect the communication between artist and viewer. For many people, content is determined by their familiarity with the subject; they are confined to feelings aroused by objects or ideas they know. A much broader and ultimately more meaningful content is not utterly reliant on the image but is reinforced by the form. This is especially so in more abstract works, in which the viewer may not recognize the image as a known object and must, therefore, interpret meaning from shapes and other elements. Images that are hardly recognizable, if representational at all, can still deliver content if the observer knows how to interpret form.

Occasionally, artists may be unaware of what motivates them to make certain choices of image or form. For them, the content of the piece may be subconscious instead of deliberate. For example, an artist who has a violent confrontation with a neighbor might subconsciously need to express anger (content) and is thus compelled to work with sharp jagged shapes, bitter acrid reds, slashing agitated marks (form), and exploding images (subject).

1.14 Käthe Kollwitz, *Young Girl in the Lap of Death*, 1934. Crayon lithograph, 42 × 38 cm. Käthe Kollwitz's natural talent for drawing was encouraged by her father, who arranged private lessons before sending her to an art school for women in Berlin. After her study of Edvard Munch's work, she boldly confronted emotionally charged images. Hunger and death were not strangers in her home because of her husband's medical practice, but the theme of death became an obsession after her son Peter was killed in WWI and her grandson Peter in WWII. It is reinforced in this composition by sharp diagonal movements, extreme contrasts of value, and the boldness of the drawing. Art © 2011 Artists Rights Society (ARS), New York/ VG Bild-Kunst, Bonn. Photo © Käthe Kollwitz Museum Köln.

Sometimes the meaning of nonobjective shapes becomes clear in the artist's mind only after they evolve and mutate on the canvas.

Although it is not a requirement for enjoying artwork, a little research about the artist's life, time period, or culture can help expand viewpoints and lead to a fuller interpretation of content. For example, a deeper comprehension of Vincent van Gogh's specific and personal use of color may be gained by reading Van Gogh's letters to his brother Theo. His letters expressed an evolving belief that color conveyed specific feelings and attitudes and was more than a mere optical experience. He felt that his use of color could emit power like Wagner's music. The letters also revealed a developing personal color iconography, in which red and green symbolized the terrible sinful passions of humanity; black contour lines provided a sense of anguish; cobalt blue signified the vault of heaven, and yellow symbolized love. For Van Gogh, color was not strictly a tool for visual imitation but an instrument to transmit his personal emotions (fig. 1.15). Color symbolism may not have been used in all his paintings, but an understanding of his intent helps explain some of his choices and the power in his work.

ORGANIC UNITY

If an artist is successful in wedding all three of the components (subject, form, and content) in a work, they become inseparable, mutually interactive, and interrelated—as if they were a living organism. When this is achieved, we can say the work has **organic unity,** containing nothing that is unnecessary or distracting, with relationships that seem inevitable (fig. 1.16).

A well-made television set displays the same principles of organic unity found in art: it has a complex but minimum number of parts necessary to function, and these parts work only when properly assembled with respect to each other. When all the parts are activated, they become organically unified. As in the sophisticated engineering of the television, this sense of reciprocal "wholeness" is also sought in art. Organic unity does not guarantee a work to be judged a "great work of art," but it does help give the work a vital feeling of completeness.

In figures 1.17A and B, we see the beginning and end state of an intaglio print by Rembrandt. Many of us would have been happy achieving the first state, but Rembrandt continued adjusting areas in search of an organic unity. As we study the two images and consider

1.15 Vincent van Gogh, *The Night Café*, 1888. Oil on canvas, 27½ × 35 in. Van Gogh used color to transmit his personal emotions and not as a tool strictly for visual imitation. He saw in the provincial café the sinful obsessions of humanity, which he expressed with reds. He used greens to represent the powers of darkness, contrasted by an atmosphere of pale sulfur like the devil's furnace. His personal symbolic application of color was constantly evolving. © Yale University Art Gallery/Art Resource, NY.

1.16 This diagram illustrates the interrelationship of subject, form, and content as described in the text. Any of these components may be the starting point for a work. For example, the inspiration for a work could begin after observing an object (subject), which might stir up passionate feelings within the artist (content) and give rise to the developing composition (form). Or, it could begin with an artist's playful manipulation of shapes and color on a canvas (form), which suggests a feeling or emotion to develop (content) and eventually becomes an image (subject). An artist's personal sadness or passion for a social issue (content) could also be the starting idea that becomes expressed through color choices (form) and results in a pattern of nonobjective marks (subject). Whatever the evolution, progression, or emphasis of the components—subject, form, and content—organic unity is the desired end.

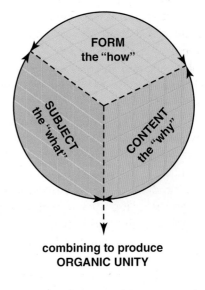

FORM
the "how"

SUBJECT
the "what"

CONTENT
the "why"

combining to produce
ORGANIC UNITY

1.17 Rembrandt Harmenszoon van Rijn, *Christ Presented to the People,* first state and last state, 1655. Print (dry point). Rembrandt searched for the most interesting and communicative presentation of his idea. In doing so, he made dramatic deletions and changes, which in this case involved scraping out a portion of the copper plate. Figure A is the first version of the work, and figure B is the last.

The Metropolitan Museum of Art, Gift of Felix M. Warburg and His Family, 1941. (41.1.36). Image © The Metropolitan Museum of Art. Art Resource, NY.

A

Subject: Rembrandt has chosen to depict the moment when Christ is presented to the Jewish chief priests, rulers, and the common people. He includes a range of figures, from the wealthy to the beggars, and the scene takes place in the courtyard of the palace or praetorium of Pilate the governor. (However, Rembrandt probably based the architecture and figures on his sketches done in the Jewish sections of Amsterdam, since Rembrandt's travels did not include Palestine.)

Form: Rembrandt's organization draws focus on the figures near the center, and the changes between the first print (A: stage 1) and the last print (B: stage 5) emphasize the Christ figure, enhance the scene's complexity, and draw the viewer into the picture. Rembrandt seems to take delight in solving compositional problems that allow him to present information in dichotomous ways. For example, could he place an image in the center of a composition and yet have that object feel higher or lower in the composition? How could the verticality be emphasized in a horizontal layout? Could it be possible to make a composition that appears to be similar and dissimilar at the same time, on both sides of a central axis? Could he darken an area to make it recede and at the same time make the object next to it advance? If an object is lightened or darkened to make it join a larger area, how could he do it without losing the object—could the object still be made to stand out?

In the first print (A), the horizontal layout is established by the plate size and the row of people moving across the bottom. But the horizontal emphasis changes to vertical in the last print (B). To do this, Rembrandt emphasizes an upward thrust in the composition by the creation of a low point of view (known as a worm's eye view), located slightly above the left sewer tunnel (notice how the angles of the lines defining the extreme right side wall appear to be pointing across in the first print (A) but more downward in the last (B). With the low viewpoint, the viewer has the feeling of looking up at the remaining composition. To further reinforce the verticality, he scrapes out the people in the center foreground of the first print (A) and replaces them with sewer tunnels and a dark shape that runs across the bottom of the picture (B). This emphasizes the vertical direction of the five wall units in the composition by allowing the central area to flow from top to bottom uninterrupted.

In addition, Rembrandt draws attention to the picture's bottom edge by creating a tension between it and the area immediately above it—due to their relative closeness and the dark shading. He anchors the dark tunnel shapes by emphasizing the ground plane under the people on either side. These ground plane lines subconsciously extend across the darkened center of the image, which helps to tie them visually to the bottom edge. The new open wall plunges to an unknown depth—further emphasizing the feeling of height.

Having emphasized the bottom of the plate (B) to increase the feeling of height, Rembrandt does the same to the top edge. Although the composition now appears even more horizontal because some of the top of the print has been removed, additional architectural detail is added across the central section, even with the top of the two recessed walls—which keeps the verticality strongly emphasized. This clustering of visual detail helps visually activate the very top of the porch area and helps make the central porch area even more important. By the last stage (B), this upward thrust is aided by the addition of an arching shape over the door immediately behind the central figures. Rembrandt has enlarged and darkened the whole area to make the central figures feel higher in the composition and more important than they were earlier.

Although this composition might appear at first glance to be similar on both sides of an imaginary vertical center line, Rembrandt works at finding ways to make all the areas similar and dissimilar at the same time. The recessed wall areas immediately to the left and right of the

B

central area are approximately the same width, yet the left side is in deep shadow and the right is bathed in light. Both sides have second-story arched window units, but to strengthen the dissimilarity, the windows on the right are noticeably higher. By the last state of the print (B), the top and bottom of the right windows have been lowered to the level of those on the left, but by removing all the glass above the figures and completely opening the window area, the windows on the right are noticeably dissimilar and still feel higher than those on the left side of the picture. All four windows contain female viewers, but the woman in the far right window is hanging out of the window frame.

Also, the extreme left and right sidewalls originate from the same point on the back wall, but they are different widths and different heights. By the last state (B), the top of the right sidewall is raised considerably with building detail. By lightening the figures in the foreground and shading the entire area with a similar gray tone, Rembrandt pulls the entire area together, making the right side of the composition more competitive visually with the left side, and does so without developing the same size or type of darkness.

After successfully stretching the composition vertically, Rembrandt works at the problem of manipulating space by pulling some areas

forward and pushing others back. In the final stage, Christ is pulled forward as the space to his right is darkened and recedes. The doorway on the ground floor to the left is deepened by the addition of five additional archways and the hint of an emerging figure in the darkest area. In the opposite doorway, emerging figures are lightened against the surrounding darkness, and the contrast of dark and light pulls them forward as they descend the stairway. The two statues above the central figures have been lightened, which pushes them back behind the central figures. The development of darks on both sides of the central balcony, even though dissimilar, also helps to bring the entire middle area forward.

Furthermore, Rembrandt's ingenious use of the balcony as a visual device allows him to create a metaphorical and physical separation between the ruling class and the common people while focusing on the main figures. With the removal of the line of people across the foreground of the first state (A), the balcony, wall, and central figures are thrust forward as if the viewer is invited to become a participant in the ongoing event. The feeling of looking up also places the viewer on the ground level with the common man.

Content: Although observers can read a number of meanings into the piece, it is

impossible to say with certainty what motivated Rembrandt to create this print. While the picture draws the viewer into the moment when Christ is presented to the people, it does so without endorsing any specific religious point of view.

We know that the print was made during a time of economic crisis in Rembrandt's life, and it reflects his lifelong interest in biblical themes. Considering the great diversity of religious doctrines of the period, it is possible that his intent was simply to develop an image with mass appeal and make a profit from the sale of this edition. However, considering Rembrandt's waning popularity, it is strange that even for the sake of increased sales, he is unwilling to provide what the buyers were finding in the work of competing printmakers—straightforward, unadorned presentation of the image. Unwilling to compromise, he seems driven to explore the use of light and dark and the solution of personal compositional problems.

"If I be lifted up" is a reoccurring scriptural theme usually associated with the concept of the crucifixion and certainly known to Rembrandt. He seems motivated, if not by that scripture, then by the idea of trying to place the main figures in the center of a horizontal composition and at the same time denying that location by emphasizing the verticality and optically elevating the platform.

the three components of a work of art, we can almost hear his critical dialogue that led to the compositional changes.

During the creative process, the initial idea that inspires the work can originate in any of the three components. Once found, it must then be developed in union with the other two components. The work can develop in any order; none is more "correct" than another.

The sense of unity may be difficult to detect in the works of some contemporary artists who blur the components. In these works, the distinctions between subject, form, and content are hazy, vague, or lost altogether because these components are sometimes treated as identical. This break with the traditional approach requires a shift in our thinking.

In **Conceptual Art,** for example, the *concept* is foremost (the product is considered negligible) and the *content and subject* seem to be the same thing. A Conceptual artist will often avoid the use of common media and form in order to convey a message or analyze an idea (e.g., using combinations of words, photography, and "found" objects of human construction). In **Process Art,** the *act* of producing is the only significant aspect of the work, thus reducing *form and content* to one entity. These two groups of artists are more concerned with their ideas and techniques, respectively, than the "look" of the final product; although they might consider their work to be intellectually "beautiful," they would probably not use this term. Styles that embrace such goals can be quite puzzling if the aims of the artist are not understood by the viewer.

How does the artist know when organic unity is really achieved? It is an intuitive understanding—often felt in the pit of the stomach—that all the pieces fit together instinctively and intellectually, that the work "makes sense." The work is finished—or is it? Having given the best of themselves,

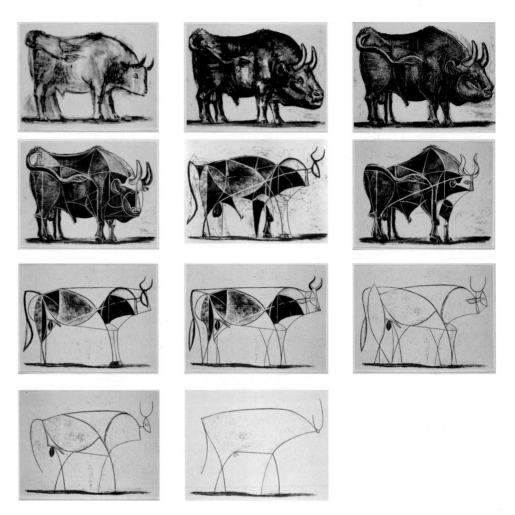

1.18 Pablo Picasso, *Bull*, states I–XI, 1945. Engraving. This illustration shows the progression of abstraction from the first state of the work to the eleventh as Picasso distills his image down to the bare essence of subject. Réunion des Musées Nationaux/Art Resource, NY. Photography by R. G. Ojeda. © 2011 Estate of Pablo Picasso/Artists Rights Society (ARS), New York.

artists are often never sure of this. Perhaps the perspective of a few days, months, or even years will give the answer.

ABSTRACTION

Let us study for a moment a process for simplifying and reorganizing information known as **abstraction.** It allows the treatment of subject matter to evolve from a purely descriptive image to one that has no reference to the natural world. For centuries, artists worked at creating representational images for the church or wealthy patrons. Artists' opportunity for self-expression was somewhat limited to what their patrons would support. Eventually, the industrial age, the rise of a well-to-do middle class with a desire for fine things, and the advance of scientific discovery altered the parameters and purpose of art. After the invention of the camera in the nineteenth century, many artists began to feel that they no longer "needed" to record reality with great accuracy (the camera could do that); instead, they felt free to reflect on their experiences in more interpretive and subjective ways. A new scientific investigation of color theory, which played various colors against each other, further removed the artist from a strictly representational interpretation of reality. Artists

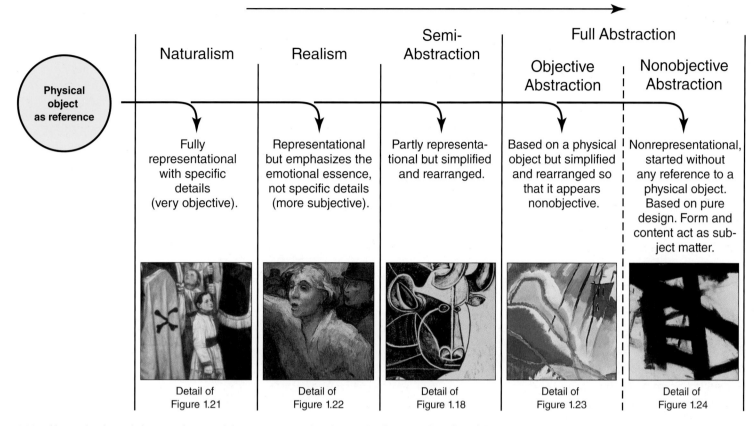

The Evolution of Abstraction

Physical object as reference

Naturalism	Realism	Semi-Abstraction	Full Abstraction	
			Objective Abstraction	Nonobjective Abstraction
Fully representational with specific details (very objective).	Representational but emphasizes the emotional essence, not specific details (more subjective).	Partly representational but simplified and rearranged.	Based on a physical object but simplified and rearranged so that it appears nonobjective.	Nonrepresentational, started without any reference to a physical object. Based on pure design. Form and content act as subject matter.
Detail of Figure 1.21	Detail of Figure 1.22	Detail of Figure 1.18	Detail of Figure 1.23	Detail of Figure 1.24

1.19 Abstraction is a relative term because it is present to varying degrees in all works of art, from full representation to complete nonobjectivity. This diagram briefly illustrates such degrees of abstraction through various historical periods—from the very descriptive to the development of nonobjective abstraction. Such progression could also happen over the lifetime of an individual artist or even within the development of a single work.

simplified images and rearranged formal elements to better communicate the essence of their experiences. This process came to be known as abstraction; as it evolved, artwork became a greater tool for self-expression.

To be sure, all visual artwork requires some degree of abstraction, however minute. The very nature of capturing life in an artistic medium makes the subject abstracted from reality. Even the most naturalistic rendering of a butterfly is an image that has been simplified from its three-dimensional existence—and captured on a flat surface. Further abstraction occurs when artists embrace the freedom and expressive qualities of process and increase the amount of changes to the image. Sometimes the subject remains a recognizable image;

sometimes it just becomes a graphical pattern or a block of elements that is far from how you would visually experience it in reality. For observers expecting a literal copying of a physical subject, a high degree of abstraction can make a work more difficult to understand and appreciate. However, abstraction is intended to make a deeper meaning more accessible and clear (fig 1.18). The degree of abstraction should not deter the viewer from looking more carefully at the artwork. Whether recognizable or not, the subject is just one component; the way it is presented or formed to give it expression is an equally important consideration in the search for meaning (see fig. 1.20).

The diagram in figure 1.19 illustrates the evolution of abstraction and shows

how the treatment of subject matter developed from a purely descriptive image to one that has no reference to the natural world. (This change will be demonstrated by looking at various historical periods in art, but such a progression could also happen over the lifetime of an individual artist or even within the development of a single work.)

In the style known as **Naturalism,** the subject has a physical reference, which the artist reproduces as close to optically perceived as possible (fig. 1.21; see also fig. 1.19). The artists that produced this style were very objective in the development of their subject matter, making the image very specific, with little personal interpretation. They used a very **descriptive** approach, stressing precise details and

1.20 Vincent van Gogh, *The Starry Night,* 1889. Oil on canvas, 29 × 36¼ in. (73.7 × 92.1 cm). *The Starry Night* was completed near the mental asylum of Saint-Remy, thirteen months before Van Gogh's death at the age of 37. His letters indicate that he wanted to create, from his imagination, a more exciting and comforting nature than one might observe from a single glimpse of reality. He was interested in exaggerated lines—warped as in old woodcuts. The compelling stylization, the staccato-like brushstrokes, the circular and swirling movement of the cosmic elements, and the flamelike cypress keep the viewer actively engaged. The Museum of Modern Art, New York. Acquired through the Lillie P. Bliss Bequest (472.1941) The Museum of Modern Art, New York, NY, U.S.A. Digital Image © The Museum of Modern Art/Licensed by SCALA/Art Resource, NY.

individual characteristics of the objects to create an image as close to reality as possible. Such emphasis was placed on the use of observable detail to re-create an object that Gustave Courbet, one of the leading artists of the movement, once said, "Bring me an angel and I will paint you an angel."

The approach became more subjective, or inventive, with the work of Honoré Daumier and those working in **Realism.** In this style, the work is still somewhat representational but not as reliant on specific detail. The subject was simplified or abstracted from what was optically seen, and it was developed to emphasize an emotional response

(fig. 1.22; see also fig. 1.19). The Realists wanted to present universal meanings rather than specific information—for example, they would paint an image that represents the conditions, the drudgery, and the hardships faced by all women of the period rather than a detailed portrait of a specific woman. A Realist's approach is more subjective and innovative, uses more experimental brushwork, and sacrifices some specific information to gain universal impressions.

As the work of artists became even more subjective, they began to simplify and rearrange their visual experiences to an even greater degree. The subject, still somewhat recognizable, was stripped

down to expressive and communicative basics, which were reordered to emphasize essential elements. The subject became *semiabstract,* although it was still reliant on an initial object (see figs. 1.18 [the first bull in the second row], 7.32, 8.44, and T.54). The intent was often to make a deeper meaning more accessible—like the **Cubists'** desire to show societal and cultural fragmentation—even if the original object is hard to recognize (see fig. T.51).

As artists continued to search for new ways to express themselves, some discovered the excitement of organizing various formal elements into works of complete abstraction. Within abstract

1.21 Gustave Courbet, *Burial at Ornans,* 1849. Oil on canvas, 10 × 22 ft. (3 × 6.7 m). Courbet was the leading early exponent of the naturalist leanings of some Realist painters. Critics harshly condemned him for painting "ugly" pictures of average people at their mundane activities. Bridgeman Art Library/SuperStock, Inc.

1.22 Honoré Daumier, *The Uprising,* c. 1852–58. Oil on canvas, 34 × 44 in. Influenced by a climate of scientific positivism, the artists of the Realist movement tried to record the world as it appeared to the eye, but they also wanted to interpret it so as to record timeless truths. This painting by Daumier shows his broadly realist renderings of a political protest. Acquired 1925. The Phillips Collection, Washington, D.C.

art are two creative approaches that are often indistinguishable unless the intent of the artist is known. The first approach, *objective abstraction,* occurs when artists base their work on a physical object, but during the working process, the finished image becomes so abstracted that it no longer resembles or even appears to represent the initial reference (fig. 1.23; see also fig. 1.19). With this approach, the effect is not always foreseen while the work is in progress.

For those working with the second approach, *nonobjective abstraction,* the image starts out as a nonrepresentational statement that is purely invented, having no reference to any physical object (fig. 1.24; see also figs. 1.19, 1.55, and 7.25). Sometimes a work suggests a meaning to the artist as it evolves; sometimes the meaning

1.23 Vasily Kandinsky, French, born Russia, 1866–1944, *Improvisation No. 30 (Cannons),* 1913. Oil on canvas, 43¹¹⁄₁₆ × 43¹³⁄₁₆ in. (111 × 111.3 cm). About 1910, the Russian Vasily Kandinsky began to paint freely moving biomorphic shapes in rich combinations of hues. His characteristic early style can be seen in this illustration. Such an abstract form of expression was an attempt to show the artist's feelings about object surfaces rather than to describe their outward appearances. Arthur Jerome Eddy Memorial Collection, 1931.511, The Art Institute of Chicago. Photo © Art Institute of Chicago. © 2011 Artists Rights Society (ARS), New York, ADAGP, Paris.

1.24 Franz Kline, *Mahoning,* 1956. Oil and paper collage on canvas, 6 ft. 8 in. × 8 ft. 4 in. (2.03 × 2.54 m). The artist was more interested in the actual physical action involved in this type of expression than in the character of the resulting painting. Collection of the Whitney Museum of American Art, New York. Purchase, with funds from the Friends of the Whitney Museum of American Art. 57.10. © 2011 The Franz Kline Estate/Artists Rights Society (ARS), New York.

is purely the pleasure of working with the elements or the artist's expression of emotion. Both approaches to abstraction require observers to interpret content from only the artist's use of media, techniques, elements, and principles of organization.

EXPANDING PERSONAL AWARENESS

When an artist views an object—a tree branch, for example—and is inspired to reproduce the original as seen, he or she is using and drawing inspiration from **optical perception.** The artist who reproduces only what he or she perceives in the "real world" is thought of as a "perceptual" artist. However, some artists see the tree branch but envision a crying child or rearing horse. When the imagination triggers this creative vision and suggests additional images, the artists are employing **conceptual perception.** Artists who are inspired by imaginative concepts are called "conceptual" artists. Leonardo da Vinci, writing in his *Treatise on Painting*, recorded an experience with conceptual perception while studying clouds: "On one occasion above Milan, over in the direction of Lake Maggiore, I saw a cloud shaped like a huge mountain made up of banks of fire. . . ." Elsewhere, he recommends staring at stains on walls as a source of inspiration. Following Leonardo, author and painter Victor Hugo found many of his ideas for drawings by studying coffee stains on tablecloths.

By attempting to see the uniqueness in everything around us, we can expand our sensitivity and response to art. The author Gertrude Stein wrote, "A rose is a rose is a rose." A literal interpretation would lead us to expect all roses to be identical, but we know that every rose has a different character, even with identical breeding and grooming. Every object is ultimately unique, be it a chair, a tree, or a person. One of the major characteristics that sets the artist apart is the ability to see (and experience) the subtle differences in things. By exposing those differences, the artist can make the ordinary seem distinctive, the humdrum exciting (fig. 1.25).

1.25 Patricia Nix, *La Primavera,* 1992–94. Mixed media on canvas, 72 × 80 in. Patricia Nix's *La Primavera* presents roses as a repeated theme, but subtle differences in texture, color, and treatment keep them fresh and unique. From the collection of Ivan Blinoff, London. Courtesy of the artist.

1.26 Nicolas Poussin, *Apollo and Daphne*, 1627, 97 × 131 cm. This painting tells the story of Apollo, a mythological deity. While walking on Mount Olympus, he spotted a beautiful nymph named Daphne. Smitten, he pursued her until she cried out for help to her father Peneus, the river god. As Apollo reached out, her feet turned to roots, her hands were covered with leaves, and her body became the trunk of a laurel tree. As a memento of his lost love, Apollo fashioned a laurel wreath— later given as the highest prize at competitions all over Greece. Alte Pinakothek © ARTOTHEK/Art Resource, NY.

All art is illusory to some extent, and some artwork is more successful than others at drawing us out of our ordinary existence into a more meaningful state. Frames, galleries, stages, exaggerated costumes or makeup, and so on all serve to set the artwork apart from the everyday world. This "aesthetic distance" helps the audience focus on the ideas presented and seems to transport them beyond the mundane, into a world of emotions and meaning. It is not just enough to "see" art but to experience and react to it.

Our ability to respond to artwork depends on maintaining an open mind. By ridding ourselves of the expectation that all forms of art should follow the same rules or have the same qualities, we can appreciate more of what we see (and be less restricted when developing ideas for our own pieces). For example, some people expect art to tell a story in a descriptive manner (fig. 1.26). Many fine works contain elements of storytelling, but not all artists have a need or an obligation to narrate. In addition, we know that many people judge a work of art by how closely it looks like something. Even the best perceptual artists, such as skillful plastic and graphic artists, try to incorporate more into a work than pure replication. Most artists feel that considerations of form are equally important to the outcome of the work, and therefore, making a "likeness" is not the only key to art. Many of the best photographers are not content to simply point and shoot. They supplement a camera's ability to capture the world with great accuracy with other formal elements; they look for the best compositional view (angle and framing), create or wait for the right lighting conditions, use filters, alter the depth of field, or make adjustments in developing (fig. 1.27).

When the artist probes below the surface of something and uses unfamiliar ways to find unexpected truths, the results can often be distressing. Exposure to a new art experience frequently causes such distress in a viewer. Under these conditions, the artist may be accused of being incompetent or a charlatan. Much of what we value in art today was once decried in this way.

1.27 Minor White, *Moon & Wall Encrustations*, 1964. Gelatin silver print. Photographers may have the edge on other visual artists when it comes to recording objective reality, but many photographer-artists are not satisfied with obvious appearances and use complex technical strategies to structure or enhance the final image. Minor White Archive, Princeton University. Bequest of Minor White. (MWA64-6). Reproduced with permission of the Minor White Archive, Princeton University Art Museum. © Trustees of Princeton University.

General acceptance of more radical art comes about when enough time has passed for the new methods to become familiar. Then, this new language loses its abrasiveness and the art's true meaning can be understood. There is no shame in feeling embarrassed, confused, or defiant at first about art that is new to you but, through continued exposure, thought, and study, you will begin to see through technique and method to a work's core meaning (fig. 1.28).

Much of the public, for example, is curious about **installations.** By creating or altering an interior or exterior setting with various media, the artist's intention is to heighten the viewer's awareness of the environmental space—to see and think of that space in a new way (fig. 1.29). Installations can range in scale from the relatively small to the enormous. They are created using any available materials, including sheet metal, fiberglass, wood, bronze, steel, plastic, stone, lasers, sound, computer-controlled projection, and mixed media. If placed outdoors, an installation may be simple (but frequently quite large) and is often in an easily viewable public location. When set in an interior location, as in a gallery, installations are often composed of multiple pieces, sometimes using all available floor and/or wall space. The positioning of the pieces can be simple, complex, ordered, or even seemingly random.

Observers react in different ways—some excited, others perplexed, some having their vision altered, and others delaying judgment. In the recent past, some installations have provoked strong, even violent reactions. Viewers have described some works as dehumanizing and irrational. This is not surprising, because the installation is

THE GATES, PROJECT FOR CENTRAL PARK, NEW YORK
Christo's and Jeanne-Claude's Plans for Their Temporary Work of Art (1979–2005)

Artistic Statement
For those who walked through *The Gates*, the saffron-colored fabric was a golden ceiling above the walkways, creating warm shadows. When seen from the buildings surrounding Central Park, *The Gates* seemed like a golden river appearing and disappearing through the bare branches of the trees and highlighting the shape of the meandering footpaths.

The sixteen-day-duration work of art was free to all, and will be remembered as a joyous experience for every New Yorker as a democratic expression that Olmsted invoked when he conceived a "central" park. The luminous moving fabric underlined the organic design of the park, while the rectangular poles were a reminder of the geometric grid pattern of the city blocks around the park. *The Gates* harmonized with the beauty of Central Park. The work of art remained for sixteen days; then the gates were removed and the materials industrially recycled.

The Gates
Number of gates: 7,500
Height of gates: 16 feet
Width of gates: varying from 5 ft. 6 in. to 18 ft.
Placement: following the edges of walkways, perpendicular to the selected 23 miles of footpaths
Spacing of the gates: 10- to 15-ft. intervals

Materials (Recycled)
Steel: 5,290 U.S. tons of steel
Vinyl tube 5 in. × 5 in.: 315,491 linear ft.
Cast aluminum reinforcements: 15,000
Steel leveling plates: 15,000
Bolts and self-locking nuts: 165,000
Vinyl leveling plate covers: 15,064
Nylon thread: woven into 1,092,200 square ft. of fabric and sewn into 7,500 fabric panels (46 miles of hems)

Work Force
Employment: hundreds of NYC residents for manufacturing and assembling the gate structures, installation workers, maintenance teams in uniform with radios working around the clock

As Christo and Jeanne-Claude have always done for their previous projects, *The Gates* was entirely financed by the artists through C.V.J. Corp. (Jeanne-Claude Javacheff, President) with the sale of studies, preparatory drawings and collages, scale models, earlier works of the fifties and sixties, and original lithographs on other subjects. The artists do not accept sponsorship of any kind.

1.28 **Christo and Jeanne-Claude, *The Gates*, project for Central Park, New York, 1979–2005.** *The Gates* represents the culmination of years of planning and hard work, spent not only in designing and organizing but also in securing the legal arrangements necessary for such a large and integrated work of art to be installed in only five days and unfurled on the same day. The photos show the saffron-colored gates installed and their earlier fabrication.
© Christo and Jeanne-Claude 2005. Photographs: Wolfgang Volz/laif/Redux.

a relatively new art form, and unusual styles of art have many times produced a general outcry. Richard Serra, a veteran of installations that are generally minimalist in nature, has had some of his work dismantled or defaced; his *Tilted Arc* was removed as the result of protests (fig. 1.29). In return, these protestations have drawn the wrath of many artists who feel that art should be given free rein, because art forms that have produced widespread criticism in the past have become accepted with the passage of time.

Despite strong reactions—both good and bad—to installations, they are now firmly a part of the art world. A well-done installation enhances viewer involvement and creates an immersing experience. These works are often extremely labor intensive—no doubt a labor of love to their creators—and cause viewers to see a particular environment in a new way. Some significant artists in this area are Ann Hamilton (see fig. 8.50), whose work is generally sensuous; Olafur Eliasson (fig. 1.30), who creates immersive environments; Anish Kapoor (see fig. 1.31), whose work is often simple and frequently disorienting; Patrick Dougherty, who twists and tilts cut branches into towering walk-through works (see fig. 6.21); and Jennifer Steinkamp, who creates interactive video/sound/space installations.

We all have the capacity to appreciate the beautiful or expressive, as evidenced by the aesthetic choices we make every day. But we must continually expand our sensitivity and taste, making them ever more inclusive. This may mean that a piece of art you dislike or find unfamiliar may not necessarily be poorly executed or devoid of meaning. However, the quality of art is always subjective and questionable. Even with training, people's tastes do not turn out to be identical. Perhaps the most reliable proof of quality comes only with time and the eventual consensus of many people.

1.29 Richard Serra, *Tilted Arc*, 1981. Cor-Ten steel (73 tons), 120 ft. long × 12 ft. high with 12/1 ft. slope toward the Federal Building. This site-specific installation was erected in Federal Plaza in New York City, commissioned by the Arts-in-Architecture program of the U.S. General Services Administration. It split the space of the Federal Plaza in half, forcing onlookers to become more aware of their own movements through the space. Unfortunately, it was not appreciated by many workers at the plaza, who complained that it interfered with the public use of the space, restricted views and access to government buildings, promoted crime, and attracted litter and rats. Many felt that "public sculpture" should be more inviting, regardless of the artist's right to create. After eight years of controversy, the sculpture was dismantled and destroyed. © 1985 David Aschkenas.

1.30 Olafur Eliasson, *I only see things when they move*, 2004. Wood, color-effect filter glass, stainless steel, aluminum, HMI lamp, tripod, glass cylinder, motors, control unit, variable sizes. This work, with its constantly changing lights and colors, creates an immersive and intoxicating environment for viewers. Installation view at Tanya Bonakdar Gallery. Photograph by Fabian Birgfeld, PhotoTECTONICS. Gift of Marie-Josée and Henry Kravis in Honor of Mimi Haas. Courtesy of The Museum of Modern Art, New York. © 2004 Olafur Eliasson.

1.31 Anish Kapoor, *Marsyas*, 2002. PVC and steel. Kapoor designed this massive sculpture (508 feet long and 114 feet high) for the Turbine Hall at the Tate Museum in London. The work is so massive, in fact, that a viewer can not see the whole piece from any one angle and must mentally construct the whole composition from several viewpoints. Installation at Courtesy, Tate.

DEVELOPING IDEAS

Creativity emanates from ideas. For the artist, a creative idea may be an all-encompassing plan, a unique set of relationships, an attitude to be conveyed, or a solution to a visual problem.

An idea may come as a "bolt from the blue," or it may be the end product of much thoughtful effort, as reflected in notes, sketches, and countless revisions of the artwork.

All artists occasionally encounter blocks on their creativity, and it can take an artist many years to break through these blocks. A beginning artist may find it difficult to even find a starting point for a project ("I don't know what to do!"). Although a familiar object or experience is usually the best starting point in such situations, the following approaches, suggested by artists, are ways to develop ideas or overcome the creative block. You may want to expand the list.

Look for stimulating ideas around you. Take a bus ride across town, or visit a restaurant and observe how people relate to each other. Study the life and heartbeat of your city or town. Look closely at nature—notice shapes, values, textures, and patterns. Remember the flattened frog skeleton you spotted on the way out of the parking lot—could it be used as a symbol for a special theme? Supplement an impulse by brainstorming anything remotely related. Doodle or experiment with any available media. Think of a pressing social issue. Make lists of all the verbs, adverbs, or adjectives that could be associated with that issue, and add color notations associated with each term. Write down a single sentence or phrase that catches your attention during a news report, poetry reading, or argument with a friend. You should note as many variations on the idea or its presentation as possible; include *visual metaphors*—ways of expressing the idea without actually depicting it directly. And, as with any good debate team, try to express an opposing concept, feeling, or setting in terms of image, color, and emotional character. In short: observe, explore, and expand. Generate as many ideas as you can—the last few may be the best.

Existing artwork can also serve as a stimulus for ideas. Try to imagine what another artist's work was trying to develop. Think about the concept or the "problem" that was being solved visually, and think about how the artist's form choices reinforced the content. It doesn't matter if you correctly pinpoint the original artist's problem or not. You can try to apply the same concept to your own subject matter. Or create a new direction to explore by altering the problem or combining several problems. Maybe you will even discover an aspect that the original artist has failed to address, and you can attempt to solve it in your own way. See how many different solutions you can develop for the same problem.

Unfortunately, the artist's block sometimes occurs right in the middle of creating the image. Some artists, when they can't quite build the bridges between nearly finished areas, feel that they must sacrifice an acceptable portion of the work in order to find the freedom to continue with the development of the remaining image. Before doing this, maintain an ongoing dialogue with yourself. Do whatever it takes to see your work with fresh eyes or from a new vantage point. Try looking at the work in a mirror, holding up your hands and blocking out portions to see sections in isolation, squinting, or turning the image upside down. Often, troublesome areas stand out when you can see them in a new way.

While most studio artists generate their own ideas, the majority of artists in commercial industries are given an initial concept. Graphic designers, product designers, architects who have client demands, or even artists working on specific commissions, are required to use a predetermined subject or content. For them, the search for ideas does not end after being given the initial goal. Quite the contrary—it is just the beginning. To expand and develop the idea, they may need to consider all the variables of the **design** of the product; study the competition; identify the age demographics to which the item must appeal; find typeface, color schemes, and layouts that reinforce most effectively the appeal to that demographic; run sample market studies of concept, design, and color; and lay out multiple

strategies for reaching their potential audience and making their product irresistible. New and exciting ideas that challenge the established paradigms for each step along the process are the backbone of a successful campaign. This search for ideas can be very logical, almost scientific, and can be used in both commercial and studio application.

CRITICAL THINKING AND ANALYSIS

At some point in the creative process (or in truth, at many points), there will come a need for analysis and evaluation. Critical-thinking skills will play a vital role in achieving a unified and successful work. Whether formal or informal, this review process, also known as a critique, identifies what works well and helps to find constructive ways to improve troublesome areas in the work.

Critiques are not restricted to any discipline and may occur in either individual or group settings. For example, after a full day's production of coffee mugs, studio potters will often pick out their five best pieces, analyze them, and try to discover those special qualities that make those five jump out as the best of the group. The same thing could be done comparing preliminary sketches for a work or studying appealing masterpieces. It is important to remember that "to critique" does not mean "to blame." Analysis and evaluation of work is not about faulting the artist for "mistakes." Unfortunately, many beginning artists let the fear of making errors prevent them from creating anything at all. Don't stop before you start.

When applied to ongoing work, critiques can happen at any point and can be repeated until the idea and creation are fine-tuned. These times of reflection and critique will become easier

and more beneficial as you study and become more familiar with the vocabulary, principles, and elements of art. If possible, participate in class critiques and/or discussions—or at least, maintain an internal dialogue. The benefits are twofold: you will learn to identify and articulate visual or conceptual problems in a work, and the experiences will become a resource for ideas. When a previously analyzed problem occurs later in your work, the solution for the stumbling block will present itself much sooner and may even be applied subconsciously.

How does one begin a critique? Unfortunately, there are no formulas. You may want to identify the three components of the work (subject, form, and content), evaluate them separately, and then examine how they work together as a whole. Analysis may seem awkward in the beginning, but asking some of the following questions may help.

- What areas feel most successful and why?
- What areas feel incomplete or troublesome, and what is the cause?
- How is the subject presented?
- Are there visual or symbolic metaphors that could have helped expand the image?
- If the image is nonobjective, what suggests the meaning?
- How are the elements used to support or destroy the image compositionally (e.g., color choices, line quality, etc.)?
- Have the principles of organization been observed (e.g., harmony versus variety, balance, etc.)?
- What is the intention behind the work?
- What is being communicated—a feeling, an idea, a personal aesthetic?
- Is it too esoteric?
- Is it too obvious?
- Where does the work succeed in integrating these components, and where is it less successful?

You may want to begin with your own feeling about each issue but then ask yourself what sets up that response and how it could be altered—are there other interpretations, viewpoints, or relationships that could have been presented? As you become more skilled at analysis, you may find it becomes less necessary to *consciously* explore a list of questions. Trust your subconscious to uncover the most relevant issues.

BASIC CONCEPTS OF TWO-DIMENSIONAL ART

Artists who work with two-dimensional art generally begin with a flat surface. The flat surface is the **picture plane** on which artists execute their images. A piece of paper, a canvas, a board, or a copper plate may function as the picture plane. This flat surface

may also represent an imaginary plane of reference on which an artist can create spatial illusions.

For example, the raw elements can be manipulated to produce either a **two-dimensional** effect (having the dimensions of height and width—like a circle, triangle, or square) or a **three-dimensional** effect (having the dimensions of height, width, and the illusion of depth—like a sphere, pyramid, or cube). In a two-dimensional work, the elements and image seem to lie flat on the picture plane, but when the elements are three-dimensional, penetration of that **plane** is implied (fig. 1.32A).

When the elements cling rather closely to the picture plane and do not leap toward or away from us dramatically in the format, we can say they are **decorative.** Although this term can also refer to ornamentation, here it refers to a spatial condition. When elements are of this nature, collectively we can say

that the **space** created by them is decorative—relatively flat or shallow.

However, when the images or elements appear to exist in front of, or behind, the picture plane, and we feel that we could dive into the picture and weave our way around and behind the art elements, the space is said to be **plastic.** Whether working with decorative or plastic space, the picture plane is used as a basis for establishing both two- and three-dimensional pictorial space.

It is important to note the difference between plastic space and the plastic arts. For example, although graphic artists may create plastic space, they are not necessarily plastic artists. Graphic artwork (drawing, painting, printmaking, photography, etc.) generally exists on a flat surface and relies on the *illusion* of the third dimension. The products of the plastic arts (sculpture, ceramics, architecture, etc.), on the other hand, have tangible mass and occupy *actual* space. With three-dimensional works

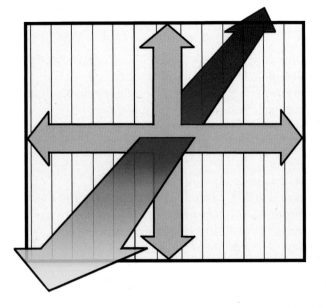

1.32A The picture plane. Movement can take place on a flat surface, as indicated by the vertical and horizontal light-blue arrows. The artist can also give the illusion of advancing and receding movement in space, as shown by the large yellow-to-dark-blue arrow.

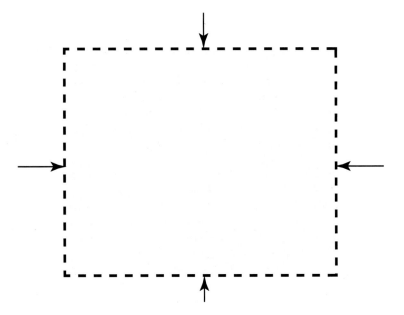

1.32B The picture frame. The picture frame represents the outermost limits, or boundaries, of the picture plane. These limits, indicated here by a broken line, represent the edges of the canvas or paper on which the artist works. The size and direction of the pictorial frame is one of the first considerations made in the composition of the work and is sometimes indicated by a drawn margin in preparatory sketches.

of art, the artist begins with the material—metal, clay, stone, glass, and so on—rather than with the picture plane, and works it as a total form against the surrounding space, without the limitations of the flat surface.

The defined boundary around the working area (or picture plane) is generally called the **picture frame** (fig. 1.32B). The picture frame should be clearly established before beginning the composition. After its shape and proportion are defined, all the art elements and their employment will be influenced by it. The problem for the pictorial artist is to organize the elements of art within the picture frame, on the picture plane.

The proportions and shapes of the frames used by artists are varied. Squares, triangles, circles, and ovals have been used as frame shapes, but the most popular is the rectangle, which in its varying proportions offers the artist an interesting variety within the two-dimensional space (figs. 1.33, 1.34, 1.35). Some artists select the outside proportions of their pictures on the basis of geometric ratios

1.33 Esphyr Slobodkina, *Composition in an Oval*, c. 1953. Oil on gesso board, 32½ × 61½ in. (82.5 × 156.2 cm). Slobodkina has used an unusual frame shape to emphasize an angular abstract painting. Now used less frequently, such frame shapes were employed more often in the past with traditional religious subjects. Grey Art Gallery. New York University Art Collection. Gift of Mr. and Mrs. Irving Walsey, 1962.

1.34 Wang Hui, *Autumn Forests at Yushan*, 1672. Ink and color on paper. This rectangular frame shape emphasizes the verticality of the image, presenting a view of both heaven and earth. These proportions were often used by classic Chinese landscape artists to capture the majestic scale of the mountainous environment. *Courtesy of the Palace Museum, Beijing.*

1.35 Elizabeth Murray, *Keyhole*, 1982. Oil on two canvases, 99½ × 110½ in. Murray uses the picture plane as physical space. The shapes that make up the picture plane contribute movement and a 3-D element to her paintings. This potentially chaotic aspect of her work is kept under control by the flattened, abstracted shapes that she uses in her imagery. Collection of Agnes Gund. © Elizabeth Murray. Courtesy Pace Gallery, New York. © 2011 Artists Rights Society (ARS), New York.

(see the "Proportion" section in Chapter 2). These rules suggest selecting lengths and widths of odd proportions (such as 2:3 or 3:5) rather than equal relationships. The results are visually pleasing spatial arrangements. Most artists, however, rely on their instincts rather than on a mechanical formula. After the picture plane has been established, the direction and movement of the artistic elements should relate harmoniously to this shape. Otherwise, they will tend to disrupt the goal of pictorial unity.

Those areas that are occupied by the objective or nonobjective images are called **positive areas**. Unoccupied spaces are termed **negative areas** (fig. 1.36A and B). Sometimes, especially with nonobjective art, images can function as both positive and negative areas, depending on perspective. (fig. 1.37). Although the positive areas may seem tangible and more explicit, the negative areas are just as important to

A

B

1.36 Paul Gaugin, *Girl with a Fan,* 1902. Oil on canvas. The subject in figure A represents a positive shape that has been enhanced by careful consideration of the negative area, or the surrounding space. In figure B, the dark areas indicate the negative shapes, and the white area designates the location of the positive image. Museum Folkwang, Essen, Germany/The Bridgeman Art Library.

1.37 Robert Motherwell, *Africa,* 1965. Acrylic on Belgian linen, 81 × 222½ in. In this nonfigurative or nonobjective work, some areas have been painted and others not. It is very simple, perhaps deceptively so. To the viewer, the darks seem to be the positive shapes, although after some looking, the effect may be reversed. The Baltimore Museum of Art. Gift of the Artist. BMA 1965.012. Courtesy of the Dedalus Foundation, Inc. Art © Robert Motherwell/Licensed by VAGA, New York, NY.

total picture **unity.** It is important for beginner artists (as well as those learning to appreciate art) to pay attention to, and consider the effects of, negative areas. Without the proper and sensitive use of negative areas, a picture may seem boring, overcrowded, busy, and/or confusing.

Traditionally, the *figure* and *foreground* positions were considered positive, while the *background* areas were considered negative. The term *figure* probably came from the human form, which was used as a major subject in artwork and implied a spatial relationship, with the figure occupying the position in front of the remaining background (see fig. 1.36A and B). More recently, abstract painters have adopted the terms *field* to mean positive and *ground* to mean negative. For example, they speak of a color field on a white ground and a field of shapes against a ground of contrasting value (see figs. 2.59 and 7.25).

TWO-DIMENSIONAL MEDIA AND TECHNIQUES

Each art **medium** (materials and tools) has intrinsically unique characteristics that affect the feeling of the work. Artists can also use various **techniques** to explore and bring out desired nuances in the chosen media—for example, a photograph has a different look than a woodcut, and a brush makes a different type of line or mark than an ink pen. Depending on what the artist wants to communicate, the choice of material and technique can fantastically enhance the expression of the work.

Artists are also stimulated by the interaction with the media and the various techniques. Painters are attracted by the smell and feel of fresh plaster resisting the brush in fresco and secco painting. Oils and watercolors

provide a different tactile excitement from gouache and tempera, as do wet or dry surfaces. For the draughtsman, the difference between a heavy pressure and a light touch can be just as compelling as the textural quality of the drawing surface. Graphite, charcoal, colored pencils, pastels, or chalk can all be blended, erased, or used aggressively (fig. 1.38). Inks, whether applied by brush, crow quill, speedball steel point, sharpened bamboo stick, or cardboard, can be exciting because of how they react to dry or dampened surfaces. For printmakers, watching the physical surface change is intriguing: in lithography, the drawing comes to life on the stone or plate as water magically resists the application of ink (see fig. 1.14); intaglio plates are etched in acid until the topography reveals the image below the plate's surface (see fig. 3.15); in woodcuts and wood engraving, the resistance of the wood provides a unique texture (see fig. 3.18); stencil or serigraphic images can be flat in decorative color and surface quality or dissolve into transparency and overlapping texture (see fig. 4.1). The examples are endless.

Over the years, many of the media and techniques have been standardized. However, artists are not restricted to standard materials or uses. With advances in technology, a deluge of new processes and materials have become available for experimentation and development. Some are extensions of traditional approaches, while others, like computer-generated imagery, are without precedent. In fact, it has become quite normal for artists and designers to make heavy use of digital hardware and computer software to edit, manipulate, and otherwise enhance images (fig. 1.39). Very often, the traditional and nontraditional are intermixed, especially in multidisciplinary works. Regardless of refinement or simplicity, all innovations have broadened the artist's vision.

BASIC CONCEPTS OF THREE-DIMENSIONAL ART

In the two-dimensional graphic arts (drawing, painting, photography, printmaking, graphic design, etc.), images generally exist in two dimensions (height and width) but can generate the *illusion* of space. In the three-dimensional arts, the added dimension is that of *actual* depth. This depth allows the viewer to observe the work from multiple angles, increasing the physical impact of the work. Because actual depth is fundamental to 3-D art, one must be in the presence of the artwork to fully appreciate it. In this text, photographic reproductions are the most convenient means of conveying the 3-D experience, but words and graphic representations of 3-D art are not substitutes for actual sensory experience. The reader is therefore strongly encouraged to observe actual 3-D artworks.

Subject, form, and content—the components of art—function in much the same manner in the plastic arts as they do in the graphic arts. The importance of each component, however, may vary in different mediums. For example, sculptors use the components for expressive purposes; architects, ceramists, and metalsmiths, while expressive, may also interpret form for the sake of utility and ornamentation.

Formal organization is more complex in three-dimensional art than in the graphic arts. Materials, developed in actual space through physical manipulation, exist in a tactile as well as visual sense. The resulting complexities expand the content or meaning of the form (fig. 1.40). It is important to note the difference between the definition of *form* as "organizing or organization" (as previously defined) and its common usage meaning the "shape" of a two- or three-dimensional object. Sculptors often use *form* to refer to

1.38 Thomas Hilty and Tamara Monk, *Phoenix,* 2006. Graphite, pencil, and acrylic, 36 × 48 in. (91.4 × 121.9 cm). This mixed-media work shows the collaborative effort of two artists. They have skillfully blended the applications of graphite, pencil, and acrylic to produce the expressive and texturally varied surfaces. Courtesy of the artists.

1.39 Phil Dunne, Who's That Girl, 2010. Digital image. The use of computers has allowed artists and designers to use an expanded palette of colors, textures, and effects. This image could never have been conceived, let alone created, before the invention of digital technology. © Phil Dunne.

1.40 Mel Kendrick, *Bronze with Two Squares,* 1989–90. Bronze (edition of three), 73 × 28 × 28 in. (185.4 × 71.1 × 71.1 cm). Meant to be experienced visually and tactilely, this sculpture is deceiving because it looks like wood but was created by manipulation and cast in bronze. The sculptor has to know his or her materials well to create this kind of trompe l'oeil effect. Courtesy of the artist.

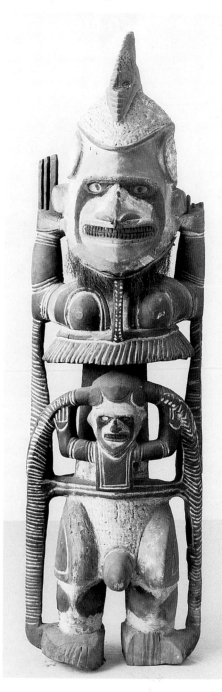

1.41 Uli figure, New Zealand. Painted wood, 59 in. (152 cm) high. To illustrate the different meanings of the term *form,* we may say that the forms in this piece of sculpture are the open and solid individual shapes, or that the form of the work consists of the total assembly of those individual parts. Hamburgisches Museum für Völkerkunde.

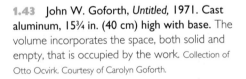

their sculpture's **shape,** defined by cavities (open negative areas) and protuberances (positive shapes; fig.1.41). Sculptures also have mass and volume. **Mass** invariably denotes a sculpture's implied weight or bulk. Mass may also refer to any solid physical object or body of matter, like clay or metal, that is not yet shaped, modeled, or cast. Stone carvers, accustomed to working with **glyptic** materials, tend to deal with a heavy, weighty mass (fig. 1.42); modelers, who manipulate clay or wax, favor a pliable mass. **Volume** is the three-dimensional space defined by an object's borders. A teapot in an empty room has a measurable volume. Mass and volume exist in relation to each other: a brick has mass within its volume. In general, positive space creates an impression of greater mass whereas negative space creates a sense of less mass (fig. 1.43). Both mass and volume indicate the presence of the sculpture's three-dimensionality, or form.

THREE-DIMENSIONAL MATERIALS AND TECHNIQUES

Over the past 100 years, the range of 3-D materials has expanded from basic stone, wood, and bronze to steel, plastic, fabric, glass, laser beams (holography), fluorescent and incandescent lighting, and so on. Such materials have revealed new areas for free exploration, while remaining grounded in the components of subject, form, and content. Still, the basic methods for working with them remain the same. There are four primary technical methods for creating three-dimensional forms: **subtraction, manipulation, addition,** and **substitution.** Although each of the technical methods is developed and discussed separately in the following sections, 3-D works are created using some combination of the four methods.

1.44 **Subtracting stone.** In the subtractive process, the raw material is removed until the artist's conception of the form is revealed. Stone can be shaped manually or with an air hammer, as shown here. Photograph courtesy of Ronald Coleman.

1.45 Michelangelo Buonarroti, *The Bearded Captive,* c. 1516–27. Marble, 8 ft. 8¼ in. (2.65 m) high. Michelangelo created heavy, massive sculptures and enlarged the sizes of human body parts for expressive purposes. The tectonic composition was in keeping with the intrinsic nature of the stone. Accademia, Florence, Italy. © Arte & Immagine srl/Corbis.

Subtraction

The subtraction method involves cutting away materials capable of being carved (glyptic materials), such as stone, wood, cement, plaster, clay, and some plastics. Artists may use chisels, hammers, torches, saws, grinders, and polishers to reduce their materials (fig. 1.44). It has often been said that when carvers take away material, they "free" the image frozen in the material, and a sculpture emerges. The freeing of form by the subtraction method produces the unique qualities of carved artwork (fig. 1.45).

Manipulation

Widely known as **modeling,** manipulation is a direct method for creating form. Clay, wax, and plaster are common media that are pliable during their working periods. Because they respond directly to human touch, they may be manipulated by hand into the finished product, leaving behind the artist's fingerprints. These pliable materials may also be mechanically shaped to imitate other materials. Special tools such as wedging boards, wires, pounding blocks, spatulas, and other modeling tools (wood and metal) are used for additional control (fig. 1.46). Because most common pliable materials are not durable, they usually undergo further technical changes. For instance, clay may be fired in a kiln to harden it (fig. 1.47) or cast in a more permanent material like bronze. The selected techniques and materials are important, because both contribute their own special quality to the final form.

Addition

Addition involves the assembling of materials like metal, wood, and plastic with the aid of welding torches, soldering guns, staplers, bolts, screws, nails, rivets, glue, and even rope (fig. 1.48; see also fig. 1.50). Methods of addition may also involve relatively sophisticated technology and, in terms of nonfunctional sculpture, may take advantage of the most recent innovations in epoxies, resins, and welding techniques. To accommodate the physical distribution of weight, stress, and tension, many sculptures also employ the use of wire armatures and other supports onto which materials may be affixed.

Substitution

Substitution, or **casting,** is a technique for reproducing an original three-dimensional model in a new material through the use of a mold. Typically,

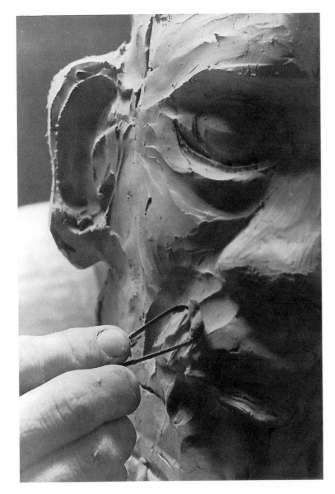

1.46 **Manipulation.** In this example of the manipulation technique, clay is removed with a loop tool. Clay may be applied to the surface with fingers, hands, or other tools. Photograph courtesy of Ronald Coleman.

1.47 David Cayton, *The Last Performance*, Ceramic, primitive firing, 18 in. (45.7 cm) high. This is an example of clay that has been fired in a primitive kiln. The heavy reduction firing has caused the clay surfaces to turn black. Courtesy of the artist.

1.48 **Welding.** In the additive process, pieces of material are attached to each other, and the form is gradually built up. Welded pieces, such as the one illustrated, are often, though not always, more open than other sculptural techniques. Sculptor John Mishler welding at his Old Bag Factory Studio, Goshen, IN. Photograph courtesy of John Mishler.

the purpose is to duplicate the original in a more permanent material. For example, a clay or wax model can be reproduced in a bronze, fiberglass, or cement cast (fig. 1.49). This may be accomplished through a variety of processes (sand casting, plaster casting, or lost-wax casting), using a variety of molds ranging from waste molds and piece molds to flexible molds. Substitution is the least creative or inventive of the technical methods because it is imitative; the creativity lies in the creation of the original, not in the casting process. Regardless of which process they employ, three-dimensional artists know that materials, tools, and techniques are not ends in themselves but necessary means for developing a three-dimensional work (see fig. 1.40).

1.49 **Substitution**. In this illustration of the substitution process, molten metal is poured into a sand mold that was made from a model. Photograph courtesy of Ronald Coleman.

AREAS OF THREE-DIMENSIONAL APPLICATION

Sculpture

The term **sculpture** has had varied meanings throughout history. The word derives from the Latin verb *sculpere,* which refers to the process of carving, cutting, or engraving. The ancient Greeks' definition of *sculpture* also included the modeling of such pliable materials as clay or wax to produce figures in **relief** (with shallow depth) or in the round (freestanding). With these materials, the Greeks developed an ideal standard of beautiful proportions for the sculptured human form (see fig. 2.43). Contemporary sculptors are no longer limited to carving and modeling because of the many new materials and techniques that have led to greater individual expression and artistic freedom. They now combine all types of materials and explore more open spatial relationships (fig. 1.50). Sculptors weld, bolt, rivet, glue, weave, sew, hammer, and stamp assorted materials

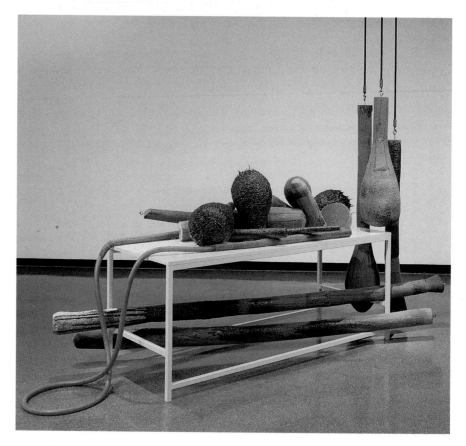

1.50 Joan Livingstone, *Seeped*, 1997–2000. Felt, stain, resin, pigment, and steel, 112 × 36 × 96 in. (284.5 × 91.4 × 243.8 cm). Modern sculpture exploits every conceivable material that suits the intentions of the artist. Courtesy of the artist and the SYBARIS Gallery, Royal Oak, MI. Photograph by Michael Tropea.

1.51 Arthur Dyson, *Lencioni Residence in Sanger, CA,* 1985. Architect Arthur Dyson designs structures that incorporate free-flowing curves and other architectural elements that integrate the residential structure with the natural environment. Courtesy of Arthur Dyson and Associates, Architects. Photo by Scot Zimmerman.

such as steel, plastic, wood, and fabric. Many images challenge the boundaries between media, as in the case of **assemblage,** where the lines between two- and three-dimensional art are crossed (see fig. 6.22).

Architecture

The architect Louis Sullivan made the oft-repeated remark that "form follows function." This concept of streamlining has influenced several decades of design, changing the appearance of architecture, tools, telephones, silverware, and even furniture. Sometimes this concept is misapplied. Streamlining a design is practical when applied to objects such as trains and cars, because it has the function of reducing wind resistance. However, while streamlining can eliminate irrelevancies from a design, it can also be taken to an undesirable extreme. The **Bauhaus** notion of the house as a "machine for living" helped architects rethink architectural principles, but it also introduced a cold and austere style against which there was an inevitable reaction.

As in sculpture, technological innovations and new building materials have also given architects greater artistic flexibility. Thanks to technical developments in steel and concrete, buildings can be large in scale without projecting massive, weighty forms. Vast interior spaces can be illuminated, and buildings can be completely enclosed or sheathed in glass, thanks to air-conditioning. Cantilevered forms can be extended into space. Freeform shapes can be created with the use of precast concrete. All these structural improvements have allowed architects to think and plan more freely. In many ways, architects today are "building sculptors," and their designs require a thorough grounding in artistic principles as well as an understanding of engineering concepts (fig. 1.51). Furthermore, computer-aided design has enabled architects to engineer

1.52 Frank Gehry, Walt Disney Concert Hall, Los Angeles, 2003. The unique design of Gehry's Walt Disney Concert Hall was only possible by using computer software during the design phase to model the building. The wildly expressionistic exterior soars, dips, and bends in a number of directions, calling to mind flowers, ships, wind, and, of course, music. © Anthony Arendt/Alamy.

1.53 Tom Muir, *Orchid Vase*, 1997. Sterling silver, 11½ × 4¾ in. (28.9 × 11.8 cm). In this beautiful presentation, organic and geometric shapes are delicately integrated. The geometric shapes of the base contrast with the flowing organic stem support which subtly balances the piece, draws the viewer's eye around the work, and highlights the presence of the orchids. Courtesy of the artist. Photograph by Tim Thayer.

highly complex and idiosyncratic buildings that could otherwise not be calculated. This may be seen in Frank Gehry's Guggenheim Museum in Bilbao, Spain, and the Walt Disney Concert Hall in Los Angeles (fig. 1.52).

Metalwork

Most of the changes in metalworking (jewelry, decorative and functional ware, etc.) have been in concept rather than technique. Traditional techniques (such as hand-welding, forging, soldering, riveting, and lost-wax or open casting) are still in use, although modern equipment has made procedures simpler and more convenient. To a large degree, cultural styles and tastes determine the designs of metalwork, and current trends in other mediums—sculpture, architecture, graphic arts, fashion—influence metalwork artists. Constant cross-fertilization occurs among the various areas of art, and metalwork is not immune to these influences. Indeed, the metalworker benefits from studying the concepts of both two- and three-dimensional art (fig. 1.53).

Glass Design

As in metalworking, glassworking makes use of modern equipment that simplifies traditional techniques. Although glassworks have been around for centuries, current glass design has evolved into a highly sophisticated art form. Many free-

1.54 Dale Chihuly, *Nepenthes Chandelier*, 2004. Blown glass, 111 × 68 × 54 in. This magnificent glass piece is most unusual and creative in its scale, coloring, shape definition, and ability to control an environmental setting. © 2011 Dale Chihuly.

form and figurative pieces have the look of contemporary sculpture. Colors augment design in a decorative, as well as an expressive, sense. Thus, the principles of art structure are integrated with the craft of the medium (fig. 1.54).

Ceramics

In recent years, as ceramic work has become, in many cases, less functional, the basic shape of the ceramic object has become more sculptural. The ceramist must be equally aware of three-dimensional considerations as well as the fundamentals of graphic art, because individual surfaces may be altered by incising, painting with colored slips, fuming, or glazing (fig. 1.55).

Fiberwork

Fiberwork has undergone a considerable revolution recently. Three-dimensional forms are becoming increasingly more common, particularly as traditional production of rugs and tapestries by hand has diminished. Woven objects now incorporate a vast array of materials into designs of considerable scale and bulk. Traditional as well as contemporary concepts of fiberwork require a fundamental understanding of both 2-D and 3-D concepts (fig. 1.56).

Product Design

Relative newcomers to the art scene, contemporary product designers create forms that are aesthetically pleasing and still fulfill their functional requirements. The same abstract quality of expressive beauty that is the foundation for a piece of sculpture underlies such functional forms as automobiles, televisions, cell phones, computers, industrial equipment, window and interior displays, and furniture (fig. 1.57). Designers of these 3-D products organize elements like shapes, textures, colors, and space

1.55 Paul Soldner, *Pedestal Piece (907)*, 1990. Thrown and altered clay with slips and low-temperature salt glaze, 27 × 30 × 11 in. (68.6 × 76.2 × 27.9 cm). The coloring resulting from the controlled firing process enhances the sculptural composition of the clay piece. Scripps College, Claremont, CA. Gift of Mr. and Mrs. Fred Marer, 92.1.154.

1.56 Eta Sadar Breznik, *Space*, 1995. Woven rayon, 157½ × 137⅞ × 137⅞ in. (400 × 350 × 350 cm). Contemporary textile design frequently goes beyond its largely two-dimensional traditions. Photograph by Boris Gaberšček, Ljubljana, Slovenia.

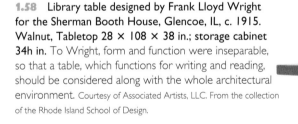

1.58 Library table designed by Frank Lloyd Wright for the Sherman Booth House, Glencoe, IL, c. 1915. Walnut, Tabletop 28 × 108 × 38 in.; storage cabinet 34h in. To Wright, form and function were inseparable, so that a table, which functions for writing and reading, should be considered along with the whole architectural environment. Courtesy of Associated Artists, LLC. From the collection of the Rhode Island School of Design.

according to the same principles of harmony, variety, balance, and proportion that are used in the fine arts.

Frank Lloyd Wright, the celebrated American architect, combined architectural engineering with art to shape his structures. The table he created for the Sherman Booth House (fig. 1.58) is a good example of this combination in product design. The sophisticated design and formal balance that Wright incorporated into this ordinary object can be seen in the highly selective repetitions, proportional relationships, and refinement of details.

The balance that exists between design, function, and expressive content varies from work to work. For instance,

1.59 David Delthony, *Lotus (rocking chair)*, 2002. Laminated plywood, 40 × 29 × 35 in. Delthony combines ergonomics and aesthetic appeal to create organic furniture that transcends function and becomes sculptural form. Courtesy of the artist.

COMBINING THE INGREDIENTS: A SUMMARY

In this chapter, we have mentioned some of the means by which an artist can achieve self-expression in a work. You have been introduced to the components, elements, and principles involved in making visual art. You have some idea of how these factors are analyzed and considered in an ongoing work, and you should be able to view your own work and the work of the "masters" with greater awareness. In the next few chapters, the fundamentals will be described in more detail, and their application will prove even more relevant to the creation of your own artwork.

Aside from satisfaction, one of the benefits gained by a better understanding of the visual arts is that it puts us in touch with some remarkably sensitive and perceptive people. Our lives are improved from contact, however indirect, with the creations of great geniuses. Einstein exposed relationships that have reshaped our view of the universe. Mozart created sounds that, in an abstract way, summed up the experiences and feelings of the human race. Though not always of this same magnitude, visual artists also expand our frames of reference, revealing new ways of seeing and responding to our surroundings. When we view artwork knowledgeably, we gain insight into the problems and solutions before us and can gather a new sense of direction for our own art.

when designing his rocking chair, David Delthony placed strong emphasis on expressing form without sacrificing comfort (fig. 1.59). At first glance, we are drawn in by the chair's dominant outer contour and its open shape. This unique piece of furniture resembles a freely expressed contemporary sculpture. Expressive form follows function in a new and creative way.

Form

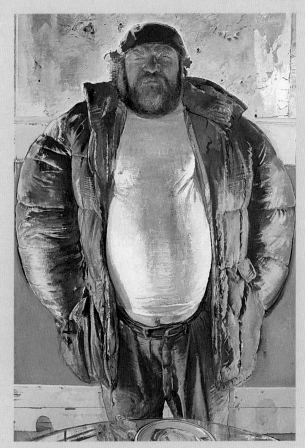

Jerome Paul Witkin, *Jeff Davies*, 1980. Oil on canvas, 6 × 4 ft. (1.83 × 1.22 m).
Palmer Museum of Art, Pennsylvania State University. Gift of the American Academy
and Institute of Arts and Letters. Hassam and Speicher Purchase Fund.

CHAPTER TWO

THE VOCABULARY OF
FORM

Form — 1. The total appearance, organization, or inventive arrangement of all the visual elements according to the principles that will develop unity in the artwork; composition. 2. In sculpture, form can also refer to the three-dimensional shape of the work.

accent

Any stress or emphasis given to the elements of a composition that brings them more attention than other features that surround or are close to them. Accent can be created by a brighter color, darker value, greater size, or any other means by which a difference is expressed.

allover pattern

A design that is formed through the systematic repetition of smaller designed units over an entire surface.

approximate symmetry

The use of similar imagery on either side of a central axis. The visual material on one side may resemble that on the other but is varied to prevent visual monotony.

asymmetry

"Without symmetry"; having unequal or non-corresponding parts. An example: a two-dimensional artwork that, without any necessarily visible or implied axis, displays an uneven distribution of parts throughout.

atectonic

Three-dimensional work characterized by considerable amounts of space; open, as opposed to massive (or tectonic), and often with extended appendages.

balance

A sense of equilibrium between areas of implied weight, attention, attraction, or moments of force; one of the principles of organization.

closure

A concept from Gestalt psychology in which the mind perceives an incomplete pattern or information to be a complete, unified whole; the artist provides minimum visual clues, and the observer brings them to final recognition.

composition

The arranging and/or structuring of all the art elements, according to the principles of organization, that achieves a unified whole. Often used interchangeably with the term **design.**

design

The organizing process or underlying plan on which artists base their total work. In a broader sense, *design* may be considered synonymous with the terms **form** and **composition.**

dominance

The principle of organization in which certain visual elements assume more importance than others within the same composition or design. Some features are emphasized, and others are subordinated. Dominance is often created by increased contrasts through the use of isolation, placement, direction, scale, and character.

economy

The distillation of the image to the basic essentials for clarity of presentation; one of the principles of organization.

form

1. The total appearance, organization, or inventive arrangement of all the visual elements according to the principles that will develop unity in the artwork; composition. 2. In sculpture, form can also refer to the three-dimensional shape of the work.

Gestalt, Gestalt psychology

A German word for "form"; an organized whole in experience. Around 1912, the Gestalt psychologists promoted the theory that explains psychological phenomena by their relationships to total forms, or *Gestalten,* rather than their parts. In other words, our reaction to the whole is greater than our reaction to its individual parts or characteristics, and our minds integrate and organize chaotic stimuli so that we see complete patterns and recognizable shapes.

golden mean, golden section

1. Golden mean—"perfect" harmonious proportions that avoid extremes; the moderation between extremes. 2. Golden section—a traditional proportional system for visual harmony expressed when a line or area is divided into two sections so that the smaller part is to the larger as the larger is to the whole. The ratio developed is 1:1.6180, or roughly 8:13.

harmony

A principle of organization in which parts of a composition are made to relate through commonality—repeated or shared characteristics, elements, or visual units. Harmony is the opposite of **variety.**

interpenetration

The positioning of planes, objects, or shapes so that they appear to pass through each other, which locks them together within a specified area of space.

kinetic (art)

From the Greek word *kinesis,* meaning "motion"; art that involves an element of random or mechanical movement.

mobile

A three-dimensional, moving sculpture.

moments of force

The direction and degree of energy implied by the art elements in specific compositional situations; amounts of visual thrust produced by such matters as dimension, placement, and accent.

motif

A designed unit or pattern that is repeated often enough in the total composition to make it a significant or dominant feature. Motif is similar to "theme" or "melody" in a musical composition.

movement

Eye travel directed by visual pathways in a work of art; one of the principles of organization. Movement is guided by harmonious connections, areas of variety, the placement of visual weights, areas of dominance, choices in proportions, spatial devices, and so on.

pattern

1. Any artistic design (sometimes serving as a model for imitation). 2. A repeating element and/or design that can produce a new set of characteristics or organization.

principles of organization

Concepts that guide the arrangement and integration of the elements in achieving a sense of visual order and overall visual unity. They are harmony, variety, balance, proportion, dominance, movement, and economy.

proportion

The comparative relationship of size between units or the parts of a whole. For example, the size of the Statue of Liberty's hand relates to the size of her head. (See **scale.**) Proportion is one of the principles of organization.

radial

Emanating from a center.

repetition

The use of the same visual effect—and/or similar visual effects—a number of times in the same composition. Repetition may produce the dominance of one visual idea, a feeling of harmonious relationship, an obviously planned pattern, or a rhythmic movement.

rhythm

A continuance, a flow, or a sense of movement achieved by the repetition of regulated visual units; the use of measured accents.

scale

The association of size relative to a constant standard or specific unit of measure related to human dimensions. For example, the Statue of Liberty's scale is apparent when she is seen next to an automobile. (See **proportion.**)

symmetry

The exact duplication of appearances in mirrorlike repetition on either side of a (usually imaginary) straight-lined central axis.

tectonic

The quality of simple massiveness; three-dimensional work lacking any significant extrusions or intrusions.

transparency

A visual quality in which a distant image or element can be seen through a nearer one.

variety

Differences achieved by opposing, contrasting, changing, elaborating, or diversifying elements in a composition to add individualism and interest. Variety is an important principle of organization; the opposite of **harmony.**

visual unity

A sense of visual oneness—an organization of the elements into a visual whole. Visual unity results from the appropriate ratio between harmony and variety (in conjunction with the other principles of organization).

FORM AND VISUAL ORDERING

We know from the last chapter that a work of art always has three essential components: subject, form, and content. These components may vary in degree of emphasis, but their interdependence is so great that no single one can exist without the others, nor can it be fully understood in isolation from the others. The entire artwork should be more important than any one of its components (fig. 2.1). In this chapter, we explore the component **form** in order to investigate

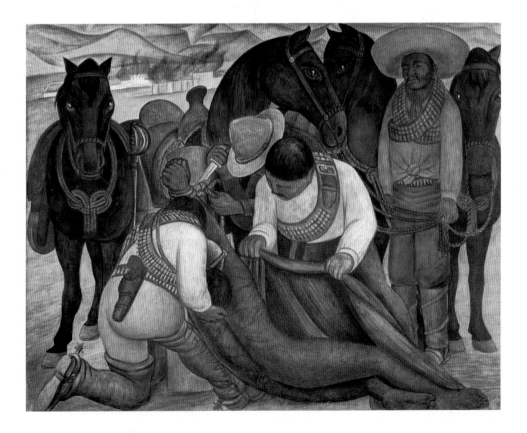

2.1 Diego Rivera, *The Liberation of the Peon,* 1931. Fresco, 6 ft. 2 in. × 7 ft. 11 in. (1.88 × 2.41 m). Here we see a political artist making use of appropriate and expected subject material. Without the effective use of form, however, the statement would be far less forceful. Philadelphia Museum of Art, PA. Gift of Mr. and Mrs. Herbert Cameron Morris. Philadelphia Museum of Art/Corbis Media. © 2011 Banco de México Diego Rivera and Frida Kahlo Museums Trust, Mexico, D.F./Artists Rights Society (ARS), New York.

2.4 Pauline Gagnon, *Secret Little Door*, 1992. Mixed media on canvas, 48 × 72 in. Repetition is introduced in this image by the theme of architectural surface and shape. But, by repeating those items in differing ways, the artist creates variety, and a potentially monotonous composition is greatly enlivened. Courtesy of the artist and Jain Marunouchi Gallery.

and hammering are all human activities that have a constantly repeated movement and beat. In visual art, that "beat" is a visual unit (an element, characteristic, or design). Consequently, the repetition of visual units will result in rhythm when strategically placed and, if necessary, suitably accented (fig. 2.6; see also fig. 9.1). These also serve to direct eye movement from one part to another.

Depending on how they are used, repetition and rhythm can confer excitement and harmony on an artwork. The rhythm of visual movement may be smoothly flowing, or it may be less regular and rather jerky. A gentle, smoothly flowing rhythm may instill a sense of peace, as in a quiet landscape (see fig. 2.63), while a very active rhythm, as in a stormy landscape, may feel rougher or suggest violent action (see fig. 4.3). The type of rhythm will depend on how regularly the units are repeated and how similar they seem. This includes the likeness of their character (e.g., rough versus smooth surface textures), their direction (horizontal versus diagonal lines), their type (regular versus irregular shapes), their value (dark versus light), their size (large versus small), and so forth. Repeating a series of extreme contrasts will create a strong beat, while subtler variations will create a quieter pulsing.

The creation of rhythm also relies on the repetition of pauses between repeating units. When a drummer plays a steady rock rhythm, the even beats are separated by spaces of silence. For a slower rhythm, the silent spaces in between the beats will be longer; for quicker rhythms, these pauses will be shorter. Furthermore, emphasizing certain beats (**accents**) can greatly change the feel of the rhythm. In the visual arts, rhythm is also created using "pauses," which are negative visual spaces. Unfortunately, artists often overlook these negative intervals—but the pauses are just as responsible for creating rhythm as the repeating element(s). The importance

resemble each other. In art, the relationships created by such resemblances give a work a degree of harmony. Additionally, carefully handled repetition can produce paths for an observer's eyes to travel. Repeated elements may also create small areas of emphasis that draw attention away from one location and to another. Conversely, the *least* related elements may achieve

subtle emphasis and draw attention to their dissimilarity.

Rhythm

One attribute of repetition is the ability to produce **rhythm.** Rhythm is a continuance, a flow, or a sense of movement that results from repeated beats, sometimes regular, sometimes more eccentric. Walking, running, wood chopping,

2.5   Paul Manes, *Eiso*, 1995. Oil on canvas, 60 × 66 in. (152.4 × 167.6 cm). The visual units in Manes's painting are ovoid saucer shapes. The repetition of this shape creates harmony. Variety develops out of differences in the shape's size and color. Courtesy of Paul Rogers/9W Gallery, New York, NY.

2.8   Bridge
curving edges
beat by changi

2.10 M. C. Escher, *Rippled Surface*, 1950. Although the subject is trees, the distinctive pictorial characteristic of this work is the pattern produced by the rippling reflections of the trees—a pattern that is developed, though not identically, in all areas of the work, creating unity.

2.11 Andy Warhol, *100 Cans*. 1962. Oil on canvas, framed: 74 × 54½ × 2¾ in. (187.96 × 138.43 × 6.98 cm); support: 72 × 52 in. (182.88 × 132.08 cm). Here, the basic pattern, or motif, is an image of a soup can. The allover pattern is constant, geometric, and static.

marks to more complex relationships of line, shape, value, texture, or color. They may be totally invented, suggested by natural objects, or inspired by man-made objects (fig. 2.9A and B). When the repetitions are irregular, the total organization may appear casual, as in the reflected-tree pattern and the soup-can pattern in figures 2.10 and 2.11. The composition can also be more controlled when more

regulated repetitions are used, as in the soup-can artwork of Pop artist Andy Warhol (see fig. 2.11). Here, the motif is easy to identify, and the allover pattern is quite regular and geometric.

However, systematic and regulated repetition does not always have to result in a predictable allover pattern. Quiltmakers often rotate their motifs and change the color, value,

texture, and placement to allow a new pattern of diagonals, squares, or diamonds to emerge from the allover pattern (fig. 2.12). In a similar manner, Chuck Close alters his repeating design unit (a diamond with circular internal shapes) by changing the color and value in each cell (motif block), and as a result, the allover pattern is a portrait of Paul III (fig. 2.13). Here,

2.6
Color
repeat
blue a

of spa
in the
(fig. 2
heads
Café (
rhythi
size or
fig. 1.7
(see fig
charge
esting
differe
ties th

2.12 Sandy Benjamin-Hannibal, *Potholders and Dervishes Plus,* 1996. Pieced cotton quilt, 108 × 96 in. Using traditional quilting techniques, Sandy Benjamin-Hannibal has repeated the basic design unit of a diamond. However, differences in color, value, and texture to the repeating motif create an allover pattern that is dynamic and vibrant. Purchase 2001 The Members' Fund and Emma Fantone Fund, 2001.32. Newark Museum, Newark, New Jersey/Art Resource, NY.

2.13 Chuck Close, *Paul III*, 1996. Oil on canvas, 102 × 84 in. (259.1 × 213.4 cm). A very interesting allover pattern emerges as a larger-than-life portrait. Because of the changing treatment in color and value, the allover pattern dominates the repeating motif, or design unit—a diamond with a series of internal circles. Image © The Cleveland Museum of Art, Mr. and Mrs. William H. Marlatt Fund, 1997.59. Photograph by Ellen Page Wilson. © Chuck Close. Courtesy of The Pace Gallery.

2.14 Don Jacot, *What Makes You Tick?* 2003. Oil on linen, 28 × 40 in. In this painting, clocks are a repeating theme, although the motif is really the *idea* of "clock" instead of one particular image that is identically duplicated numerous times. Notice the variety of style, size, and shape involved with the repetition. Courtesy of Louis K. Meisel Gallery.

it is quite obvious that the allover pattern (a face) would be impossible if the motif were repeated without alteration.

Many studio artists prefer an even subtler use of motif. Instead of repeating similar patterns, these artists repeat an *idea* or *theme*. For example, in Don Jacot's *What Makes You Tick?* the clocks are the repeating theme (fig. 2.14). The clocks are not repeated over and over exactly alike but rather are constantly changed and accented in differing ways. This is similar to the famous theme in Beethoven's Fifth Symphony ("ta-ta-ta-TUM"), which is repeated throughout the composition but constantly changes in terms of tempo, pitch, volume, and instrumentation.

Sometimes the theme (motif) develops for an artist over a long series of works. Consider thirty paintings by an artist, each of which deals with a cat in some different attitude or position.

In each individual painting, the cat would be the subject, but in considering the total series, the cat becomes the artist's repeating theme, idea, or motif. Two examples from a larger series may be seen in Impressionist artist Claude Monet's *Waterloo Bridge* paintings (see fig. 7.27) and the work of Piet Mondrian (see figs. 1.5–1.8).

Closure (Visual Grouping)

In the early part of the twentieth century, Max Wertheimer, a German **Gestalt** psychologist, began to investigate how the viewer sees form, pattern, or shape in terms of group relationships rather than as individual items. He discovered that several factors, such as nearness, size, and similarity in shape, help the mind relate objects visually. When the arrangement of visual units suggests that they are part of a larger pattern or shape, people mentally "fill in" missing gaps and tend to see incomplete patterns as complete or uni-

fied wholes. We will be referring to this mental process as **closure**.

Closure occurs when an artist provides a minimum of information or visual clues and the observer mentally completes the pattern. The following examples demonstrate this concept. In figure 2.15A, some viewers will see an *X* formed by the black circles, and others will see a + created by the blue squares. In figure 2.15B, the mind connects those objects that help us see the configuration of an arrow. The four triangles with concave hypotenuses in figure 2.15C seem to create a complete circle, but remove some triangles or move them out of alignment and the circle becomes harder to "see" or is destroyed completely. (These four shapes also demonstrate how negative areas can become "positive" shapes: when the positive black shapes appear to connect into a circle in figure 2.15C, the negative central area becomes important, and we see the central area as a positive circle.) However, the same small shapes that created the circle can be rearranged to suggest a serpentine line instead (figure 2.15D).

With the concept of closure, the whole (the collective pattern or organization) is greater than its individual parts. In practice, this means that when images are evenly spaced across a pictorial field, they must be experienced individually—such as the circles, rectangles, and triangles in figure 2.16A. But as they are moved closer together and the negative spaces are reduced, it becomes easier to see a developing circular shape in the upper half and a horizontal line in the lower half (fig. 2.16B). At this stage, the growing awareness of the larger groupings becomes more important than any one individual triangle, circle, or rectangle. As the individual shapes are moved closer, they appear to "bond" together at some point *before* they physically touch each other (fig. 2.16C). How close do the objects have to come before they optically link? Recognition of the

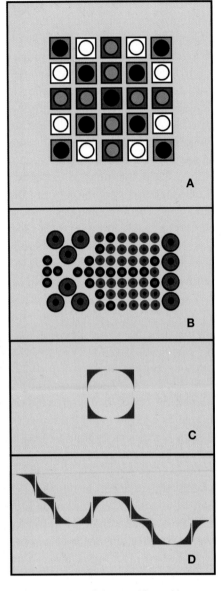

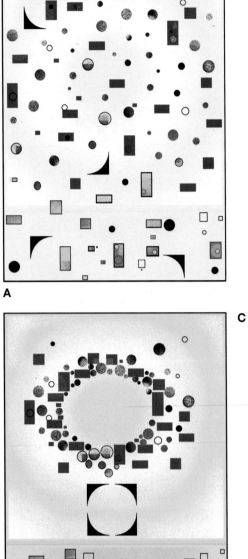

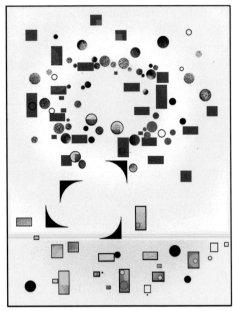

A

B

C

2.15 **Examples of closure.** The total configuration is more important than the individual components, as our minds "see" incomplete patterns as complete wholes. (A) The similar shapes are mentally connected to see an X or a + instead of small circles and squares. (B) The similar shapes optically join to form an arrow. (C) The shapes seem to form a circle within a square. (D) The shapes optically connect into a serpentine object.

2.16 (A) Individual shapes without any implied organization. (B) Individual shapes moving closer together and beginning to establish a visual grouping. (C) Shapes close together, with closure suggesting patterns of an oval, a circle, and a horizontal bar.

visual connection is a matter of experience that improves with practice but requires an awareness of the adjusted negative space. (Try to discover how the mind fills in the missing information.

Determine at what point shapes begin to join visually. Can a third shape be made to join a grouping of two? Is more or less space needed between the units to do so? Try to determine what

spacing creates the most tension between the units and if any particular spacing becomes too static.)

In the final image (fig. 2.16C), all the various shapes have a harmonious relationship because of their spacing. The individual circles, rectangles, and triangles have become related, although variations in the negative intervals between shapes allow the new groupings to appear dense in one location while fading away in another. The sense of harmony may be further enhanced by similarity in color, surface texture, shapes, direction, linear quality, and the like. Shapes also visually join more easily wherever their edges are made to align.

Admittedly, with closure many factors are at work, including proximity and similarity. For Wertheimer, this visual ordering helped explain how artists organize structure and create pattern in their work.

Visual Linking

While closure unifies shapes that share an implied group relationship, bringing these elements so close together that they physically touch suggests other ways of unifying a composition. When this occurs, the shared space itself becomes the cohesive factor. We will study the concept as it applies to shared edges, overlapping, transparency, and interpenetration.

Shared Edges

Shapes that share a common edge (contacting, touching, or abutting) are often united because the shared edge imposes common spatial relationships that help draw them together. For example, shapes with shared edges tend to be on the same limited spatial plane or share a similar spatial or pictorial depth. The Cubists and other recent artists like Gunther Gerzso (fig. 2.17, see also fig. T.51) have used this idea quite successfully. Shapes of the same size and related color or value will further unite compositions dealing with flat or limited space.

This harmonizing technique, however, can somewhat restrict the illusion of three-dimensional images. When

2.17 Gunther Gerzso, *Personage in Red and Blue*, 1964. Oil on fabric, 39⅜ × 28¾ in. (100.33 × 73 cm). In this painting, shapes are united by shared edges as well as similar color and textural development. Though the sense of space is shallow, it is heightened by the contrast of value. Courtesy of the Gene C. Gerzso 1999 Trust.

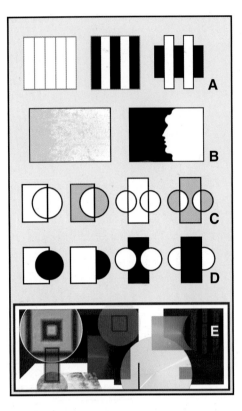

connected shapes are of the same size and value, they limit the ability to create spatial references (fig. 2.18A, *left*). Changing the value makes them more distinct, but their spatial depths become more ambiguous—sometimes advancing, sometimes receding (fig. 2.18A, *center*). However, altering both the value and size of the connected shapes begins to establish a spatial reference in which the shapes more easily pass behind or in front of each other (fig. 2.18A, *right*). Additional variations in shading also serve to enhance the illusion of depth, however shallow (see fig. 2.17). (When connected shapes no longer share the same depth, harmony can be further established, if needed, through some other method—such as similar use of texture or color.)

Although sharing spatial relationships will pull areas of a composition together, there may be additional complications with using shared edges. When shapes with a common border share a similar value level or color, the dividing edge where they merge is often obscured—visually they become one new shape (fig. 2.18B, *left*). In addition, connected shapes seem to retain their individual character when the common dividing edge is rather nondescript, but when the edge begins to suggest something recognizable, the suggested image becomes a positive shape, and a specific spatial reference is created that forces the remaining shape to recede as a negative area (fig. 2.18B, *right*). Differences in value or texture further exacerbate the situation. M. C. Escher

2.18 (A) Denied or implied spatial references involving *shared edges*. (B) Dissolved and altered spatial references involving *shared edges*. (C) Little spatial reference created by *overlapping shapes*. (D) Greater spatial reference created by *overlapping shapes*. (E) Shapes related by *transparency*.

2.19 M. C. Escher, *Day and Night*, 1938. Woodcut in two colors, 15½ × 26¾ in. (39.3 × 67.9 cm). In this print, Escher effectively incorporates shapes with shared edges, structured ambiguity, and stable figure/ground relationships in the transition from light to dark. His use of variety (separation and elaboration) helps make the light and dark ducks stand out as figures against the opposite-value background.

2.20 Jerry Uelsmann, *Untitled (rowboat, ocean, and clouds in cupped hands)*, 1996. Gelatin silver print, 16 × 20 in. Overlapping images share the same space in this work, commenting on the relationship between humans and nature. Despite the digital revolution, Uelsmann still prefers to create images like this one using analogue techniques in a darkroom. *Courtesy of Jerry N. Uelsmann.*

explored this phenomenon, using it to his advantage when he made patterns of dark ducks fly through patterns of light ducks (fig. 2.19). As the ducks fly farther away from the central part of the image, the detail becomes more and more distinct, whereas the "duck" shapes toward the middle take on the imagery of the landscape.

Overlapping

With overlapping, the areas involved are also drawn together by a common relationship, and the shared item is a bit more involved than a simple edge; it becomes a shared area. As long as the colors, values, and textures are the same or related, the overlapping tends to unite the areas involved (fig. 2.18C). However, the space defined may be shallow and rather ambiguous—one time the circle is seen on top; the next time the square is seen on top. The Futurists

often achieved this effect by overlapping multiple views of the same object (see fig. 9.9).

Overlapping does not always mean limited space or cohesive relationships. A difference in treatment may cause visual separation of the two shapes and deeper spatial references, in which the overlapped object is seen as the receding shape (fig. 2.18D). Color and value choices may exaggerate or minimize the spatial effect.

In an artistic context, independent symbolic information can not only overlap but even occupy the same shared physical space. For example, in Jerry Uelsmann's *Untitled (rowboat, ocean, and clouds in cupped hands)*, very different images are brought together through overlap (fig. 2.20). Using darkroom techniques, Uelsmann combines human and natural subjects to create a unique visual experience.

Transparency

An artist can also add harmony to images that occur in the same area through the use of **transparency** (see fig. 2.18E; see also figs. 1.56 and 8.9). When a shape or image is seen through another, harmony is created through the shared area itself, the layers of space they both pass through, and the surface treatment of all the images (highlights, shading, color, texture). Like simple overlapping, this technique tends to limit visual depth but still serves as another harmonious device.

Interpenetration

When several images not only share the same area but also appear to pass through each other, they are brought into a harmonious relationship not only by the common location but also by the physical depth of the space in which they all appear (see figs. 8.10 and 8.11).

2.21 Clouret Bouchel, *Passing Through,* 2001. Digital imagery, 7 × 10½ in. (17.8 × 26.7 cm). This is an example of interpenetration, with lines, shapes, and planes passing through one another. Courtesy of the artist.

Whether shallow or deep, illusionistic or stylized, the space itself pulls the various images into a visual harmony. Notice that in figure 2.21 there are two series of shapes. Some seem to plunge toward the left end and the rest toward the right end of the composition. Even though the two sets of planes are treated in very different textures and colors, the sharing of the internal space created by the **interpenetration** of shapes helps unify this work.

Linking through Extensions (Implied and Subjective Edges/Lines/Shapes)

A variety of dissimilar images and shapes can be made to relate by being visually linked through the use of *extensions*. Like the invisible signals that connect our cell phones to towers and then to each other, the extensions in a composition help the artist organize and bring all parts of that structure into a harmonious relationship.

While we have seen harmony achieved through shared edges, overlapping shapes, transparency of surface, or forms passing through each other, the related items are relatively close to each other. However, the concept of extensions—implied edges, lines, or shapes—provides the artist with a system of visual alignment that can relate shapes much farther apart from each other.

By simply extending the edge of a shape across the composition, the artist can establish new objects, images, or shapes in locations some distance away. Placing new shapes along the implied extended edge links distant shapes, thereby harmonizing the areas. Artists often use such alignment to integrate an entire composition and create space by implied tension.

Extensions reveal "hidden" relationships. They harmonize by setting up related directional forces, creating movement, and repeating predictable intervals between units. The directional impulse of these invisible, implied lines or shape edges suggests—sometimes subconsciously—an expectation that something will be discovered in a new area and pulls the eye toward this new location. These impulses integrate a work as they wind through the composition along the contours of information (fig. 2.22A and B).

2.22A Johannes Vermeer, *Diana and the Nymphs,* c. 1655–56. Oil on canvas, 33½ × 41 in. (97.8 × 104.6 cm). Here, Vermeer uses extended edges to interlock the images, find the location for new forms, relate shapes, and create directional movement across the painting. Royal Cabinet of Paintings, Mauritshuis. The Hague, Netherlands, Scala/Art Resource.

2.22B This overlay shows some of the extended edges with solid lines of various weights and their extensions by dots and dashes. Notice how the implied direction is often interrupted or disguised by subtle changes.

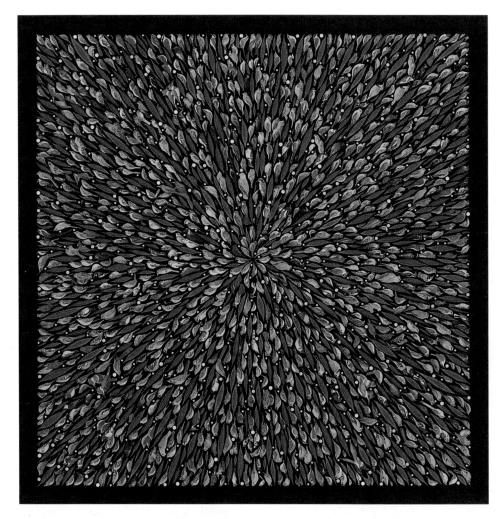

2.36 Fred Tomaselli, *Bird Blast,* 1997. Pills, hemp leaves, photocollage, acrylic, resin on wood panel, 60 × 60 in. (152.4 × 152.4 cm). With radial balance, there is frequently a divergence from some (usually central) source. Here, too, the linear development of the red leaves and the birds seems to explode from the center of the composition. Gift of Douglas S. Cramer. The Museum of Modern Art, New York, NY. U.S.A. Digital image © The Museum of Modern Art/Licensed by SCALA/Art Resource, NY.

2.37 Marc Chagall, *I and the Village,* 1911. Oil on canvas, 6 ft. 3⅝ in. × 4 ft. 11⅝ in. (1.92 × 1.51 m). The fairy-tale world of the imagination is found in this example by Chagall, an artist who evades fixed classification. Recent—for the time—technological concepts (X-rays and flight) are reflected in the freely interpreted transparent objects and in the disregard for gravity. © 2011 Artists Rights Society (ARS), New York/ADAGP, Paris. The Museum of Modern Art, New York, NY. Mrs. Simon Guggenheim Fund. Digital image © The Museum of Modern Art/Licensed by SCALA/Art Resource, NY.

Asymmetrical Balance (Informal/Occult Balance)

Balance created through **asymmetry** achieves equilibrium of the elements that is "felt" or implied among all parts of the work. Asymmetry is also sometimes referred to as an *informal* or *occult* balance because it is hidden, somewhat mysterious, and intended to be experienced across the entire composition (figs. 2.38 and 2.39; see also figs. 2.32 and 8.42).

As the name suggests, asymmetry does not involve a central axis or any degree of symmetry but rather balances forces horizontally, vertically, and diagonally in all directions. Visual units that have very different moments of force (degrees of emphasis) may be made to balance each other depending on the position of the units. The visual center of balance may thus be in any location. For example, a "felt" balance might be achieved between a small area of strong color and a large empty space. The placement of that colored area would depend on its qualities such as size, shape, and so forth, as well as the size of the negative area around it. There are no rules for achieving asymmetrical balance. If, however, the artist can establish the opposing forces and their tensions so that they seem to balance each other within a total work, the result will be vital, dynamic, and expressive.

As an artist works on an image, the sense of compositional balance changes each time an element is added, subtracted, or altered—one adjustment may require subsequent modification in other areas. Asymmetrical artwork

A

B

2.47 Georges Seurat, *Circus Sideshow (La Parade),* 1887–88. Oil on canvas, 39¼ × 59 in. (99.7 × 149.9 cm). (B) When this Seurat painting is divided by a diagonal from upper left to lower right (large dashes), it crosses the large square where a golden rectangle would be subdivided by a heavy horizontal line. Smaller golden rectangles are created in the vertical rectangle on the right. These small rectangles may be further divided by intersecting diagonals. This could continue indefinitely. In addition, when another large square is established on the right side of the picture (small dotted lines) and a diagonal is drawn from lower left to upper right, the left side may be broken down into smaller golden rectangles that mirror those on the right side of the diagram. Notice how Seurat has used these lines and their intersections for the strategic placement of figures and imagery. The Metropolitan Museum of Art, Bequest of Stephen C. Clark, 1960. (61.101.17) Photograph © The Metropolitan Museum of Art. Art Resource, NY.

2.48 Claes Oldenburg and Coosje van Bruggen, *Saw, Sawing*, 1996. Steel, epoxy resin, fiber-reinforced plastic, urethane and polyvinylchloride foams, painted with polyester gelcoat, 50 ft. 8 in. × 4 ft. 9 in. × 40 ft. (15.4 × 1.5 × 12.2 m). This clearly recognizable object far surpasses the scale expected of it. Courtesy Oldenburg van Bruggen Studio. Photography by Spatial Design Consultants Co., Ltd., Yokohama.

2.49 Jerome Paul Witkin, *Jeff Davies*, 1980. Oil on canvas, 6 × 4 ft. (1.83 × 1.22 m). If there was ever a painting in which one subject dominated the work, this must be it. Most artworks do not need this degree of dominance, but Witkin evidently wanted a forceful presence—and he got it. Palmer Museum of Art, Pennsylvania State University. Gift of the American Academy and Institute of Arts and Letters. Hassam and Speicher Purchase Fund.

imposing man, is presented with a bulky torso in simple, light values, surrounded by the darker forms of the head, arms, jacket, and pants. The artist has positioned the white torso in the center of the composition for primary attention and has sized the figure's image so that it seems to burst the limits of the painting's format. Witkin's exaggerated enlargement and relative scaling came from his perceptions of the subject, resulting in an overpowering portrait.

Another way artists have used inordinate proportion or scaling is to indicate rank, status, or importance of religious, political, military, and social personages. *Hierarchical scaling* is a term used to describe this system, whereby figures of greatest importance are made relatively larger to denote their status. In the painting *Madonna of Mercy*, Piero della Francesca doubled the size of his Madonna figure in order to elevate her to a lofty object of reverence (fig. 2.50). The proportions in this painting, and others like it, are subjective in their intent rather than representational (fig. 2.51).

The physical size of the work can also be utilized for expressive purposes. The artist Chuck Close tends to overwhelm

us with paintings of enormous human heads (fig. 2.52). Resulting from their overall size—the portraits range from five to eight feet in height—there is a proportional enlargement of facial details, such as hairs and skin pores. The view of the artist in his studio illustrates the overpowering scale of these enlargements (see fig. 2.13). The heads, at first heroic, become intimidating and, in some respects, even frightening.

Dominance

While developing an image, an artist strives for interest by creating differences that emphasize the degrees of importance of its various parts. These differences result from compositional considerations within the medium—some features are emphasized, and others are subordinated. This creates both primary focal points and secondary areas of interest that help move the eye around the work.

Areas become dominant when they are emphasized by contrasts that make them stand out from the rest. Contrast draws attention like the spotlight in a dramatic production or crescendo in a musical piece. In general, the greater the contrast, the greater the emphasis and the more dominant an area becomes.

The following methods of emphasis can be used to achieve **dominance**: (1) *isolation*—a separation of one part from others; (2) *placement*—"center stage" is most often used, but another

2.50 Piero della Francesca, *Madonna of Mercy* (center panel of triptych), 1445–55. Oil and tempera on wood, height about 4 ft. 9 in. (1.44 m). The figure of Mary extends her arms to make a shelter of her cape for the smaller figures at her feet. The positioning of the worshipful figures who surround the central figure helps give a sense of depth to the scene. The artist's use of hierarchical scaling also strengthens the feeling of the maternal and merciful power of the Madonna. Italian Civic Museum, Sansepolcro, Italy/SuperStock, Inc.

2.51 Nancy Spero, *Artemis, Acrobats, Divas and Dancers*, 1999–2000. Glass and ceramic mosaic. Comparing the *Madonna of Mercy* (fig. 2.50) from 1445–55 with the female figure in Spero's *Artemis, Acrobats, Divas and Dancers* reveals a variety of ways to impart dominance. Even though the *Madonna* was made for a sacred space while Spero's *Artemis* resides in the profane space of a New York City subway stop, both use centrality to establish dominance. Francesca's *Madonna* also uses scale relationships within the painting to establish her importance. Staring directly at the viewer, Artemis spreads her arms in a gesture of independence, using her cape as an extension of her body. Gazing downward, the Madonna also spreads her arms but to envelop her dependents in a gesture of protection, making her cloak a refuge. While different, each pose expresses dominance. Public commission for MTA Arts for Transit, New York, NY. © Nancy Spero. Courtesy Galerie Lelong, New York.

2.52 Chuck Close working on *John*, 1992. Oil on canvas, 100 × 84 in. The colossal size of the head in Close's painting requires an examination and interpretation of every textural and topographical feature of the model's face. Courtesy of PaceWildenstein. Photograph by Bill Jacobson.

2.53 Milton Glaser, *Dylan Poster*, 1966. Offset lithograph, 33 × 22 in. (83.8 × 55.8 cm). Glaser created an area of dominance in this poster through the use of size and color. The psychedelic hair becomes the focal point, contrasting with the black silhouette. Furthermore, the swirling rhythms of the hair create a pattern that mirrors Bob Dylan's music. © Milton Glaser, Inc.

position can be dominant, depending on the surroundings; (3) *direction*—a movement that draws focus; (4) *scale or proportion*—larger sizes normally dominate, but unusual scale or proportion also attracts attention; (5) *character*—a significant difference in general appearance is striking (such as a change in line quality). These methods of dominance can be enhanced by exaggerating contrast in the various elements—color, value, texture, and so forth.

Artwork that neglects varying degrees of dominance seems to imply that everything is of equal importance, resulting in a confusing image that gives the viewer no direction and fails to communicate. This does not mean that areas of secondary dominance are insignificant to an overall composition. Those subordinate areas are actually

just as vital, as they produce the background against which the dominant parts are emphasized.

Artists have two important considerations when dealing with dominance. First, they must see that each part has the necessary degree of importance; and second, they must incorporate these parts, with their varying degrees of importance, into the balance of the entire work. In doing this, artists often find that they must combine different methods to achieve dominance. One significant area might derive impor-

tance from its change in value, whereas another might rely on its busy or exciting shape (figs. 2.53, 2.54, and 2.55).

Movement

Many observers do not realize that in looking at artwork, they are being "taken on a tour." The tour director is, of course, the artist, who makes the eye travel through visual pathways and settle on areas of rest. The roadways leading to the rest stops have certain speed limits established by the artist,

2.54 Poteet Victory, *Symbols of Manifest Destiny*, 1999. Oil and mixed media on canvas, 60 × 40 in. (152.4 × 101.6 cm). In this work, the yellow-orange striped rectangle becomes dominant because of the contrast of light against dark and warm color against cool color. Courtesy of the artist.

and the rest stops are of a predetermined duration.

The way an artwork dictates these visual pathways is called **movement.** These paths are, in fact, transitions between optical units, and the time required to negotiate them depends on the amount of harmony and variety applied to each. The eye movements dictated by these transitions are produced by the direction of lines, shapes, and shape edges (or contours) that seem to relate and connect to one another. The lines, shapes, and shape contours are generally pointed at one another or in the same general direction. They may be touching but are normally interrupted by gaps over which the eyes skip as they move about. Sometimes "leaps" are necessary, requiring strong directional thrusts and attractions.

The optical units that attract our attention contain vital information. In works that lack multiple areas of great emphasis, a single figure may be the dominant unit, as in the *Mona Lisa* (see fig. 5.12). Although extreme eye movement is not required throughout this composition, secondary material within the image may be of considerable interest and used to create its own pattern of movement. In other works, there may be several units of great interest that are widely separated, and it thus becomes critical that the observer's vision be directed to them. There is usually some hierarchy in these units,

2.55 Giambattista Tiepolo, *Madonna of Mt. Carmel and the Souls in Purgatory*, c. 1720. Oil on canvas, 82⅔ × 256 in. (210 × 650 cm). The movement weaves its way through this work because the lighting gives the figures dominance. © SCALA/Ministero per i Beni e le Attivita culturali/Art Resource, New York.

with some calling for more attention than others. Their degree of dominance usually determines the amount of time spent at each location.

The written word is read from side to side, but a visual image, whether two-dimensional or three-dimensional, can be read in any direction. The movement of the viewer's eyes is dictated by the artist, who must ensure that all areas are exploited with no static or uninteresting parts. Carefully handled repetition and subtle variations entice eye movement from one part of the composition to another. Areas of related values or colors may appear to move across a composition as a value pattern (fig. 2.56), while the pauses and beats of visual rhythms can create subtle changes that draw the eye along. By varying the negative space between individual shapes, movement can occur where groupings appear dense in one location and fade away in another. The movement should be self-renewing, constantly drawing the eye back into the work.

Artists can not only control eye movement across the surface of the composition but also direct movement into the depth of the pictorial space. Historically, the illusion of spatial positioning has been based in linear perspective. Perspective is effective but not necessary. There is also "intuitive" space, which can suggest depth by using certain artistic devices—for example, overlapping, transparency, or a series of successively smaller objects that recede into the distance (see Chapter 8).

Some art, particularly kinetic (moving) sculpture, involves the physical movement of the work itself. As parts of the sculpture move about, the viewer stays to watch their changing relationships—this begins to incorporate the element of time into its movement (see Chapter 9, "Time and Motion"). However, most sculpture and picture surfaces are physically static, and

2.56 Lorraine Shemesh, *Propeller*, 2002. Oil on canvas, 67½ × 71½ in. Shemesh controls the movement through this painting with an interesting value pattern of light and dark colors. This movement is enhanced by an undulating repetition of shapes, the intersecting of curved lines, and the visual rhythms and patterns that they create. Private collection, courtesy Allan Stone Gallery, New York City.

movement must be developed through the artist's configuration of compositional parts.

Economy

As a work develops, the artist may realize that the solutions to various compositional problems are resulting in unnecessary complexity. This situation is frequently characterized by broad aspects of the work deteriorating into fragmentation, and it commonly results from the artist's working on one segment of the composition at a time. Although this may be a

necessary phase in developing the work, such isolated solutions may result in a lack of visual unity in the overall composition.

Sometimes order may be restored by returning to essentials, eliminating elaborate details, and relating the particulars to the whole. This sacrifice is not easily made or accepted because, in returning to essentials, interesting discoveries and effects must often be sacrificed for legibility and a more direct expression. However, by applying the principle of economy, the work may regain a sense of unity.

Employing the principle of **economy** means composing with efficiency—expressing an idea as simply and directly as possible with no arbitrary or excessive use of the elements (fig. 2.57). Economy has no rules but rather must be an outgrowth of the artist's instincts. If something works with respect to the whole, it is kept; if disruptive, it may be reworked or rejected.

Economy is sometimes associated with the term *abstraction*. Abstraction (simplification and rearrangement) implies an active process of selecting the essentials that strengthen both the conceptual and organizational aspects of the artwork. In some measure, the artistic style dictates the kind of abstraction, though all art requires abstraction to some degree.

Although the early Modernists Pablo Picasso and Henri Matisse were among those most influential in the trend toward economical abstraction, economy is easy to detect in many contemporary art styles (fig. 2.58; see also figs. 4.1 and T.51). The hard-edged works of Ellsworth Kelly, the "field" paintings of Barnett Newman and Morris Louis, and the analogous color canvases of Ad Reinhardt all clearly feature economy (fig. 2.59; see also figs.

2.59   Barnett Newman, *Covenant,* 1949. Oil on canvas, 3 ft. 11¾ in. × 4 ft. 11⅝ in. (1.21 × 1.51 m). This example is characteristic of Newman, an early Color Field painter. Such works generally feature carefully placed stripes superimposed on a flat color. Hirshhorn Museum and Sculpture Garden, Smithsonian Institute, Washington, DC. Gift of Joseph H. Hirshhorn, 1972. Photograph by Lee Stalsworth. © 2011 Barnett Newman Foundation/Artists Rights Society (ARS), New York.

7.15 and T.78). The absence of elaboration results in a very direct statement.

In economizing, one runs the risk of being monotonous. Sometimes embellishments must be preserved or added to avoid this pitfall. But if the result is greater clarity, the risk (and the work) may be well worth it.

SPACE: RESULT OF ELEMENTS AND PRINCIPLES

The artist is always concerned about space as it evolves in an artwork. Some people regard space as an element (such as when working with sculpture), but for those working in a two-dimensional medium, it results as the elements are put into action and altered by the various principles of organization. In this section, we will only briefly cover some general aspects of spatial organization; Chapter 8 will explain in greater detail the different types of space and what the artist must do to achieve them.

In transferring our three-dimensional world to the canvas, the painter faces problems that have been dealt with in various ways in different historical periods. If the illusion of spatial phenomena is to be represented in the artwork, the artist must use the art elements to produce the effect sought. Quite often the artist uses the frame as a window into the space, terminating at some point or continuing to infinity. Such space is called *three-dimensional* or *plastic* because all of this seems to be condensed into the picture plane. These surfaces have their limits, but the illusion of depth gives a further dimension—a sense that actual 3-D space is involved. Artists *not* interested in developing the illusion of volume and depth may choose to work with a flat or shallow two-dimensional interpretation known as *decorative space.*

When considering space in a work, an artist usually looks for consistency of relationships. Nothing can throw an artwork so "out of kilter" as a jumbled spatial order. An artist who begins with one kind of space, say, a flat two-dimensional representation of a figure, should continue to develop 2-D concepts throughout the piece and in the succeeding stages of the artwork. Consistency contributes immeasurably to visual unity.

THREE-DIMENSIONAL FORM AND THE PRINCIPLES OF ORGANIZATION

The organizational principles used in three-dimensional art are the same as those used in two-dimensional art. However, three-dimensional forms, with their unique spatial properties, call for somewhat different applications of the principles.

Three-dimensional artists deal with forms that have multiple views (fig. 2.60). Composing is more complex. What might be a satisfactory solution for an arrangement with one view might be only a partial answer in a work seen from many different positions. Adjustments of adjacent areas must be intriguing enough to urge the viewer to move around the work, but changes to one area should not ruin the successful results of another. A series of calculated adjustments are required to totally unify a piece.

Compositionally, a three-dimensional work may be **tectonic** (closed, massive, and simple), with few and limited projections, as in figure 2.61, or **atectonic** (open, to a large degree), with frequent extensive penetrations and thin projections, as in figure 2.62. Both tectonic and atectonic arrangements can be found in nearly all 3-D art, and each of these arrangements can be used individually to achieve different expressive and spatial effects.

Harmony and Variety

We know that harmony and variety are indispensable concerns in the creation of two-dimensional artworks. Their careful consideration is equally

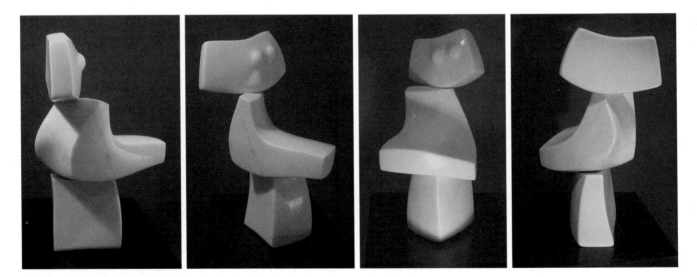

2.60   Shawn Morin, *Treasure Mountain Dove*, 2003. Colorado yule marble, 26 × 17 × 15 in. This sculpture encourages the viewer to move around the work. Relationships of shape and form are constantly changing with each new position. The change in the appearance from one view to the next represents the sculptor's challenge during creation—to make adjustments to the components in one view without destroying the structure of the next. Photos courtesy of the artist.

2.62 Kenneth Snelson, *Dragon*, 2000–3. Stainless steel, 30.5 × 31 × 12 ft. (9.3 × 9.5 × 3.65 m). Kenneth Snelson has developed sculptures that are "open," or atectonic. Based on technical principles related to the geometry of atoms, helixes, and weaving, his works are often referred to as "floating compression" or "tensegrity" installations. This work, *Dragon*, uses a steel cable to suspend individual steel tubes in the air with only minimal ground support. Courtesy of the artist. Photo © Jan Cook.

2.61 James DeWoody, *Big Egypt,* 1985. Black oxidized steel, 72 × 30 × 30 in. (182.9 × 76.2 × 76.2 cm). In this example of a tectonic arrangement, James DeWoody has cut planes that project in and out of his surfaces without penetrating voids or opening spaces. This is sometimes referred to as "closed" composition. Courtesy of the Arthur Roger Gallery, New Orleans, LA.

as important in 3-D works, although applying them is more complex due to the added dimension of depth. One must keep in mind that to fully view a three-dimensional work such as sculpture, the viewer must circumnavigate the work, which has an almost infinite number of viewpoints. The multiple viewing angles of a 3-D work produce an inherent degree of variety, and this must be balanced with harmony for the benefit of the work's totality.

Extensions are an important consideration in producing harmony and in leading the viewer around a sculpture. These subjective edges, lines, and shapes suggest directions around the work in the same way extensions unify 2-D work. They imply connections with other such lines and shapes, thus creating a continuous movement encircling the work. The *repetition* of elements—line, shape, color, value, and texture—helps establish harmony and adds to the sense of visual flow (fig. 2.63).

The sculptor can calculate this movement to give a sense of rhythm that is either agitated or comparatively calm. Predictable rhythm incorporates proportional transitions that give flow to a work (fig. 2.64). If the sculptor considers some areas as significant, *closure*—employing the proximity of certain shapes or lines—may be used to draw attention to those passages. There are instances where the tension between close forms is emphasized and the work harmonized by the

2.63 John Mishler, *Wind Seeker,* Stainless steel, paint, and bearings, 14 × 5 × 6 ft. (4.3 × 1.5 × 1.8 m). The repetition of the grasslike shapes, their graceful curves, and the shared markings of the polished surfaces help create harmony in this sculpture. In addition, the upward thrust and implied connection of the extended shape edges add to the unity and create visual movement within the piece. Commissioned for the Wolf Ranch Mall, Georgetown, TX. Courtesy of John Mishler.

2.64 Sebastian, *Variación Nuevo Mexico,* 1989. Painted steel, 27 × 24 × 24 ft. The rhythmical repetition of the stepping planes in Sebastian's sculpture creates an exciting, flowing movement. Photograph by Jonathan A. Myers, 2008. Funded by the City of Albuquerque, 1% for Art Program and The Albuquerque Museum, 1987 General Obligation Bonds. In commemoration of the Sister City relationship between Albuquerque and Chihuahua, Mexico.

application of *interpenetration,* with one form passing through another. These areas, however, should not imprison a viewer. An observer should always feel free to move continuously about the work.

Some sculptors make use of transparent materials, such as glass (fig. 2.65), rather than opaque media. The superimposition of such material creates genuine *transparency.* This can suggest space, albeit usually in a limited way. Architects, who are increasingly sculptural in their visions,

sometimes make use of *overlapping* to produce harmony among the sections of their building structures. Additionally, in sculpture, there are instances of *interpenetration,* notably in large metal pieces or works with reflective surfaces.

Variety, as in 2-D works, is achieved by increasing the dissimilarities between areas or by reducing or reversing the means by which harmony is produced. Contrasts in shapes, textures, values, colors, and lines will all increase the amount of variety, even if there is

only a small change—the aim being, of course, to create greater interest.

The ultimate goal is an effective combination (sometimes a precarious balance) of both harmony and variety. This goal is a concern of all three-dimensional artists, whatever the nature of the work. It might be added that sculptural work in *low relief* (having shallow surface depth) is closely related to 2-D work, whereas *high-relief* sculpture is somewhat of a hybrid production, necessitating considerations similar to those of freestanding 3-D artworks.

2.65 Lucas Samaras, *Mirrored Room*, 1966. Mirrors on wooden frame, 9 × 9 × 10 ft. (2.44 × 2.44 × 3.05 m). This is an example of Environmental Art, which, by its size and structure, may actually enclose the observer within the form of the work. Gift of Seymour H. Knox, 1966. Albright-Knox Art Gallery, Buffalo, NY/Art Resource, NY. Courtesy Pace Gallery, New York.

Balance

When considering balance and the effects of spatial positioning in three-dimensional art, we need to examine some special conditions. For example, when balancing a 3-D piece of work, the added dimension of depth affects its multiple views. Although a sphere appears symmetrical from any view, a rectangular box may appear symmetrical only when one of its sides is seen straight-on. If the rectangular box is seen at an angle, the multiple views seen in depth may influence the sense of balance.

Three types of balance are possible in actual space: symmetrical (fig. 2.66), asymmetrical (fig. 2.67), and radial (fig. 2.68). Of the three, symmetrical and radial balance are considered formal and regular. Radial balance is spherical, with the fulcrum in the center. The parts that radiate from this point are usually similar in their formations. However, artists more commonly make use of asymmetrical balance because it

2.66 Donald Judd, *Untitled,* 1969/1982. Anodized aluminum, 6 × 27 × 24 in. (15.2 × 68.6 × 61 cm). In this minimal work, Judd is primarily interested in perceptually explicit shapes, reflective surfaces, and vertical interplay. There is a rhythm between shapes and negative space, and the work invites the eye to travel from one square to the next. Collection Walker Art Center, Minneapolis. Gift of Mr. and Mrs. Edmond R. Ruben, 1981. Art © Judd Foundation. Licensed by VAGA, New York, NY.

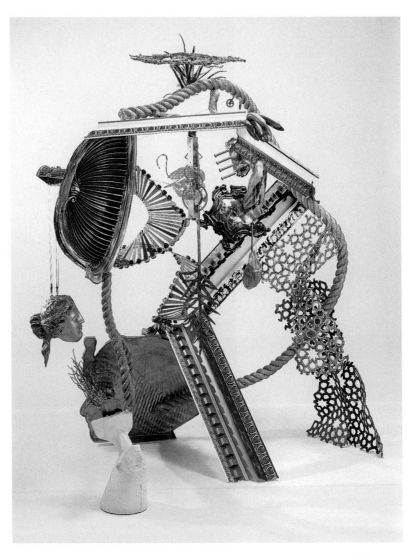

2.67 Nancy Graves, *Unending Revolution of Venus, Plants, and Pendulum,* 1992. Bronze, brass, enamel, stainless steel, and aluminum, 97 × 71½ × 56½ in. (2.46 × 1.82 × 1.44 m). In this sculpture, we see a variety of form parts. We also see an excellent example of an asymmetrically balanced sculpture. © Nancy Graves Foundation/ Licensed by VAGA, New York, NY. Photograph by Sam Kwong.

provides the greatest individual latitude and variety.

Proportion

When we are viewing a three-dimensional work, the effect of proportion (the relationship of the parts to the whole) is fundamental in determining the basic form, for it sets the standard for relationships and permeates the other principles. Experiencing a 3-D work that can not only be seen but also touched or caressed, stood on, walked on, or passed through puts special emphasis on the relation of the parts to the whole. A sense of proportion must apply continually in a 3-D work as we look at it from multiple views.

The actual size of a 3-D work when compared to the physical measurement of the human figure is referred to as its *scale*. Scale is most dramatic at the extremes, whether the works are small enough to be held in the palm of the hand or immense enough to tower

2.68 Mark di Suvero, *Eviva Amore,* 2001. Steel, Size unknown. The fulcrum of this sculpture is at the center of the work, identified by the circular shape, as the diagonal beams radiate in outwardly thrusting directions. Art © Mark di Suvero. Photo courtesy of Raymond and Patsy Nasher Collection, Dallas, Texas. Photographer: Tim Hursley.

above or engulf the viewer (see figs. 1.28 and 1.31). Small jewelry and miniaturized models (maquettes) are considered small scale. Larger works made for public places—like malls, parks, religious temples, mosques, or cathedrals—can be awe-inspiring in their size (see fig. 2.62).

Dominance

While developing a 3-D image, an artist strives for interest by creating differences through contrast that call attention to significant parts, making them dominant. As with 2-D organization, the emphasis or degree of contrast for the visual elements is varied to ensure that a hierarchy of importance is established; some fea-

tures are emphasized, and others are subordinated. This creates both primary focal points and secondary levels of interest that help move the eye around the work (see figs 2.63, 2.67, and 2.70). These differences result from compositional considerations within the medium.

Movement

Two types of movements are used by three-dimensional artists. Implied movement, the most common type, is illusionary (fig. 2.69; see also fig. 2.64), but actual movement—as with **kinetic** sculpture—involves the physical movement of the work itself. As parts of the sculpture move about, the viewer stays to watch their changing relationships.

This infuses the element of time into the composition and emphasizes those moving parts, thereby elevating their degree of dominance.

The actual movements found in kinetic art are set into motion by air, water, mechanical devices, or computer programs. Alexander Calder, an early innovator and the father of **mobile** sculptures, at first used motors to drive his pieces but later made use of air currents (fig. 2.70). Many contemporary sculptors also work with wind, water, and air propulsion. Jean Tinguely (see fig. 9.27), Arthur Ganson (see fig. 9.28), and José de Rivera (see fig. 3.31) use motors. Other artists today use computer software to control various electronic elements of their works (see fig. 2.71).

3.24 Steve Magada, *Trio*, c. 1966. Oil on canvas, size unknown. The gestural lines in this work evoke the energy of the performers. Photograph courtesy of Virginia Magada.

3.25 Giovanni Battista Tiepolo, *Study for Figure of Falsehood on the Ceiling of the Palazzo Trento-Valmarana, Vicenza*, no date. Pen and brown ink, 6⅜ × 6 in. (16.2 × 15.4 cm). This gestural drawing clearly illustrates the dramatic motion of drawing as an activity. Artists often try to sustain this effect beyond the initial stage of a sketch. Princeton University Art Museum. Bequest of Dan Fellows Platt, Class of 1895 ×1948-863.

figures 3.27 and 3.28, one can see the shared qualities of fluid movement and unique gesture. The written calligraphic line can be made to take on the quality of the object being described (see figure 3.28) or instill a sense of space, leaping upward and outward (see figure 3.27). This wide application of line includes the creation of value and texture, illustrating the impossibility of truly isolating the elements of art from one another.

In the lithograph *Jane Avril*, the artist Henri de Toulouse-Lautrec creates calligraphic lines with a gestural character

3.26 Annie Cicale, *Untitled*, 2001. **Pen and ink drawing, 7 × 10 in.** In the words of the artist, "Beautiful writing, called calligraphy, captures the power of the written word and elevates it so that the writing becomes an image as powerful as the words." Like the individual styles of painters or sculptors, such beautiful calligraphy evolves only after years of practice. Courtesy of the artist.

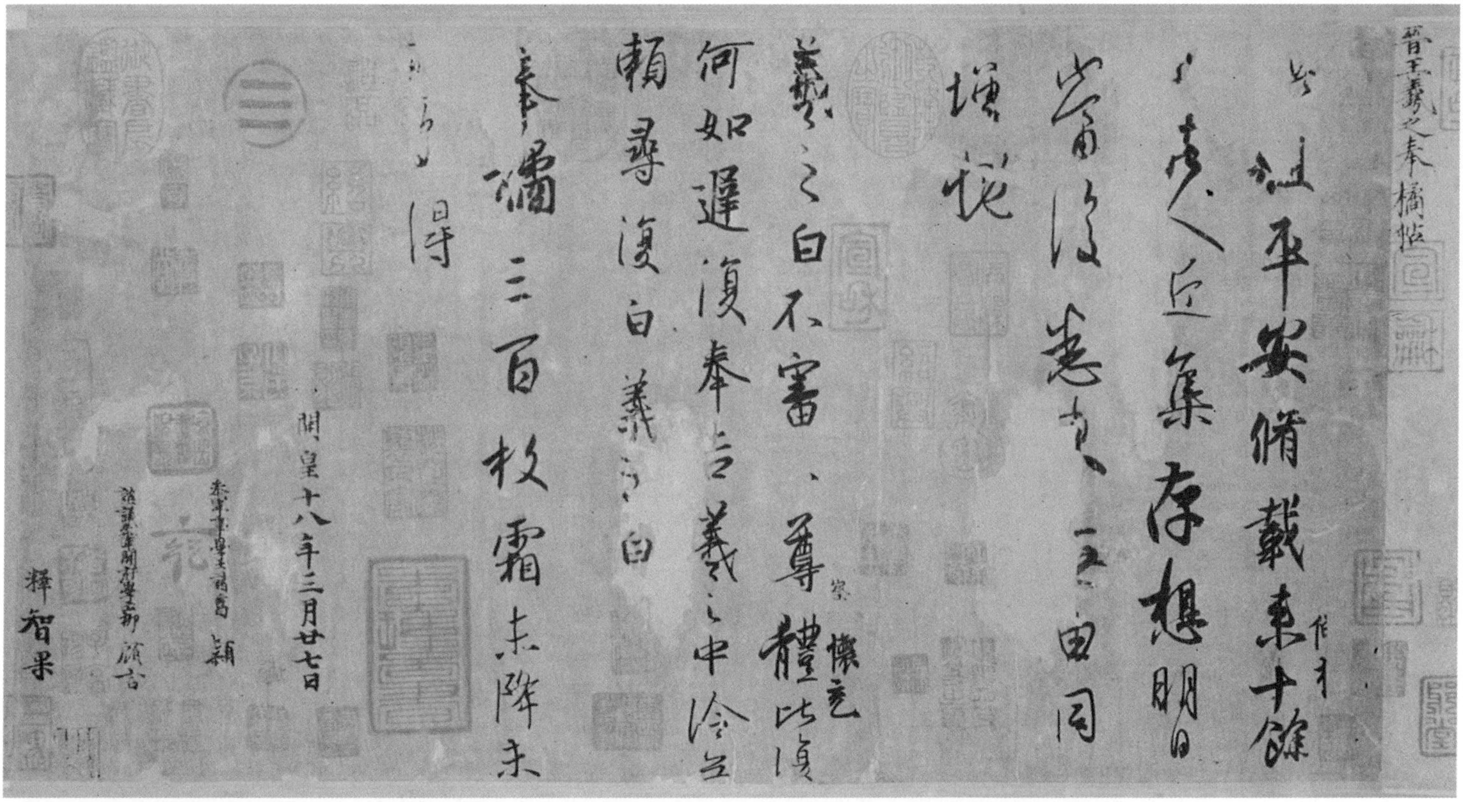

3.27 Wang Hsi-chih, from Three Passages of Calligraphy: "Ping-an," "Ho-ju," and "Feng-chu," Eastern Ch'in dynasty, fourth century (321–379 C.E.), *Calligraphy*. **Ink on paper.** Certain meanings intrinsic to line arise from its character. These meanings are the product of the medium, the tools used, and the artist's method of application. Calligraphy is esteemed in China as an art form equal to painting. Created with brush and ink on paper (the Chinese invented paper), the lively, abstract ideographs of Chinese calligraphy appear to leap upward and outward, "like a dragon leaping over heaven's gate." National Palace Museum, Taipei, Taiwan, Republic of China.

3.28 Wu Zhen (attributed to), *Bamboo in the Wind*, early-fourteenth-century hanging scroll, Yuan dynasty, China. Ink on paper, 29⅝ × 21⅜ in. (75.2 × 54.3 cm). Wu Zhen uses meticulous, controlled brushwork to describe the flowing linear (calligraphic) qualities of the bamboo tree.
Museum of Fine Arts, Boston, Chinese and Japanese Special Fund, 15.907. Photograph © 2013 Museum of Fine Arts, Boston.

3.29 Henri de Toulouse-Lautrec, *Jane Avril*, first plate from *Le Café Concert*, 1893. Lithograph, printed in black, 10½ × 8⁷⁄₁₆ in. (26.7 × 21.4 cm). The lines in this image seem to have been drawn with great freedom, communicating the graceful action of the subject. Gift of Abby Aldrich Rockefeller. (167.1946) The Museum of Modern Art/Licensed by SCALA/Art Resource, NY.

that captures the spirit of the dance (fig. 3.29). The calligraphic line in this print also becomes a broken **implied line,** a variation in application that further suggests spatial change, movement, and animation. An implied line seems to fade, stop, and/or disappear and then reappear as a continuation or an extension of the same line, edge, or direction. You can see this effect in figure 3.29 as you follow the line of the skirt around. It suggests movement

and asks the viewer to complete missing sections (see the "Linking through Extensions" section in Chapter 2).

Line has many objective and subjective implications. In its role of signifying ideas and conveying feelings, line moves and lives, pulsating with significant emotions. It describes the edges or contours of shapes, it diagrams silhouettes, and it encompasses spaces and areas—all in such a way as to convey a variety of meanings. These meanings

are created as an artist manipulates a line's physical properties.

The qualities of line can be described in terms of general states of feeling—somber, tired, energetic, brittle, alive, and the like. An infinite number of conditions of varying subtlety can be communicated by the artist. The various attributes of line can act in concert toward one goal or can serve separate roles of expression and design. Gently curving lines, long lines, thin lines, and lines placed low in the frame may all contribute to the feeling of calmness in a composition. However, in a work of art, as in the human mind, such feelings are rarely so clearly defined. The viewer's recognition of these qualities is a matter of feeling, which means that the viewer must be receptive and perceptive and have a reservoir of experiences to draw on.

For the artist, an intuitively sensitive use of line evolves when one is empowered by a thorough understanding of line's physical properties and understands the relationship between line and the other elements. When these properties are internalized, an artist can use line to create spontaneously, using mind and body to express an idea or feeling. Whether line is used to create a sketchy interpretation, express a deep emotion, reveal the gesture of an action, or record factual information, it remains a basic means of communication and one of the first elements employed.

THREE-DIMENSIONAL APPLICATIONS OF LINE

For the 3-D artist, line is a visual phenomenon that, for the most part, does not actually exist in nature or in the third dimension. What we visually interpret as line is primarily a change in value, color, or texture that indicates the meeting of planes or the outer edges of shapes. When two planes come together, they form a ridge, or an edge known as an **arris**. Whether we are looking at tree bark or cracks in the sidewalk, this edge can be perceived as a line when it is enhanced by a cast shadow (fig. 3.30). That line can fade away as the ridge, or arris, is softened and rounds over. In three-dimensional art, the spatial characteristics of line are physical, as they literally move in space with measurable

3.30 Bill Barrett, *Kindred*, 2001. Bronze, 10 ft. high × 9 ft. wide × 5 ft. deep. The contour lines in this sculpture come alive as it is "washed" with values ranging from highlights to deep shadows. Other internal lines occur along the arris (edge) where two planes meet abruptly and a contrasting shadow is cast. The sharper the edges, the greater the contrast. Where those edges are softened, the line becomes indistinct—dissolving completely in some locations. Just as line can be used to harmonize a graphic image, line used in 3-D work can control the eye movement and unify the form. Commissioned by the University of Michigan School of Social Work, Ann Arbor, MI. Photo by Tanya C. Hart Emley.

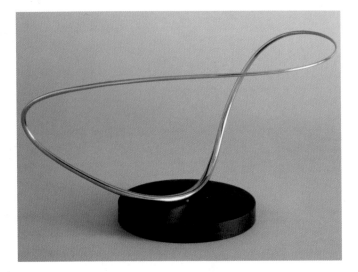

3.31 José de Rivera, *Construction 8*, 1954. Stainless steel forged rod, 10 × 16 × 13 in. (25.4 × 40.6 × 35.5 cm) including base. The concept of attracting observers to a continuous series of rewarding visual experiences as they move about a static three-dimensional work of art led to the principle of kinetic, or mobile, art, as with this sculpture set on a slowly turning motorized plinth. Gift of Mrs. Heinz Schulz. The Museum of Modern Art, New York, NY. Digital Image © The Museum of Modern Art/ Licensed by SCALA/Art Resource, NY.

3.32 Richard Lippold, *Variation within a Sphere, No. 10, the Sun*, 1953–56. 22-karat gold-filled wire, 11 × 22 × 5½ ft. (3.35 × 6.70 × 1.68 m). The development of welding and soldering techniques for use in sculpture made the shaping and joining of thin linear metals possible, as in this work by Lippold. Metropolitan Museum of Art, Fletcher Fund, 1956, (56.106.1) Photo © Metropolitan Museum of Art /Art Resource, NY. Art © 2011 Estate of Richard Lippold/Artists Rights Society (ARS), New York.

distances between them. These three-dimensional lines can carry a great deal of energy, swooping and swirling in space (fig. 3.31).

Materials like string, wire, tubes, solid rods, and the like have been used for their linear quality and have added to the repertoire of the plastic artist. The use of these materials creates a more obvious instance of line, referencing characteristics of two-dimensional art within three dimensions. Such linear explorations of space can be seen in the works of artists such as Richard Lippold (fig. 3.32), Alexander Calder (see. fig. 2.70), and Kenneth Snelson (see fig. 2.62).

Incising line in clay or in any other soft medium is similar to the graphic technique of drawing, but in addition to being made visible by cast shadows,

line may be experienced tactilely because of the inscribed valleys and ridges. In three-dimensional art, incised lines are used to accent surfaces for interest and movement. Italian artist Giacomo Manzu employed such lines to add sparkle to relief sculpture (fig. 3.33).

3.33 Giacomo Manzu, *Death by Violence*, 1950. Bronze cast from clay model, 36⅝ × 25¼ in. (93.5 × 64 cm). This is a study for one of a series of panels for the doors of Saint Peter's (Vatican, Rome). The confining spatial limitations of relief sculpture are evident. To create a greater feeling of mass, Manzu used sharply incised modeling that is similar to the engraved lines of the printmaker's plate. The crisp incising creates sharp value contrasts that accentuate movement as well as depth. © David Lees/Corbis.

Shape

CHAPTER FOUR

Hayao Miyazaki, *Ponyo*, 2008.
© Photos 12/Alamy

THE VOCABULARY OF SHAPE

Shape — An area that stands out from its surroundings because of a defined
or implied boundary or because of differences of value, color, or texture.

actual shape
A positive area with clearly defined boundaries
(as opposed to an implied shape).

amorphous shape
A shape without clear definition: formless, indistinct, and of uncertain dimension.

biomorphic shape
An irregular shape that resembles the freely
developed curves found in living organisms.

Cubism
The name given to the painting style invented by
Pablo Picasso and Georges Braque between 1907
and 1912, which uses multiple views of objects
to create the effect of three-dimensionality while
acknowledging the two-dimensional surface
of the picture plane. Signaling the beginning of
abstract art, Cubism is a semiabstract style that
continued the strong trend away from representational art initiated by Cézanne in the late 1800s.

curvilinear shape
A shape whose boundaries consist of predominantly curved lines; the opposite of **rectilinear.**

decorative (shape)
Ornamenting or enriching but, more importantly
in art, stressing the two-dimensional nature of an
artwork or any of its elements. Decorative art
emphasizes the essential flatness of a surface.

equivocal space
A condition, usually intentional on the artist's
part, in which the viewer may, at different times,
see more than one set of relationships between
art elements or depicted objects. This may be
compared to the familiar "optical illusion."

geometric shape
A shape that appears related to geometry; usually simple, such as a triangle, rectangle, or circle.

implied shape
A shape that does not physically exist but is
suggested through the psychological connection of dots, lines, areas, or their edges. (See
Gestalt in the Glossary.)

kinetic (art)
From the Greek word *kinesis*, meaning
"motion"; art that includes the element of actual
movement.

mass
1. In graphic art, a shape that appears to stand
out three-dimensionally from the space surrounding it or creates the illusion of a solid body
of material. 2. In the plastic arts, a physical bulk
of material. (See **volume.**)

objective
That which is based, as closely as possible, on
physical actuality or optical perception. Such art
tends to appear natural or real; the opposite of
subjective.

perspective
Any graphic system used to create the illusion of
three-dimensional images and/or spatial relationships in which the objects or their parts appear
to diminish as they recede into the distance.
(See the discussion of atmospheric perspective
and linear perspective in Chapter 8.)

planar (shape)
Having to do with planes; shapes that have
height and width but no indication of thickness.

plane
1. An area that is essentially two-dimensional,
having height and width. 2. A two-dimensional
pictorial surface that can support the illusion of
advancing or receding elements. 3. A flat sculptural surface.

plastic (shape)
1. Element(s) used in such a manner as to create the illusion of the third dimension on a
two-dimensional surface. 2. Three-dimensional
art forms, such as architecture, sculpture, and
ceramics.

rectilinear shape
A shape whose boundaries consist of straight
lines; the opposite of **curvilinear.**

shape
An area that stands out from its surroundings
because of a defined or implied boundary
or because of differences of value, color, or
texture.

silhouette
The area between or bounded by the contours,
or edges, of an object; the total shape.

subjective
That which is derived from the mind, instead
of physical reality, and reflects a personal bias,
emotion, or innovative interpretation; the opposite of **objective.**

Surrealism
A style of artistic expression, influenced by
Freudian psychology, that emphasizes fantasy
and whose subjects are usually experiences
revealed by the subconscious mind through the
use of automatic techniques (rubbings, doodles,
blots, cloud patterns, etc.). Originally a literary
movement that grew out of Dadaism, Surrealism
was established by a literary manifesto written
by André Breton in 1924.

three-dimensional
Possesses, or creates the illusion of possessing,
the dimensions of depth, height, and width. In
the graphic arts, the feeling of depth is an illusion, while in the plastic arts, the work has actual
depth.

two-dimensional
Possesses the dimensions of height and width,
especially when considering a flat surface or picture plane.

void
1. An area lacking positive substance and consisting of negative space. 2. A spatial area within an
object that penetrates and passes through it.

volume
A measurable amount of defined, three-dimensional space. (See **mass.**)

INTRODUCTION TO SHAPE

Shapes are often referred to as the building blocks of art structure. Like the bricks, stones, and mortar used to construct architectural edifices, shapes in art build strength into the structure of the composition. With careful placement and treatment, shapes also create various illusions of depth and dimensionality and engage the viewer through their expressive nature.

As artists begin their work, they frequently have some preliminary vision of shape, whether planning composition-wide patterns or just thinking about individual subjects. The artist may have a clear concept in mind for an abstract image and know instinctively what shapes will give that idea substance and structure. Or he or she may prefer an evolving process in which shapes gradually reveal themselves through experimentation.

Sketches that start with rambling lines or hatch marks may suggest ideas that evolve into more defined shapes. As lines crisscross and connect to one another, spaces become enclosed and appear as shapes, while areas of contrast emerge from the background and materialize into other shapes. With this progression, the act of doodling turns shapes with vague beginnings into refined images that capture the viewer's imagination.

Whatever the development, **shape** may be defined as an area distinguished from its surroundings by an outer edge or boundary. Whether explicitly precise or simply implied, that edge exists as either a contour line that encloses the area or as a contrast in value, texture, or color between the shape and its surroundings (fig. 4.1).

SHAPE TYPES

The configuration of a shape's outer edge helps give it a character that distinguishes it from others. When the shapes used by an artist imitate observable phenomena, they may be described as **objective,** naturalistic, representational, or realistic, depending on the context. However, when shapes are more imaginary or seem to have been invented by the artist, they are often called **subjective,** abstract, nonobjective, or nonrealistic (see the "Abstraction" section in Chapter 1). Shapes may also belong to a number of other categories or families of shape type, according to the configuration of their edges.

Man, in his need to make order from the chaos of the natural world, devised shapes that were structured, precise, and often sharply defined. Known as **geometric shapes,** these include circles, ovals, squares, rectangles, triangles, hexagons, pentagons, and other mathematically derived shapes. Although geometric shapes may have a variety of configurations, they generally retain the character of being **curvilinear** (made of curved lines), **rectilinear** (straight-lined), or some combination thereof. Architecture, machinery, and other man-made technologies abound with standardized geometric shapes. However, as man-made as these shapes seem, they do occur in nature as well.

4.1 Henri Matisse, *The Burial of Pierrot,* Plate VIII from *Jazz,* 1947. Pochoir (stencil printing), 16¼ × 25⅛ in. (41.2 × 63.5 cm). Matisse's biomorphic shapes, which are abstracted from organic forms, stand out from the background area due to the contrasts in color and value. Though decorative in nature, the shapes give the composition a sense of energy and movement. SCALA/Art Resource, NY. Photograph by Archives Matisse. © 2011 Succession H. Matisse/Artists Rights Society (ARS), New York.

4.2 Juan Gris (José Victoriano González), *Breakfast*, 1914. Cut-and-pasted paper, crayon, and oil over canvas, 31⅞ × 23½ in. (80.9 × 59.7 cm). Gris, a Cubist, not only simplified shapes into larger, more dominant areas but also gave each shape a characteristic value, producing a carefully conceived light-dark pattern. He also made use of open-value composition, where the value moves from one shape into the adjoining shape, as we see in this example. The Museum of Modern Art, New York, NY. U.S.A. Acquired through the Lillie P. Bliss Bequest. Digital image © The Museum of Modern Art/Licensed by SCALA/Art Resource, NY.

4.3 Dorothea Tanning, *Guardian Angels*, 1946. Oil on canvas, 35 × 57½ in. Here, Tanning combines a realistic rendering of form with the fantastic. Like other Surrealists, Tanning was interested in the inner psychic life of human beings. Courtesy New Orleans Museum of Art: Museum Purchase, Kate P. Jourdan Memorial Fund, 49.15 © 2011 Artists Rights Society (ARS), New York/ADGP, Paris.

They can be seen in spiral seashells, honeycombs, snowflakes, flowers, and precious stones like quartz and diamonds. Whatever the origin, visual artists often find inspiration in geometric shapes and use them to manifest ideas in an ordered way (fig. 4.2; see also figs. 4.23 and T.77).

In contrast to the regulated, often severe nature of geometric shapes are the flowing qualities of **biomorphic shapes**. Biomorphic shapes are made from rounded, curving, and sometimes undulating edges and suggest living organisms or natural forces (fig. 4.3).

We can see these irregular shapes in the human form as well as in stones, leaves, puddles, plant life, and clouds. Such shapes may also be referred to as *organic* or *natural*, because the term *biomorphic* was coined in the early twentieth century. Sculptors and pictorial artists often use biomorphic, or organic, shapes in their respective media to represent human, plant, and animal forms and the natural world in general. Architects and designers also use biomorphic forms to add a natural or human element to otherwise very

geometric shapes (fig. 4.4). In addition, biomorphic shapes can be used to symbolize abstract thoughts, ideas, and concepts, or simply give a decorative quality to flat surfaces (fig. 4.5; see also figs. 3.11, 4.1, and 4.22).

Although the most obvious shapes are created by distinct and continuous boundaries, such unequivocal contours are not absolutely necessary for a shape to be seen. Instead, the edges need only to be suggested. We know from our study of closure (a Gestalt concept explained in Chapter 2) that the mind

4.4 Joan Miró, *The Painting*, 1933. Oil on canvas, 68½ in. × 6 ft. 5¼ in. (174 × 196.2 cm). Some shapes in this work seem to be veiled references to unlikely creatures and deserve the term *biomorphic* because of their organic configuration. Loula D. Lasker Bequest (by exchange). (229.1937) The Museum of Modern Art, New York, NY. Digital image © The Museum of Modern Art/Licensed by SCALA/Art Resource, NY. © 2011 Artists Rights Society (ARS), New York/ADGP, Paris.

4.5 Hayao Miyazaki, *Ponyo*, 2008. In this still from Miyazaki's film *Ponyo*, biomorphic shapes abound—in the ocean waves, the clouds, the little girl, and the bubble that covers her. These rounded shapes convey a comforting aesthetic, as well as a visual reminder of the natural world in which the story takes place. © Photos 12/Alamy

SHAPE AND EXPRESSIVE CONTENT

While a shape's physical characteristics may be easily defined, its expressive character is rather difficult to pinpoint, because viewers react to the configuration of shape on many different emotional levels. In some cases, our responses to shapes are commonplace; in others, our reactions are complex and individual because of our own personality and experiences. The familiar Rorschach (inkblot) test, which was designed to aid psychologists in evaluating emotional stability, perfectly demonstrates our emotional sensitivity to shapes. The test indicates that shapes provoke emotional responses on different levels. Thus, the artist might use specific abstract or representational shapes to provoke a desired emotional response. By using the knowledge that some shapes are inevitably associated with certain feelings and situations, the artist can set the stage for a pictorial or sculptural drama. The full meaning of any shape, however, can be revealed only through the relationships developed throughout an entire composition.

Whether viewing inkblots or artwork, our reaction to shape is often quite primal and subconscious. Some shapes convey relatively standard meanings. Squares, for instance, commonly express perfection, stability, solidity, symmetry, self-reliance, and monotony. Similarly, circles may suggest self-possession, independence, and/or confinement; ovals may suggest fruitfulness and creation; stars could suggest reaching out.

The psychological association of abstract shapes may be especially appealing to certain artists. Particularly in the twentieth century, numerous movements were based on the use of specific abstract configurations. The Surrealists of the early 1900s, for example, were interested in the mystic origins of being and in the exploration of subconscious revelations, such as in

4.22 Charles Burchfield, *Orion in December,* 1959. Watercolor and pencil on paper; sheet: 39⅞ × 32⅞ in. Burchfield believed that an artist must paint not what he sees in nature but what is there. To do this, he invented his own symbols, drawing from the sights and sounds around him to represent the force and beauty of nature. In this wonderful scene, the primeval forest soars—perhaps as a Gothic cathedral—stars symbolize ecstasy, and Orion, the hunter in Greek mythology, hovers, merging heaven and earth. Along the bottom, crackling ice-covered shrubs twist and move as if in a frigid breeze and repeat the patterns of the starlit sky. Smithsonian American Art Museum, Washington, DC/Art Resource, NY.

dreams. These artists lived in a time of increasing awareness of the microscopic world, the growth of Freudian psychology, and the revival of interest in pure abstraction (in which shapes function symbolically), and biomorphic shapes became a key component in their works. Such shapes worked well in **Surrealism** (see fig. T.66) and may be seen in the paintings by Burchfield (fig. 4.22) and Miró (see fig. 4.4).

Other artists, like Matisse and Braque, worked with abstracted organic forms in a less symbolic manner (see figs. 4.1 and 4.18).

In contrast, the precise, machinelike quality of geometric shapes appealed to artists working with **Cubism,** who used them in their analytical dissection and reformulation of the natural world (see fig. 4.33A and B). Following the Cubists, the Futurists were influenced by the stylization of machinery and created pristine, clear-cut shapes and shape relationships that expressed the power and speed of the mechanized world (see fig. T.59). Later, the Minimalists and the Conceptualists of the 1970s and 80s also used simple geometric shapes to further reduce images to their basic elements of meaning (see figs. 2.71, 2.72, and 4.31).

While the configuration of a shape greatly affects our interpretation of it, additional characteristics of the shape can also affect its psychological impact. Color, value, texture, spatial depth, and the application of particular media can affect whatever feelings that arise in such works of art. Depending on how they are treated by the artist, shapes may feel static, stable, active, or lively, or seem to contract or expand. For example, the work of Charles Sheeler (fig. 4.23), Dorothea Rockburne (fig. 4.24), and Joseph Albers (fig. 4.25) all use similar geometric shapes, but differences in color, value, and their application change the shapes' meanings

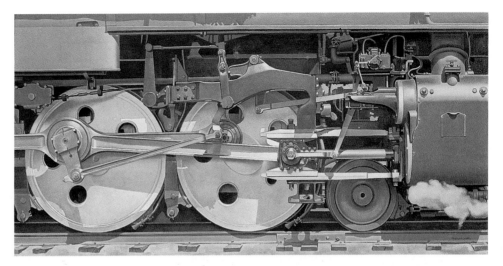

4.23 Charles Sheeler, *Rolling Power*, 1939. Oil on canvas, 15 × 30 in. (38.1 × 72.6 cm). While commenting on the abstract quality of his images, Sheeler remarked, "I had come to feel that a picture could have incorporated in it the structural design implied in abstraction and be presented in a wholly realistic manner." Courtesy of Smith College Museum of Art, Northampton, MA. Purchased, Drayton Hillyer Fund, 1940.

4.24 Dorothea Rockburne, *Mozart and Mozart Upside Down and Backward*, 1985–87. Oil on gessoed linen, hung on blue wall, 89 × 115 × 4 in. (226.06 × 292.1 × 10.16 cm). In this painting, Dorothea Rockburne is representative of the Neo-Abstractionist painters, who leaned toward the geometric abstraction of the 1950s. Though based on a seemingly simple scheme, on closer examination, this piece reveals a labyrinth of interlocking rectilinear shapes. Courtesy of André Emmerich Gallery, a Division of Sotheby's, on behalf of the artist. © 2011 Dorothea Rockburne/Artists Rights Society (ARS), NY.

4.26 Helen Frankenthaler, *Madame Butterfly,* 2000. Woodcut print, triptych, 41¼ × 79 in. (104.8 × 200.7 cm). Many shapes are not meant to represent or even symbolize. Here, for example, the shape extremities, the softly changing values of the larger shapes, and the brown wood-grained ground act against the horizontal violet and white components and the outer frame shape. The artist provokes a momentary feeling of excitement within an otherwise quiet mood.

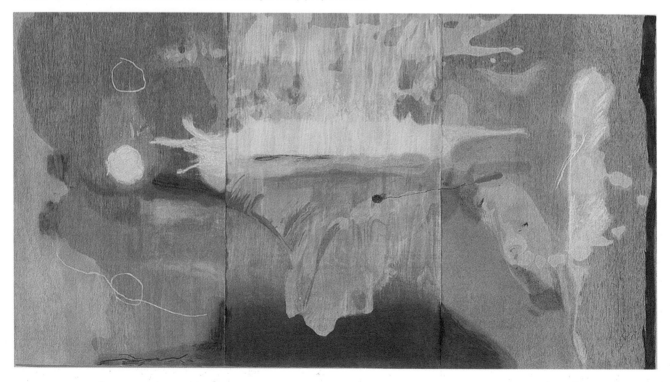

4.27 Fernand Léger, *Three Women (Le Grand Déjeuner)*, 1921. Oil on canvas, 6 ft. ¼ in. × 8 ft. 3 in. (183.5 × 251.5 cm). The Cubist painter Léger commonly used varied combinations of geometric shapes in very complex patterns. Here, because of his sensitive design, he not only overcomes a dominant, hard-edged feel but also imbues the painting with an air of femininity. © 2011 Artists Rights Society (ARS), New York/ADGP, Paris. The Museum of Modern Art, New York, NY. Mrs. Simon Guggenheim Fund. Digital image © The Museum of Modern Art/Licensed by SCALA/Art Resource, NY.

and create a different sense of space. In figures 4.23 and 4.24, shapes imply spatial depth through the use of blended colors and values. However, in figure 4.25, the sense of space is achieved in a different manner; although Albers's shapes appear flat, that flatness is contradicted by the contrast of color and value, which make various squares advance or recede, and a tunneling effect is made by placing the squares closer to the bottom edge of the picture frame. In other examples, the quality of the shape's edge is important; the

terms *soft edge* and *hard edge* are used to indicate the degree of clarity or sharpness used to define the image (figs. 4.26 and 4.27).

Our reactions to abstraction and/or representation also affect how we interpret any work of art. Many people can accept Sheeler's artwork, even when the abstraction is more pronounced, because the subject is still recognizable (see figs 1.13 and 4.23). However, other people react adversely to simple, nonobjective shapes like those in Albers's paintings (see fig. 4.25). Unfortunately,

viewers who value representational artwork because they can easily interpret the subject matter often fail to see the intellectual metaphor and visual effects of the shape relationships; they don't appreciate how *form itself* may be the subject matter.

Conception and imagination have always been part of artistic expression. It is usually a matter of degree as to how much artists use their imagination and how much they use their perceptual vision in the selection and creation of their shapes (figs. 4.28 and

shapes become so important that they often dominate the width, thickness, and weight of the materials that define them (see fig. 3.31).

Like their two-dimensional counterparts, three-dimensional shapes also play a large role in establishing dominance (emphasis) within sections of a work. The relative dominance of a shape may be altered by contrasts in size, color, value, visual detail, or textural emphasis (see figs. 2.63 and 4.30). A shape may become dominant by making it different from other shapes that surround it. Because the degree of dominance is established by the degree of contrast, the amount of change within a shape family helps to establish the amount of importance given to each shape. Less variety makes them more easily harmonized. With **kinetic** forms (mobiles), the length of time an observer concentrates on the work may also be increased through the physical motion of various portions of the sculpture—the constantly changing relationship of shapes may hold the viewer's attention longer than immobile works of art.

Sculptors, architects, or product designers, whose work involves actual space, may have an advantage over the graphic artist when it comes to spatial design. However, when sculptors (plastic artists) do their initial planning using graphic means, they must be aware that the 2-D picture plane is limited in how it can predict their three-dimensional intentions. Some artists and designers (and most architects) now use 3-D modeling software to plan their work, enabling them to rotate the design and see it from multiple perspectives.

Value

Peter Milton, *Points of Departure III: Twentieth Century Limited,* 1998. Etching and engraving, 24½ × 38½ in.

© Peter Milton. Courtesy of Davidson Galleries.

CHAPTER FIVE

THE VOCABULARY OF
VALUE

Value — 1. The relative degree of lightness or darkness. **2.** The characteristic of color determined by the degree of lightness or darkness or the quantity of light reflected by the color.

achromatic value
Relating to differences of lightness and darkness, without regard for hue and intensity.

cast shadow
The dark area that occurs on a surface as a result of something being placed between that surface and a light source.

chiaroscuro
1. The distribution of lights and darks in a picture, usually in an attempt to develop the illusion of mass, volume, or space. 2. A technique of representation that blends light and shadow gradually to create the illusion of three-dimensional objects in space or atmosphere.

chromatic value
The value (relative degree of lightness or darkness) demonstrated by a given color.

closed-value composition
A composition in which values are contained within the edges or boundaries of shapes. The value pattern reveals the subject(s) and is dependent upon the positioning of the subject(s).

decorative (value)
Ornamenting or enriching but, more importantly in art, stressing the two-dimensional nature of an artwork or any of its elements. Decorative value stresses the essential flatness of a surface.

high-key value
A value that has a level of middle gray or lighter.

highlight
The portion of an object that, from the observer's position, receives the greatest amount of direct light.

local value
The relative lightness or darkness of a surface, seen in the objective world, that is independent of any effect created by the degree of light falling on it.

low-key value
A value that has a level of middle gray or darker.

open-value composition
A composition in which values are not limited by the edges of shapes and therefore flow across shape boundaries into adjoining areas. The value pattern created is unrelated to the location of the subject(s).

plastic (value)
Value used to create the illusion of volume and space.

sfumato
A technique devised by Leonardo da Vinci of softly blending areas from light to dark, creating subtle transitions. Images often have vague outlines and a hazy or smoky appearance. *Sfumato* is derived from the Latin *fumo*, meaning "smoke." Leonardo described sfumato as "without lines or borders, in the manner of smoke beyond the focus plane."

shadow
The darker value on the surface of an object that suggests that a portion of it is turned away from or obscured by the source of light.

shallow space
The illusion of limited depth. With shallow space, the imagery moves only a slight distance back from the picture plane.

silhouette
The area between or bounded by the contours, or edges, of an object as defined by a contrast of value; the total shape.

tenebrism
A technique of painting that exaggerates or emphasizes the effects of chiaroscuro. Larger amounts of dark value are placed close to smaller areas of highly contrasting lights—which change suddenly—in order to concentrate attention on important features.

value
1. The relative degree of lightness or darkness. 2. The characteristic of color determined by the degree of lightness or darkness or the quantity of light reflected by the color.

value pattern
The arrangement or organization of values that control compositional movement and create a unifying effect throughout a work of art.

INTRODUCTION TO VALUE RELATIONSHIPS

From the rising of the sun to the soft glow of the moon, we see images as light against dark or dark against light. The greater the contrast, the easier the image can be seen—although an extreme contrast of light and dark is not always necessary for an object to be understandable.

In the visual arts, an area's relative lightness or darkness is referred to as its **value**. Contrasts in value allow us to see lines and shapes, sense depth and dimensionality, and perceive surface textures. Our eyes are also guided through a composition by the patterns of those value contrasts, which encourage us to focus on particular locations in the work. Careful value choices even affect our psychological or emotional reactions. Value has both compositional function and great expressive capability. An understanding of value is fundamental to the study of art because it applies to all the elements.

This chapter is primarily concerned with **achromatic values**, which consist of white, black, and the limitless degrees of gray without color. The achromatic value scale in figure 5.1 illustrates the change from white to black in evenly gradated steps. Although there could be an infinite number of steps between any two values, the chart shows a few, with the same number of steps from middle gray to white and from middle gray to black.

Many beginning artists do not realize that when they are working with color, they are working with value as well. The comparative lightness or darkness of a color is its **chromatic value**. A standard yellow, for example, is of far greater lightness than a standard violet, although both colors may be modified to the point that they become virtually equal in value. (Chapter 7, "Color," covers this in more detail.) The relative values of various colors are often easier to compare after they have been translated into their corresponding achromatic values. The value scale in figure 5.1 can be a useful tool for finding the appropriate level of gray for any color.

An artist can create an image with contrasting values, similar values, or any combination along the value scale. Sometimes, a designer will use the extreme contrast of black and white for dramatic effect (fig. 5.2). Other times, to harmonize a piece, an artist can choose to work with values that are closely related. The artist selects values within a limited range rather than use the full value spectrum. A work that uses predominantly dark values, ranging from middle gray to black, may be said to have **low-key values** (fig. 5.3). When a

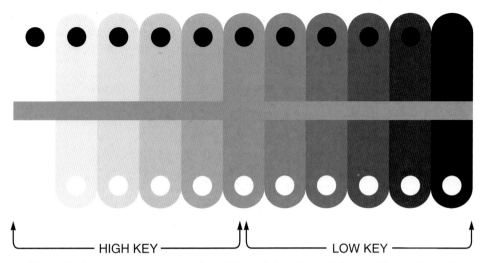

HIGH KEY   LOW KEY

5.1 This scale shows a value gradation from light to dark against middle gray. To use the scale, make a colored photocopy, and remove the black and white circles in each gray stripe using a paper punch. To find the achromatic value for any color, slide the photocopy back and forth over the color, comparing the value of the gray stripes to the color seen through the punched holes. Search until you find the stripe where the value of the gray and the color appear to be the closest—neither being darker or lighter. That will be the correct achromatic value for that color. The location of the stripe relative to middle gray will also indicate if the color's value is high key or low key. Note: it is often easier to compare value and color while squinting.

5.2 Barbara Morgan, *Cadenza (Light Drawing)*, 1940. Gelatin silver print, 17⅞ × 15 in. (45.5 × 38.2 cm). This work features an intense contrast between light and dark values. The extreme whiteness of the swirling line glows and dances against the deep black background. Digital Image © The Museum of Modern Art/Licensed by SCALA/Art Resource, NY. The Museum of Modern Art, New York, NY.

5.3 Käthe Kollwitz, *Whetting the Scythe* (K1.90x/xiib), original 1905. Edition published by Otto Felsing in 1921. Plate 3 of the *Peasants' War* series. Etching, 11¾ × 11¾ in. (298 × 298 mm). Käthe Kollwitz brilliantly used low-key values—middle gray to black—to create a dramatically menacing mood in her composition, which is quite appropriate for the subject matter: peasants preparing for revolt. Notice how the lightest of those values is reserved for small areas of highlight, while the majority of the work consists of darker tones. Photograph © Whitworth Art Gallery, The University of Manchester, UK/The Bridgeman Art Library International. Art © 2011 Artists Rights Society (ARS), New York/VG Bild-Kunst, Bonn.

5.4 Robert Bauer, *Centinela III*, 2004. Graphite on gessoed paper, 15 × 18¼ in. In this image the artist has developed what appears at first glance to be quite a full and broad array of value. But a closer examination reveals that the range of value is limited to the lightest values on the achromatic scale— from white to middle gray. Known as high-key composition, it holds the viewer's attention by the skillful organization of areas of related value and juxtaposing extremes of the limited value range employed. © Robert Bauer. Courtesy of Forum Gallery, New York.

work contains mostly light values, ranging from white to middle gray, it is said to have **high-key values** (fig. 5.4). With both approaches, a limited amount of the opposite values may be introduced for accents, but those contrasting accents should not destroy the dominant feeling of lightness or darkness. The "key" selected can be used to establish a general mood for the work—a preponderance of dark (low-key) areas creates an atmosphere of gloom, mystery, drama, or menace, whereas a composition that is basically light (high-key) will produce quite the opposite effect.

Martha Alf, *Pears Series 11 #7*, 1978. 4B pencil on bond paper, 11 × 14 in. At a casual glance, these values appear blended by rubbing drawing materials, but close examination reveals that Martha Alf created this image using delicately drawn lines so fine that they are not recognized as individual lines. Rather, the marks combine to produce areas of strong highlights and shadows that define the pears and their surroundings. This results in crisp and sparkling surfaces. Newspace Gallery, Los Angeles. Photograph by George Hoffman.

5.6 Peter Milton, *Points of Departure III: Twentieth Century Limited*, 1998. Etching and engraving, 24½ × 38½ in. This very large and complex intaglio print uses a full range of achromatic values to capture the essence of another era. As seen here, etching and engraving techniques can create a wide range of line qualities, as well as sharp value contrasts and more subtle gradations of light to dark. © Peter Milton. Courtesy of Davidson Galleries.

VALUE AND ART MEDIA

Although any medium can show rich darks, sparkling whites, and the complete range of grays, some media lend themselves more naturally than others to the development of a full range of value. Artists working in drawing, printmaking, or photography, for example, have long experimented with value, using the tools, materials, and techniques of that medium to explore its effects.

For the *draftsman*, the range of value in a drawn line could be the result of the chosen surface or the pressure exerted on it. In a pencil line, for example, the degree of value could be determined by the hardness of the graphite, the force with which it is used, or the surface quality of the paper (see fig. 3.8D).

Value can also be created by placing lines of the same or different qualities (wet or dry, pencil or chalk, direct or blended) alongside or across each other to produce generalized areas of value. These marks may be so delicate that they are barely noticeable (fig. 5.5) or so aggressive that they reveal the energy driving the artist. In addition to hatching and cross-hatching, a wide range of grays and gradual changes in value

5.17 Jack Beal, *Still Life with Tools*, 1979. Pastel on black wove paper, 75.9 × 101.7 cm (sheet). Beal transforms ordinary tools into mysterious objects with his tenebristic use of pastel. The objects in the wheelbarrow seem to glow, elevated from their prosaic origins. Jalane and Richard Davison Collection, 1990.511.2. The Art Institute of Chicago. Photography © The Art Institute of Chicago.

5.18 Signed: Khem Karan, *Prince Riding an Elephant*, Mughal, period of Akbar, c. 1600. Opaque watercolor and gold on paper, 12¼ × 18½ in. (31.2 × 47 cm). Historically, South Asian artists have usually disregarded the use of light (illumination) in favor of decorative-value compositions. The Metropolitan Museum of Art, Rogers Fund, 1925. (25.6B.4) Photograph © 1988 The Metropolitan Museum of Art /Art Resource, NY.

northern-Italian painters and instituted this so-called dark manner of painting in Western Europe. The tenebrists and their followers were fascinated by the peculiarities of lighting, particularly the way that lighting affected mood or emotional expression. They deviated from standard light conditions by placing the implied light sources in unexpected locations, thereby creating unusual visual and spatial effects (fig. 5.15). Rembrandt continued to adapt and perfect the techniques of this effect, which he learned from migratory artists from Germany and southern Holland (fig. 5.16). The strong contrasts lent themselves well to highly dramatic—even theatrical—work, and *value* became a defining characteristic in Baroque painting. The extreme darkness of tenebrism eventually fell out of style but, recently, artists like Jack Beal have revived interest in the style for its expressive properties (fig. 5.17).

DECORATIVE VALUE

Art styles that stress **decorative** or **shallow space** usually ignore conventional light sources or neglect representation of light altogether. If lighting effects appear, they are incorporated based on their contribution to the total form of the work, not to highlight a specific object. The lack of lighting—either natural or "staged"—is characteristic of the artwork of primitive and prehistoric tribes and traditional East Asians and from certain periods of Western art, notably the Middle Ages. In addition, the work of many contemporary artists is completely free of illusionistic lighting; instead, such artists concentrate on pictorial invention, imagination, and formal considerations. Emotional impact is not necessarily sacrificed (as witnessed in medieval art), but the emotion speaks primarily through the form and is consequently less obvious.

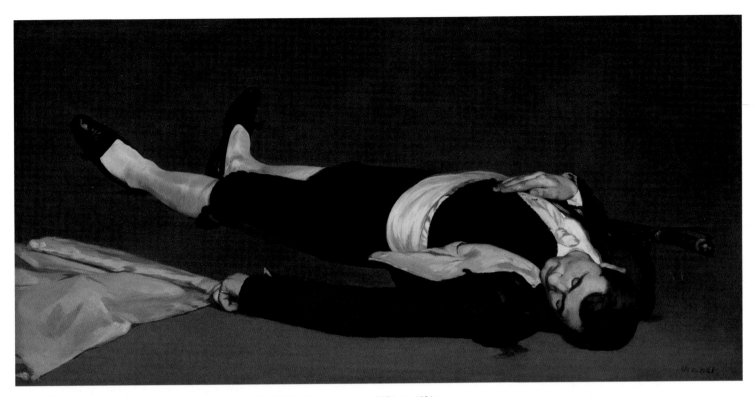

5.19 Édouard Manet, *The Dead Toreador*, probably 1864. Oil on canvas, 29⅞ × 60⅜ in. (75.9 × 153.4 cm). Manet, a nineteenth-century naturalist, was one of the first artists to break with traditional chiaroscuro, making use, instead, of flat areas of value. These flat areas meet abruptly, unlike the blended edges used by artists before Manet. This was one of the great technical developments of nineteenth-century art. Widener Collection. © 1998 Board of Trustees, National Gallery of Art, Washington DC.

The trend away from illumination values (lights and darks from a single light source) gained strength in the nineteenth century, partly because of growing interest in Middle Eastern and East Asian art forms (fig. 5.18). The interest in nondramatic lighting was also given a scientific, Western interpretation when the naturalist Édouard Manet observed that multiple light sources tend to flatten object surfaces and neutralize the plastic qualities of objects, thereby minimizing gradations of value (see fig. 5.10B). As a result, he laid his colors on canvas in flat areas, beginning with bright, light colors and generally neglecting shadow (fig. 5.19). Some critics have claimed this to be the great technical advance of the nineteenth century, because it paved the way for nonrepresentational uses of value and helped revive interest in the shallow-space concept.

The use of carefully controlled shallow space can be seen in the works of the early Cubists and their followers (see fig. T.51). Those painters gave order to space by arranging flat planes that abstracted the subject matter. Initially, the planes were shaded individually and semi-naturalistically, although giving no indication of any one light source. Later, each plane took on a characteristic value and, in combination with others, produced a carefully conceived shallow space. Eventually, this shallow spatial effect was developed by focusing on the advancing and receding characteristics of value (see fig. 4.2). The explorations of these early-twentieth-century artists led to increased attention on the intrinsic significance of each

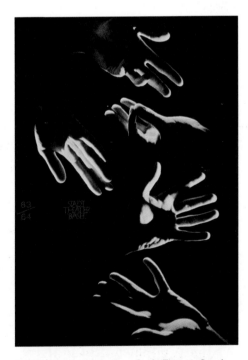

5.20 Armin Hofmann, *Stadt Theater Basel, 63/64*, 1963. Offset lithograph, 50¼ × 35½ in. (127.6 × 90.1 cm). The contrast between light and dark is the dominant element in this poster, creating a sense of drama. Gift of the artist. Digital image © The Museum of Modern Art/Licensed by SCALA/Art Resource, NY.

5.21 Nicolas Poussin, study for *Rape of the Sabines*, c. 1633. Pen and ink with wash, 6½ × 8⅞ in. (16.4 × 22.5 cm). Preparatory, or "thumbnail," sketches give the artist the opportunity to explore movement, ground systems, value structure, and compositional variations. In Poussin's sketch, it seems likely that the artist was striving for rhythmical movement within the horizontal thrust of the composition. Devonshire Collection, Chatsworth. Reproduced by permission of the Duke of Devonshire and the Chatsworth Settlement Trustees. Photograph: Photographic Survey Courtauld Institute of Art.

5.22 Barry Schactman, *Study after Poussin*, 1959. Brush and ink with wash, 10 × 7⅞ in. (25.4 × 20 cm). Loose, rapid sketches can also be used to explore value patterns, color structure, and movement. Yale University Art Gallery, New Haven, CT. Transfer from Yale Art School.

and every element. Value was no longer forced to serve primarily as a tool to create depth and space, although it continued to be used in this way. Artists began to think of value as a vital and lively part of a work, one that was worthy of being the primary focus itself (fig. 5.20). Indeed, there are many ways that value contributes to a work—it creates relative dominance, indicates deep or two-dimensional space, establishes mood, and produces spatial unity.

VALUE PATTERN AND COMPOSITION

Although most viewers recognize the importance of subject in an artwork, they often overlook the importance of the areas of value that are strategically woven through the composition. These organized areas of light and dark create a **value pattern,** which becomes the compositional skeleton that supports the image. The value pattern provides the underlying movement, tension, and foundation on which the subject is built. When properly integrated into the final work, the value pattern reinforces the subject. It should neither distract from the image nor separate itself as an overpowering entity or isolated component.

Before starting the final image, many artists explore possible variations for a composition's value pattern by making small studies known as *thumbnail sketches*. These small-scale preliminary value studies allow artists to see how variations in value can change the subject and its overall impression. In figures 5.21 and 5.22, for example, Nicolas Poussin and Barry Schactman develop large rhythmical dark shapes across the bottom of the composition while intermingling smaller receding toned shapes in the middle areas.

Although thumbnails are beneficial in compositional planning, they may be difficult to relate to the final work because of their scale. Small drawings may look exciting because of the way the areas of value are drawn—with rapid, sketchy strokes full of textural detail. But when enlarged many times, these small strokes may become flat shapes that no longer have the same visual appeal. The artist must then adjust and refine these enlarged value areas to recapture the original intention.

Artists who embrace the use of value pattern can benefit from its subconscious movement and direction. This is true regardless of whether the final work is in black and white or color. Unfortunately, pure, intoxicating color

A

B

5.23 Gerrit Greve, *Monet's Water #3*, 1996. Oil on canvas, 24 × 36 in. A common weakness when using color is a lack of awareness of the pattern created by the colors' values. Black-and-white photographs of artwork can reveal this problem very clearly. When figure A is translated into achromatic values (B), it becomes apparent that the range of lights and darks is quite limited. In this case, the artist probably intended for a limited value range, but this phenomenon may surprise a beginning artist who thinks only in terms of color. Even a composition of closely related hues benefits from the careful consideration of its value pattern. © Gerrit Greve/Corbis.

5.24 Andrew Stevovich, *Internet Café*, 2006. Oil on linen, 28 × 32 in. In this painting, a closed-value composition, the color values lie between prescribed and precise limits, primarily object edges and contours. Courtesy of Andrew Steovich and Adelson Galleries.

often "blinds" people from seeing how chromatic values relate to the overall organization. Black-and-white photographs of colorful work help reveal any related weaknesses (fig. 5.23A and B).

While integrating value structure into an image, an artist should be aware of two approaches for developing the value pattern: closed-value and open-value compositions. In **closed-value compositions,** values are contained within the edges or boundaries of shapes. This sets those shapes apart from surrounding areas and often serves to clearly identify them. The pattern created by these values is dependent on the positioning of the subject(s) (fig. 5.24). In **open-value compositions,**

5.25 DeLoss McGraw, *Mother and Child "Bleak and Lonely Heights" in August Moving Sunlight,* 2002. Gouache on paper, 20 × 30 in. This is an example of what is basically an open-value composition. A light-valued yellow moves across the upper half, occasionally interrupted by a rocking horse, black rectangle, and ladder. A dark red shape moves across the lower third through the baby, the woman's dress and legs, the wagon, and the background. A linear accent or subtle change of color defines the subject in those areas. A few closed areas—like the wheels and ladders—are strategically placed for contrast. Courtesy of ACA Galleries, New York.

values cross over shape boundaries into adjoining areas, and a line or subtle change in texture or color is often necessary to make the shapes visible. The pattern made by these values is not in any way dependent on the location of the subject(s); this independent patterning of lights and darks helps integrate the shapes and unify the composition (fig. 5.25; see also fig. 4.2).

With both open-value and closed-value compositions, the emotive possibilities of value schemes are easy to see. The artist may employ closely related values to generate hazy, foglike effects (see figs. 5.4 and 8.4). Sharply defined shapes are enhanced by dramatically contrasting values (see figs. 5.5 and 5.14). Thus, value can run the gamut from decoration to vivid expression. It is a multipurpose tool for establishing contrasts, controlling eye movement, creating the illusion of space, and conveying a vast range of emotion.

THREE-DIMENSIONAL APPLICATIONS OF VALUE

Although artists working with three-dimensional forms do not have to create the illusion of mass through the rendering of light and dark surfaces, they are certainly aware of the relationship between lighting and dimensionality. As the artist physically manipulates three-dimensional shapes, contrasting lights and shadows are produced on the forms. The presence of light occurs when a surface area is exposed by a source of light. Conversely, dark or shadowy areas occur when a surface faces away (or is hidden) from a light source. Each basic form reacts differently to the light. As we see in figure 5.26, gently curved surfaces reveal an evenly flowing value gradation, whereas an abrupt change of value occurs on a sharp edge. Any angular change of two juxtaposed surfaces, however slight, results in contrasts of value. The sharper the angular change, the greater the contrast (see figs. 3.30, 4.33, 4.35, and 5.8).

When any part of a 3-D work blocks the passage of light, shadows result. (This includes an area that has been heavily textured, although shadows cast by the textures themselves will make the area appear darker when compared to smoother passages.) The pattern of lights and darks changes as the position of the viewer, the work, or its source of illumination changes. If a work has a great deal of shape variation and/or penetration, the shadow patterns are more likely to define the work, regardless of the position of the light source. For most 3-D work, the light source is relatively constant, and the highlights and shadows change only as the viewer moves positions. However, kinetic sculpture (such as mobiles) creates continuous changes in the relationship of light and shadow because the light source, in effect, changes as the object itself moves (see fig. 2.70). Many sculptors are interested in creating these kinds of relationships.

Value changes can also be achieved by painting a 3-D work. It is much easier to see shadow patterns that are cast on an object painted with light values than on a piece that has been painted with dark values (see fig. 1.40). The lighter values work best on pieces that depend on secondary contours; darker values are most successful in emphasizing the major contour, or **silhouette** (see figs. 4.33A and B and 4.37). Strong contrasts between image and background also create the silhouettes that define thin linear 3-D structures (see figs. 3.31 and 3.32).

For the three-dimensional artist, a good light source and the value range created by it are important compositional tools. Light and shadows aid in

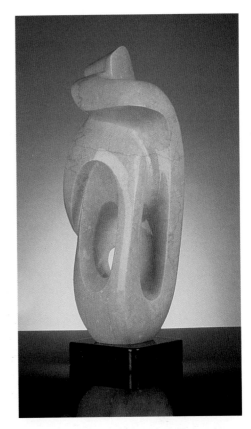

5.26 Julie Warren Martin, *Marchesa*, 1988. Italian Botticino marble, 28 × 12 × 10 in. (71.1 × 30.5 × 25.4 cm). A piece of sculpture "paints" itself with values. The greater the projections and the sharper the edges, the greater and more abrupt the contrasts. From the Collection of Kirby and Priscilla Smith. Courtesy of the artist.

describing a work's dimensionality and spatial setting; enhance the effectiveness of the design pattern; and contribute to the psychological, emotional, and dramatic expression of the artist.

Texture

CHAPTER SIX

Henrique Oliveira, *Tapumes*, 2009. Wood, 4.7 × 13.4 × 2 m.
Installation at Rice Gallery, Houston. Courtesy of the artist and Galeria Millan, Sao Paulo, Brazil. Photograph by Nash Baker.

THE VOCABULARY OF
TEXTURE

Texture — The surface character of a material that can be experienced through touch or the illusion of touch. Texture is produced by natural forces or through an artist's manipulation of the art elements.

abstract texture
A texture derived from the appearance of an actual surface but rearranged and/or simplified by the artist to satisfy the demands of the artwork.

actual texture
A surface that can be experienced through the sense of touch (as opposed to a surface visually simulated by the artist).

assemblage
A technique that involves grouping actual items (three-dimensional objects) in a display. The items may be found or specially created, and they are often displayed "in situ"—that is, in a natural position or in the middle of a room rather than on a wall.

atmospheric perspective
The illusion of depth produced in graphic works by lightening values, softening details and textures, reducing value contrasts, and neutralizing colors in objects as they recede.

collage
A technique of picturemaking in which real materials possessing actual textures are attached to the picture-plane surface, often in combination with painted or drawn passages.

genre paintings
Paintings with subject matters that concern everyday life, domestic scenes, family relationships, and the like.

invented texture
A created texture whose only source is the artist's imagination. It generally produces a decorative pattern and should not be confused with **abstract texture.**

paint quality
The intrinsic character of a painting material—thickness, glossiness, and so forth—which can enrich a surface through its own textural interest.

papier collé
A visual and tactile technique in which scraps of paper having various textures are pasted to the picture surface to enrich or embellish those areas. The printing of text or images on those scraps can provide further visual richness or decorative pattern.

pattern
1. Any artistic design (sometimes serving as a model for imitation). 2. A series of repeated elements and/or designs that are usually varied and produce interconnections and obvious directional movements.

simulated texture
A convincing copy or translation of an object's texture in any medium. (See **trompe l'oeil.**)

tactile
A quality that refers to the sense of touch.

texture
The surface character of a material that can be experienced through touch or the illusion of touch. Texture is produced by natural forces or through an artist's manipulation of the art elements.

trompe l'oeil
Literally, "deceives the eye"; the copying of nature with such exactitude as to be mistaken for the real thing. (See **simulated texture.**)

INTRODUCTION TO TEXTURE

Texture is a universal experience that often occurs on a subconscious level. Whether running your toes through grass or putting on a sweater, you feel the unique tactile quality of those materials, even if you are not consciously aware of it. For example, when you hold this book, you feel the slippery smoothness of the pages, the sharp corners, and the ridged effect of the stacked pages. Look around, and you will see many other textures—some that are inviting, others that are repelling. In fact, everything has a texture, from the rough surface of tree bark to the soft fluffiness of a carpet, from the hard glossiness of a window pane to the jagged edge of broken glass. Look for art that is around you and see what textures it displays. Is the texture obvious? Does it make you want to touch the work? Although pieces of art have definite textures when touched, they also can give the appearance of textures in solely a visual way. Indeed, our world is full of a variety of textural experiences.

THE NATURE OF TEXTURE

Texture may be unique among the art elements because it immediately engages two sensory processes. It is more intimately and dramatically known through the sense of touch, but we can also *see* texture and, thus, predict its feel. In viewing a picture or a piece of sculpture, we may recognize objects through the artist's use of characteristic shapes, colors, and value patterns—but we may also react to the artist's

6.1 Dennis Wojtkiewicz, *Kiwi Series #1*, 2005. Oil on canvas, 36 × 66 in. (91.4 × 167.6 cm). This painting is an excellent example of our sight being able to activate other senses. Here, the presentation of the translucent fruit and fuzzy skin is so convincing that we have a visual and a tactile reaction—and for some, a sensation of taste. Courtesy J. Cacciola Gallery, New York, NY.

6.2 A cross section of four materials shows (*from left to right*): a hard, smooth, glossy surface; a rippled metallic surface; rough cinderblock; and weathered wood. The textures of these objects can be clearly seen due to the highlights and shadows formed by the light shining on each surface, suggesting how the actual objects would feel if they were stroked. The far left, being flat, produces no shadows but shows reflections. The middle left texture produces both shadow and reflection. In the cinderblock, shadows are cast among the small stones, and in the wood, alongside the weathered undulations.

rendering of the surface character of those objects. In such a case, we have both visual and **tactile** experiences (fig. 6.1).

Whether an artwork is 2-D or 3-D, our response to the textural qualities of the work is an important part of the viewing experience, and an

understanding of the nature of texture is vital. The feel of an object's surface—its physical texture—depends on the degree to which the surface is broken up in its treatment: the more broken, the rougher the texture. This not only determines how we feel it but

also how we see it. Rough surfaces intercept light rays, producing an often irregular pattern of lights and darks; glossy surfaces reflect the light more evenly, giving a smoother appearance (fig. 6.2). As we see these patterns of different values, our memory of touching surfaces with similar characteristics triggers a tactile response or sensory reaction. Thus, we can predict an object's feel without ever touching its surface.

TYPES OF TEXTURE

The artist can use four basic types of texture: actual, simulated, abstract, and invented.

Actual Texture

Actual texture is the "real thing"—a surface that can be experienced through the sense of touch. It is not an illusion created by drawing or painting. Historically, actual texture has been a natural part of three-dimensional art; wood, glass, and fibers, for example, have inherent textures that are incorporated into the work (although those textures may be manipulated). For many works of art, the design depends heavily on the actual texture of the medium, especially in the textile arts as well as in ceramics, jewelry, and so forth (see figs. 1.53, 1.54, and 1.56). Architects, for example, often rely on the feel of the materials for inspiration and direction and then balance the varying textures through careful composition (see figs. 1.51 and 1.52).

Painters, too, can utilize the actual texture of their materials, and quite often their work seems to cross the boundary from two- into three-dimensionality. As artists begin to paint or draw on canvas, they change the textural quality of that surface. In some cases, as with charcoal or graphite, the change is subtle—little is done to the "feel" of the surface. In other cases, like *impasto* painting, the thickness and texture of the applied paint can be quite heavy and modeled. This buildup of material alters the way the surface "feels" to the touch, and often, the paint is textured enough to create its own highlights and shadows.

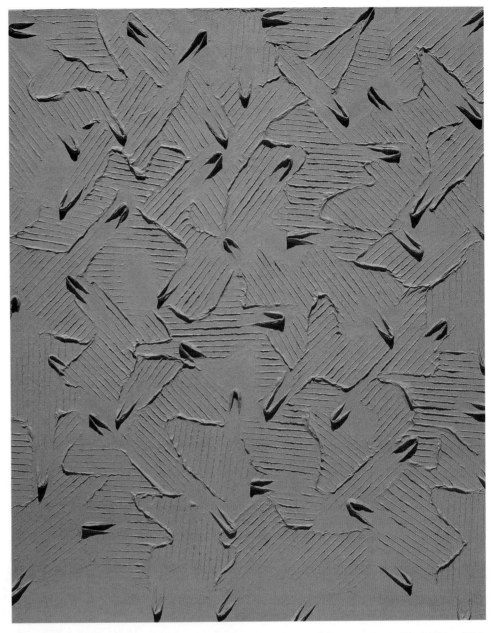

6.3 Seo-Bo Park, *Ecriture No. 940110,* 1994. Mixed media with Korean paper, 26 × 18 in. (65.3 × 46 cm). The massing of paint is clearly evident, particularly in the central portion. Some shapes seem to have been effected by a comblike instrument. Courtesy of Jean Art Gallery, Seoul, Korea.

The textural enrichment can be employed in the creation of specific subject matter, but many times it is used to simply enliven an area with interesting visual detail. In Seo-Bo Park's *Ecriture No. 940110,* the paint is applied in projecting mounds and ridges that begin to create their own patterns (fig. 6.3). Other artists, like Van Gogh in his *Starry Night,* apply the pigment in heavy ribbons directly from the tube of paint, with the furrows of paint reinforcing the subject matter in the picture (see fig. 1.19). The creation of actual texture in both cases is enhanced by the **paint quality,** which is the intrinsic character of the painting materials. The artist controls the paint's thickness, glossiness, and textural richness through the addition of various

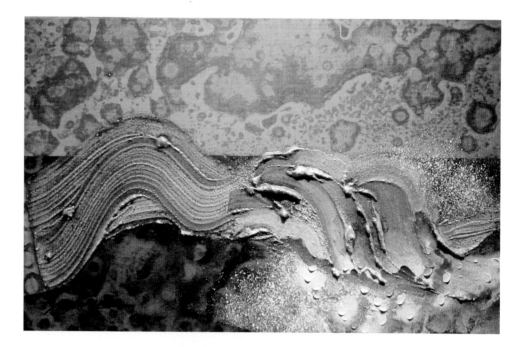

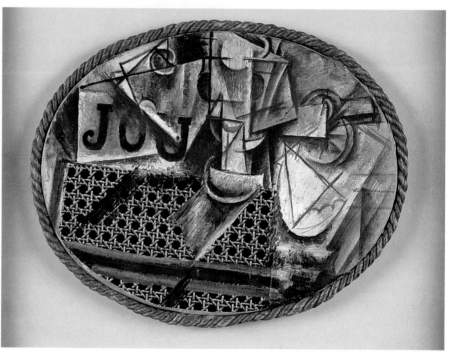

6.4 Robert Mazur, *Nightwave*, 2007. Acrylic on canvas, 18 × 30 in. (45.7 × 76.2 cm). In this painting, invented textures are used to suggest the subject matter. Wet-on-wet resists symbolize sky and water, while heavily aggregated paint textures applied by fingers, brush, and modified palette knife represent crashing waves. Collection of Mr. and Mrs. Edward Plocek. Courtesy of the artist.

6.5 Pablo Picasso, *Still Life with Chair Caning*, 1912. Oil on pasted oilcloth, rope, oval, 10⅝ × 13⅜ in. (27 × 34.9 cm). With this work, Picasso pioneered the development of the papier collé and collage forms—art created by fastening actual materials with textural interest to a flat working surface. These art forms may be used to simulate real textures but are usually created for decorative purposes. Musée Picasso, Paris, France. © 2011 Estate of Pablo Picasso/Artists Rights Society (ARS), New York. Bridgeman-Giraudon/Art Resource, NY.

varnishes, binders, and aggregates in the form of sand or marble dust (fig. 6.4).

In the early twentieth century, the concept of actual texture was expanded to include the addition of various textural materials along with the application of paint. In 1908, Picasso pasted a piece of paper to a drawing. This is the first known example of **papier collé,** a practice that was later expanded to include the use of tickets, portions of newspapers, menus, and the like (see fig. 4.2). Papier collé soon led to **collage,** an art form in which actual objects—rope, chair caning, and other articles of greater substance than paper—were used. Sometimes these objects were used in combination with printed pictures of textures, to juxtapose the experience of actual texture with simulated texture (fig. 6.5).

The problem created by mixing objects and painting is: what is real—the objects, the artistic elements, or both? Do the painted objects have the same reality as the genuine objects? Whatever the answers, the early explorations of the Cubists (the style of Picasso and Braque, about 1907–1912) stimulated other artists to explore new attitudes toward art and made them more

6.6 Ilse Bing, *My World*, 1985. Mixed media, 14 × 17 × 3¾ in. (35.6 × 43.2 × 9.5 cm). The inspiration behind the use of burlap in this artwork stems ultimately from the first collages of Picasso and Braque—then a revolutionary, but now a fairly commonplace, technique. © Ilse Bing, courtesy of Edwynn Houk Gallery, New York.

conscious of surface (fig. 6.6). Today, many artists use actual textures created from combining paint with a wide range of materials other than aggregate, ranging from nails to paintbrushes (fig. 6.7; see also fig. 9.13).

Simulated Texture

Every surface has characteristic light and dark features as well as reflections. When these are skillfully reproduced in an artist's medium, the imitations may be mistaken for the surfaces of real objects. The surface character that looks "real" but in fact is not is said to be a **simulated texture** (fig. 6.8).

Simulated textures are useful for making things identifiable; moreover, we experience a rich tactile enjoyment when viewing them. The Dutch and Flemish artists produced amazing naturalistic effects in still-life and **genre paintings.** Their work shows their dedication to and passion for the

use of simulated texture. Interior designers employ this technique when painting faux (fake) surface treatments imitating stone or veined marble. Simulated textures are often associated with **trompe l'oeil** paintings, which attempt to "fool the eye" with photographic detail convincing enough that it might be mistaken for the real thing (fig. 6.9; see also fig. 6.1). Simulation is a copying technique, a skill that can be quite impressive in its own right. However, a viewer must see past the richness of detail to experience everything else the composition has to offer.

Abstract Texture

Instead of trying to reproduce or exactly imitate the textures of their subjects, many artists prefer to abstract them. **Abstract textures** usually display some hint of the original texture, but they have been modified to suit the artist's particular needs. The result is

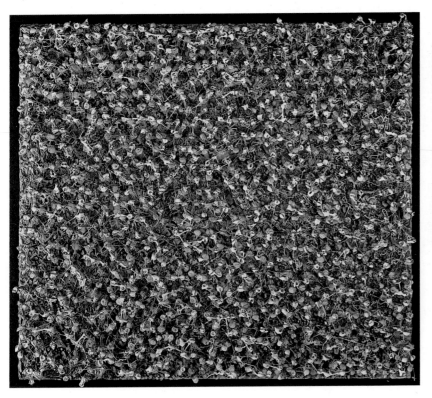

6.7 Gary Lawe, *I Remember Being Free*, 1998. Lucite, acrylic, encaustic, and nails, 24 × 30 in. (61 × 76 cm). The admixture of nails with the varied paint media creates an actual textured surface that is rich in its inherent visual and tactile qualities. Courtesy of the artist Gary Lawe and the Don O'Melveny Gallery, West Hollywood.

6.8 Andrew Newell Wyeth, *Spring Beauty*, 1943. Drybrush watercolor on paper, 20 × 30 in. (50.8 × 76.2 cm). Skillful manipulation of the medium can effectively simulate actual textures. Sheldon Memorial Art Gallery, University of Nebraska, Lincoln, NE. The F. M. Hall Collection 1944.H-247. © Andrew Wyeth.

6.9 Gary Schumer, *Split Table Still Life*, 1992. Oil on canvas, 64 × 76 in. (162.6 × 193 cm). In this painting, the artist is concerned with the simulation of textures ranging from plywood and plexiglass to cloth, ceramic, and metal. As with all trompe l'oeil painting, the wealth of detail can obscure other compositional offerings—such as the compelling value pattern and the Cubist-like twisting and layering of spatial planes. Courtesy of the artist, Private Collection.

6.10 Roy Lichtenstein, *Cubist Still Life with Playing Cards*, 1974. Oil and magna on canvas, 96 × 60 in. (243.8 × 152.4 cm). The wood grain in this work is not abstracted beyond recognition; it is clearly derived from wood, though simplified and stylized. © Estate of Roy Lichtenstein.

often a simplified version of the original, emphasizing the pattern or design (fig. 6.10). Abstract textures normally appear in works where the degree of abstraction is consistent throughout. In these works, the textures function in a decorative way; there is no attempt to "fool the eye," but they enrich the work in the same way that simulated textures do. Besides helping the artist to simplify his or her material, abstract textures can be used to accent some areas or diminish others (i.e., to achieve relative dominance) and to control eye movement. Thus, they can be a potent compositional tool.

Invented Texture

Invented textures are textures without precedent; they do not simulate, nor are they abstracted from reality. They are purely the creation of the artist's imagination and usually appear in abstracted and nonobjective works (fig. 6.11).

6.11 Brian Fridge, *Vault Sequence No. 10*, 2000. Black-and-white silent video, four minutes, DVD, edition 2 of 5. *Vault Sequence* is a seven-minute video of the inside of the artist's refrigerator freezer. Through the medium of video, the artist creates invented texture. The time-based aspect of this medium creates images that would otherwise not be seen. The video camera's eye reveals mini-universes. Courtesy of Brian Fridge, the Modern Art Museum of Fort Worth, and Dunn & Brown Contemporary.

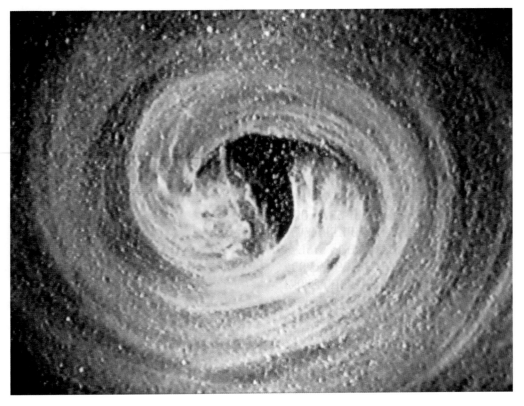

Color

CHAPTER SEVEN

Paul Cézanne, *Apples and Biscuits*, c. 1879–1882. Oil on canvas, 46 x 55 cm.
Musée de l'Orangerie, Paris, France/Lauros-Giraudon, Paris/SuperStock, Inc.

Color — The visual response to different wavelengths of sunlight identified as red, green, blue, and so on; having the physical properties of hue, intensity, and value.

academic
Art that conforms to established traditions and approved conventions as practiced in formal art schools. Academic art stresses standards, set procedures, and rules.

achromatic
Relating to color perceived only in terms of neutral grays from light to dark; without hue.

additive color
Color created by superimposing light rays. Adding together (or superimposing) the three primary colors of light—red, blue, and green—will produce white. The secondaries are cyan, yellow, and magenta.

analogous colors
Colors that are closely related in hue. They are usually adjacent to each other on the color wheel.

chroma
1. The purity of a hue, or its freedom from white, black, or gray (and wavelengths of other color). 2. The intensity of a hue. 3. Computer programs often refer to chroma as *saturation*.

chromatic
Pertaining to the presence of color.

chromatic value
The relative degree of lightness or darkness demonstrated by a given color.

color
The visual response to different wavelengths of sunlight identified as red, green, blue, and so on; having the physical properties of hue, intensity, and value.

color tetrad
Four colors, equally spaced on the color wheel, containing a primary and its complement and a complementary pair of intermediates. This has also come to mean any organization of color on the wheel forming a rectangle that could include a double split-complement.

color triad
Three colors, equally spaced on the color wheel, forming an equilateral triangle. The twelve-step color wheel is made up of a primary triad, a secondary triad, and two intermediate triads.

complementary colors
Two colors directly opposite each other on the color wheel. A primary color is complementary to a secondary color, which is a mixture of the two remaining primaries.

high-key color
Any color that has a value level of middle gray or lighter.

hue
The generic name of a color (*red, blue, green*, etc.); also designates a color's position in the spectrum or on the color wheel. Hue is determined by the specific wavelength of the color in a ray of light.

intensity
The saturation, strength, or purity of a hue. A vivid color is of high intensity; a dull color is of low intensity.

intermediate color
A color produced by a mixture of a primary color and a secondary color.

intermediate triad
A group of three intermediate colors that are equally spaced on the color wheel and form an equilateral triangle; two groups of intermediate triads are found on the color wheel: red-orange/yellow-green/blue-violet and red-violet/blue-green/yellow-orange.

local (objective) color
The color as seen in the objective world (green grass, blue sky, red barn, etc.).

low-key color
Any color that has a value level of middle gray or darker.

monochromatic
Having only one hue; may include the complete range of value (of one hue) from white to black.

neutralized (color), neutralization (of color)
Color that has been grayed or reduced in intensity by being mixed with any of the neutrals or with a complementary color (so that the mixture contains all three primaries, in equal or unequal amounts).

neutrals
1. The inclusion of all color wavelengths will produce white, and the absence of any wavelengths will be perceived as black. With neutrals, no single color is noticed—only a sense of light and dark or the range from white through gray to black. 2. A color altered by the addition of its complement so that the original sensation of hue is lost or grayed.

patina
1. A natural film, usually greenish, that results from the oxidation of bronze or other metallic material. 2. Colored pigments and/or chemicals applied to a sculptural surface.

pigment
A color substance that gives its color property to another material by being mixed with it or covering it. Pigments, usually insoluble, are added to liquid vehicles to produce paint and ink. They are different from dyes, which are dissolved in liquids and give their coloring effects by staining or being absorbed by a material.

primary color
A preliminary hue that cannot be broken down or reduced into component colors. Primary colors are the basic hues of any color system that in theory may be used to mix all other colors.

primary triad
The three primary colors on the color wheel (red, yellow, and blue), which are equally spaced and form an equilateral triangle.

secondary color
A color produced by a mixture of two primary colors.

secondary triad
The three secondary colors on the color wheel (orange, green, and violet), which are equally spaced and form an equilateral triangle.

shade (of color)
A color produced by mixing black with a hue, which lowers the value level and decreases the quantity of light reflected.

simultaneous contrast
When two different colors come into direct contact, the contrast intensifies the difference between them.

spectrum
The band of individual colors that results when a beam of white light is broken into its component wavelengths, identifiable as hues.

split-complement(s)
A color and the two colors on either side of its complement.

subjective color
1. That which is derived from the mind, instead of physical reality, and reflects a personal bias, emotion, or interpretation.
2. A subjective color tends to be inventive or creative.

subtractive color
The sensation of color that is produced when wavelengths of light are reflected back to the viewer after all other wavelengths have been subtracted and/or absorbed.

tertiary color
Color resulting from the mixture of all three primaries, two secondary colors, or complementary intermediates. Tertiary colors are characterized by the neutralization of intensity and hue. A great variety of tertiary colors, created by mixing differing amounts of the parent colors, are found on the inner rings of the color wheel, which lead to complete neutralization.

tint (of color)
A color produced by mixing white with a hue, which raises the value level and increases the quantity of light reflected.

tonality, tone (color)
1. A generic term for the quality of a color, often indicating a slight modification in hue, value, or intensity—for example, yellow with a greenish tone. 2. The dominating hue, value, or intensity; for example, artwork containing mostly red and red-orange will have an overall tonality of red (the dominant *hue*), and areas of color might have a dark tonality (indicating the dominant *value*) or a muted tonality (indicating the dominant *intensity* level).

value (color)
1. The relative degree of lightness or darkness. 2. The characteristic of color determined by its lightness or darkness or the quantity of light reflected by the color.

value pattern
The arrangement or organization of values that control compositional movement and create a unifying effect throughout a work of art.

THE CHARACTERISTICS OF COLOR

Color, the most universally appreciated element, appeals to children and adults instantly. Infants reach out for brightly colored objects, and older children watch in fascination as yellow mixed with blue magically becomes green. People generally find color exciting and attractive. They may question art for many other reasons but rarely object to the use of color, provided that it is harmonious in character. In fact, a work of art can frequently be appreciated for its color style alone.

Color is one of the most expressive elements because it affects our emotions directly. When we view a work of art, we do not have to rationalize our feelings about its color; instead, we have an immediate emotional reaction to it. Pleasing rhythms and harmonies of color satisfy our aesthetic desires. We like certain combinations of color and reject others. In representational art, color identifies objects and creates the illusion of space. In nonrepresentational art, the use of color conveys a concept, idea, or emotional experience. The study of color is based on scientific theory—principles that can be observed and easily systematized. In this chapter, we will examine these basic characteristics of color relationships to see how they help give form and meaning to the subject of an artist's work.

LIGHT: THE SOURCE OF COLOR

Color begins with and is derived from light, either natural or artificial. Where there is little light, there is little color; where the light is strong, color is likely to be intense. When the light is weak, such as at dusk or dawn, it is difficult to distinguish one color from another. Under strong sunlight, as in tropical climates, colors seem to take on additional intensity.

Every ray of light coming from the sun is composed of waves that vibrate at different speeds. The sensation of color is aroused in the mind by the way our sense of vision responds to the different wavelengths. This can be

7.1 As a beam of light passes through a glass prism, the rays of light are bent, or refracted, at different angles according to their wavelengths. The rays of red have the longest wavelengths and are bent the least; those of violet have the shortest wavelengths and have the greatest refraction. In this rainbow array of hues, called the *spectrum,* we see bands of red, orange, yellow, green, blue, blue-violet (or indigo), and violet. © David Parker/Photo Researchers, Inc.

7.2 The projected additive primary colors—red, blue (a color named by industry and scientists that is actually closer to violet), and green—create the secondary colors of cyan, yellow, and magenta when two are overlapped. When all three primaries are combined, white light is produced. © Eastman Kodak Company.

demonstrated by observing the way a beam of white light passes through a glass prism and then reflects off a sheet of white paper. The rays of light bend, or refract, as they pass through the glass at different angles (according to their wavelengths) and then reflect off the white paper as different colors. We see these colors as individual stripes in a narrow band called the **spectrum.** The colors easily distinguishable in this band are red, orange, yellow, green, blue, blue-violet, and violet (scientists use the term *indigo* for the color artists call *blue-violet*). These colors also blend gradually; thus, we can discern several intermediate colors between them (fig. 7.1).

Additive Color

The colors of the spectrum are pure, and they represent the greatest intensity (brightness) possible. If we could reverse the process mentioned in the previous paragraph and recombine all these spectrum colors, we would again have white light. When artists or physicists work with rays of colored light, they are using **additive color,** and by mixing only a select few of the spectrum colors, they may produce various other colors of light. Red, blue, and green are known as the *additive primaries.* These three colors of light are so basic that they themselves cannot be created from other mixtures, but when they

are combined, they form the *additive secondaries*—magenta, yellow, and cyan. As seen in figure 7.2, magenta is produced where red and blue light overlap; yellow is produced where red and green light overlap; and cyan is produced where green and blue light overlap. In the center of that figure, white light is created where the red, blue, and green light rays overlap (magenta, yellow, and cyan thereby also overlap)—demonstrating again that white light may be created by the presence of all color wavelengths.

Televisions and computers both use this additive-color mixing process. Most modern TVs and color monitors consist of small pixel groups

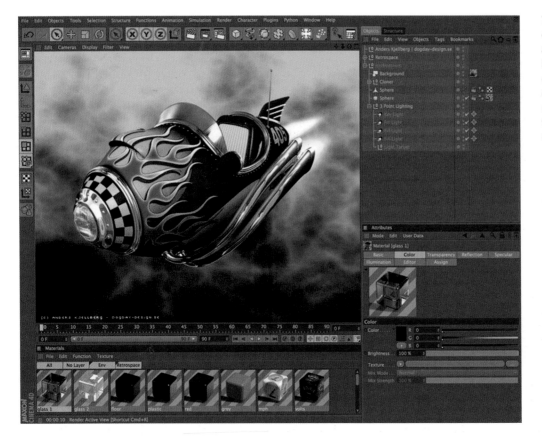

7.3 Color adjustments in computer design, rocket design. Filmmakers have always sought to push technological boundaries. Today, designers on films can use numerous software programs to create objects and people digitally, testing out various looks and coloring before finalization. © Anders Kjellberg/dogday-design.se. Courtesy of MAXON (maxon.NET).

that emit red, blue, and green light. Arranged in nearly imperceptible horizontal and vertical lines, these units can illuminate each color singly or in various combinations to produce the sensation of every color possible. At viewing distance, the eye merges the glowing pixels to perceive one complete image (a viewer sees thirty images per second). Numerous technologies (including the cathode ray tube, liquid crystal display, plasma display, and digital light projection) offer innovative methods for transmitting images, but all use additive color in their methodology. Some quickly flash the colored lights to make an image; some use a steady stream of constantly changing lights. In general, the more frames displayed per second, the smoother the movement appears onscreen. The image may seem jumpy at 18 frames per second but smooth at 30 frames per second—although as many as 120 frames may be needed in high-end video rendering to make the image seem more realistic for computer games and special effects. Normally, our brains can process only about 75 frames per second; the extra information is coalesced to make each image more complete.

Computers are now regularly employed as an important tool in additive-color mixing. Not only can software programs allow the artist to create color images, many with the illusion of three-dimensional space and scale, but they also assist the artist in developing ideas. Computer-generated models let the user move about in the image, trying multiple spacing and color relationships. Today, artists and designers for films and video games find these programs to be indispensable in their work (fig. 7.3).

Other artists, such as James Turrell, specifically explore the properties and characteristics of additive color in their works (fig. 7.4). These artists explore the nature of light, often encountering strange effects. Combinations of colors, for example, can heighten or even change the perception of a color. In Turrell's work, the color of the sky is influenced by the structure's continuously changing ambient lighting. Using both space and the principles of additive color, Turrell explores the psychological and spiritual phenomena that occur when we perceive light.

Increasingly, an artist needs to be familiar with the additive-color system. In addition to computer art, it is used in theater, video production, computer animation, video games, digital billboards, slide and multimedia presentations, laser light shows, and landscape and interior lighting. In each case, art-

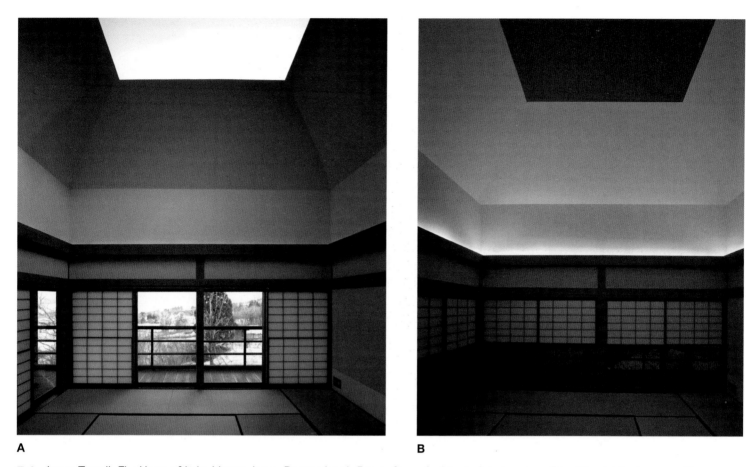

A   **B**

7.4 James Turrell, *The House of Light*, Niigata, Japan. Designed with Future Scape Architects. Interior view of traditional tatami room with Turrell-designed retractable roof. In this Skyspace, Turrell combines principles of architecture, sculpture, lighting, and color to create a meditative atmosphere. The work is meant to be experienced slowly, quietly, and over time. A square hole in the ceiling frames the ever-changing sky above. In addition, the interior space is equipped with ambient lighting that further alters the tint of the sky's color. © View Pictures Ltd/SuperStock, Inc.

ists and technicians work with light and create color by mixing the light primaries—red, blue, and green.

Subtractive Color

Because all the colors are present in a beam of sunlight (white light), you may be wondering how certain objects can appear to be one color or another. Any colored object has certain physical properties, called *pigmentation* or *color quality,* that enable it to absorb some color waves and reflect others. The wavelengths that are reflected back to our eyes allow us to perceive that object as a particular color. A green leaf, for ex-

ample, appears green to the eye because the leaf *reflects* only the green waves in the ray of light; the other wavelengths are absorbed, or subtracted, by the pigments in the leaf. An artist's **pigments** have this same property and when applied to the surface of an object, carry the same characteristics. The artist may also modify the surface pigmentation of an object through the use of dyes, stains, and chemical treatments, such as those applied to sculpture.

Regardless of how the surface pigmentation is applied or altered, the sensation of color is created when the object's surface reflects certain wavelengths; the surface absorbs all

wavelengths *except* those of the color perceived. When color is experienced through *reflected* light, we are dealing with **subtractive color** rather than actual light rays and additive color. When an area appears white, all the light wavelengths of color are reflected back to the viewer—none is subtracted (or absorbed) by the area. However, when a color pigment covers the surface, only the wavelengths of that color are reflected back to the viewer—all others are subtracted (or absorbed) by the pigment. As a result, the sensation of that specific color is experienced.

If all the pigment colors were to be blended together, they would (in theory) cancel each other out, and the mixture would *absorb all* wavelengths. In theory, the mixture would appear black—no color reflected. However, in actual practice on the palette, the combination of all pigment colors results not in black but in dark gray, which hints at some color presence but feels "muddy." This occurs because adulterants and imperfections in the pigments, inks, and dyes make it impossible for the surface to absorb all wavelengths. As a result, the area may reflect a mixture of various colors and/or a certain amount of white.

The theory of subtractive color, then, helps explain how we perceive most colored objects and images; the colors we see are reflected wavelengths, as all others have been absorbed. The following sections, therefore, will be concerned with the artist's typical palette of pigments and the color made visible by subtraction (reflected light).

ARTISTS' PIGMENTS AND THE TRIADIC COLOR SYSTEM

As previously mentioned, the spectrum contains red, orange, yellow, green, blue, blue-violet, and violet, with hundreds of subtle color variations. This range of color is available in pigments as well. Beginning artists are likely to use only a few simple, pure colors. They may not realize that simple colors can be varied or that mixing them can create an even wider range of color.

In traditional processes (using pigments and subtractive color), three colors cannot be created through mixing: red, yellow, and blue. These are known as the **primary colors** (fig. 7.5). When two or more of these primaries are mixed, in equal or unequal amounts, they can produce all of the possible colors.

Mixing any *two* primaries in more or less equal proportions produces a **secondary color**: red and yellow result in orange; yellow and blue create green; and blue and red produce violet (see fig. 7.5).

Intermediate colors are mixtures of a primary color with a neighboring secondary color. Combining yellow and green, for example, will create the intermediate color yellow-green (fig. 7.6). Because a change in the proportion of

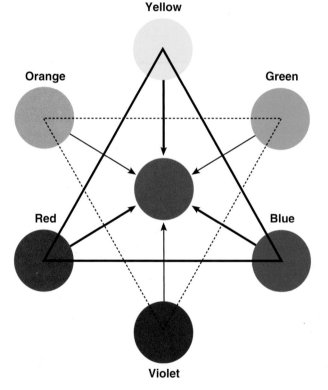

7.5 Primary and secondary colors. A primary triad is shown by solid lines. When the yellow, red, and blue of the primary triad are properly mixed together, the resulting color is a neutralized gray. A secondary triad is connected by dotted lines. When secondary colors are also properly mixed together, the resulting color is gray.

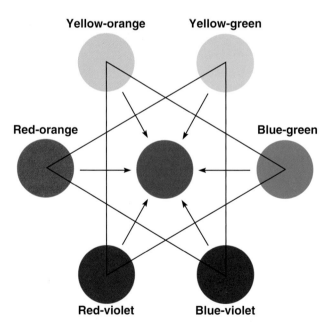

7.6 Intermediate colors. Intermediate colors are created by mixing a primary with a neighboring secondary color (see fig. 7.5). As illustrated here, intermediate colors form two intermediate triads. When the colors of an intermediate triad are mixed together in appropriate proportions, the resulting color is usually a neutralized gray. Unbalanced mixtures produce tertiary colors, which are found in the center rings of figure 7.7.

primary or secondary color used will change the resultant color, many subtle variations are possible; the yellow-green can be made to lean more toward yellow or more toward green.

If we study the theoretical progression of mixed color from yellow to yellow-green to green and so on, we discover a natural order that can be presented as a color wheel (fig. 7.7). Our ability to differentiate subtle variation allows us to see a new color at each position. Note that the primaries, secondaries, and intermediates are found on the outermost ring, where the hues are at spectrum intensity.

Although the number of possible colors is actually infinite, we generally recognize the wheel (or its outermost ring) as having twelve colors, which can be divided and organized into **color triads.** This system of organization is known as the *triadic color system.* The three primary colors are spaced equally apart on the wheel, with yellow usually on the top because it is lightest in value. These colors form an equilateral triangle called a **primary triad** (see fig. 7.5). The three secondary colors are placed between the primaries from which they are mixed; evenly spaced, they create a **secondary triad** composed of orange, green, and violet (see fig. 7.5). Intermediate colors placed between each primary and secondary color create equally spaced units known as **intermediate triads** (see fig. 7.6). The placement of all the colors results in the twelve-step color wheel.

As we move around the color wheel, there is a change in the wavelengths of the light rays that produce the colors. The closer together colors appear on the color wheel, the closer their relationships are; the farther apart, the more contrasting in character they are. The colors directly opposite each other afford the greatest contrast and are known as **complementary colors** (see fig. 7.17). The complement of any color—based on the triadic

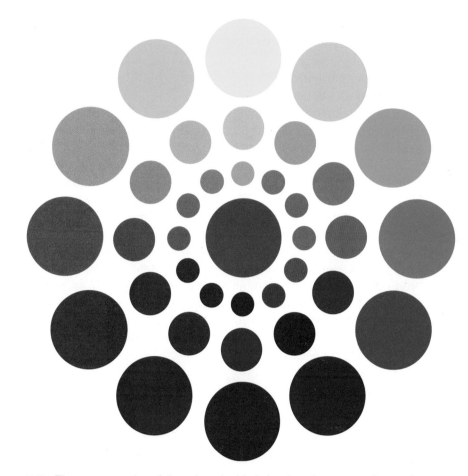

7.7 The outermost ring of the color wheel includes the primary, secondary, and intermediate colors at their greatest intensity (brightness); only twelve steps are shown here, although the number of possible hues is actually infinite. The inner rings contain the tertiary colors, which result from the mixture of one primary with its complement. As each color progresses from the outermost ring toward the center of the wheel (and toward its complement), it loses intensity and becomes more neutralized (grayed). Complete neutralization occurs in the center circle. Only two steps are shown between the outermost ring and complete neutralization, but the number of possible steps is actually infinite.

system—is the combination of the other two colors in its triad. For example, the complement of red (a primary color) is green—an equal-parts mixture of the remaining points in the primary triad (in this case, yellow and blue). Thus, we see that a color and its complement are made up of the three triadic colors. Another example: The complement of yellow is violet—a mixture of blue and red. The complement of any secondary color may be found by knowing what primaries created that secondary; for example, orange is created from red and yellow, so the remaining member

of the primary triad (blue) will be orange's complement.

When a color is mixed with its complement, it becomes **neutralized** (grayed), and a **tertiary** color is produced. Tertiary colors are also created by mixing any two secondary colors or by combining non-analogous intermediate colors. In practical terms, this involves the intermixing of all three primaries in varying proportions and creates the browns, olives, maroons, and so on found on the inner rings of the color wheel (see fig. 7.7). Between the initial color in the outermost ring and complete neutralization in the center, there are actually an infinite number of possible steps, but, for the sake of space, we have presented only two inner rings in our illustration. This will be more fully explained in the coming section called "Intensity."

It should be noted that the color illustrations presented here are created by inks and should be used as guides rather than absolutes. The actual mixing of pigments will reveal, for instance, that each manufacturer's "red" is different and that the color of your mixed "green" depends on what you use as primaries; lemon yellow mixed with ultramarine blue will create a different green than one that uses cadmium yellow and cobalt blue. Color-mixing experiments will disclose much about opacity, staining power, and the adulterants mixed in by manufacturers.

We will see later in this chapter that photographers, printers, and some other artists use alternative systems for organizing color (see "The Evolution of the Color Wheel"). Those systems involve a different set of primaries and secondaries from those mentioned here. However, for the majority of this chapter when we discuss color, we will be concerned with the triadic color system of the painter's palette.

Neutrals

Not all pigments, of course, contain a perceivable color. Some, like black, white, or gray, do not look like any of the colors of the spectrum. No color quality is found in these instances; they are **achromatic.** They differ merely in the quantity of light they reflect. Because we do not distinguish any one color in black, white, and gray, they are also called **neutrals.**

Even though we may not realize it, neutrals do reflect varying amounts of the color wavelengths. One neutral, white, could be thought of as the presence of *all* color, because it occurs when a surface reflects all the color wavelengths to an equal degree. Black, then, could be thought of as the *absence* of color, because it results when a surface absorbs all the color rays equally and reflects none of them. Absolute black is rarely experienced except in such places as deep caves or ocean depths. Therefore, most blacks will contain some trace of reflected color, however slight.

Any gray is an impure white, because it is created by only partial reflection of all the color wavelengths. If a great amount of light is reflected, the gray is light; if very little light is reflected, the gray is dark. The neutrals are concerned with the *quantity* of light reflected, whereas color involves the *quality* of light reflected.

THE PHYSICAL PROPERTIES OF COLOR

Regardless of whether the artist works with **chromatic** paints, dyes, or inks, every color used must be described in terms of three physical properties: hue, value, and intensity (figs. 7.8 and 7.9).

Hue

Hue is the generic color name—*red, blue, green,* and so on. It is determined by the specific wavelength of the color in a ray of light (fig. 7.10; see also fig. 7.1). Hue also designates a color's position in the spectrum or on the color wheel. Each hue exists in many subtle variations, although the differences in wavelengths are so small that they can still bear the same simple color name. Many reds, for example, differ in character from the theoretical red of the spectrum, yet we recognize the hue "red" in all of them. A color's hue can be changed by adding it to another hue; this actually changes the wavelength of light. An unlimited num-

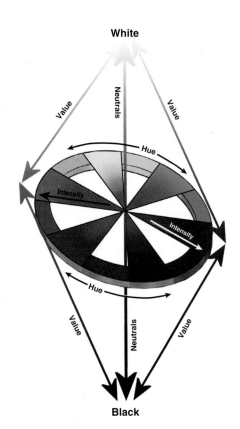

7.8 This diagram demonstrates the relationship between the three physical properties of color: hue, value, and intensity. Based on this, we can imagine all the color variations existing on a three-dimensional solid (a double cone). As the colors move circularly around the solid, they change in hue. When the hues move upward or downward on the solid, they change in value. As the colors on the outside move towards the center, they become more neutralized (closer to the achromatic neutrals) and lose their intensity.

ber of steps (variations) may be created by mixing any two hues—many steps exist between yellow and green, for example. Yet, for the sake of clarity, artists recognize the hues as those identified on the twelve-step color wheel.

Value

The second physical property of color, known as **value,** indicates the relative degree of lightness or darkness in an image. More specifically, **chromatic value** refers to the lightness of darkness of a color—or the quantity of light a color reflects. A large amount of light is

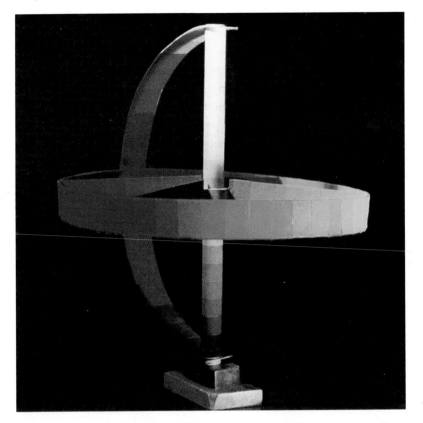

reflected from yellow, whereas a small amount of light is reflected from violet. Each color at its maximum intensity has a normal value that indicates the amount of light it reflects. It can, however, be made lighter or darker than normal by adding white or black. When a hue is mixed with varying amounts of white, the colors produced are known as tints. When a hue is mixed with varying amounts of black, the resulting colors are called shades. Many value steps can exist between the lightest and darkest appearance of any one hue.

Although a wide range of chromatic values can be produced by simply adding black or white, value changes can also be made by mixing a pigment of one hue with a pigment of another hue that is darker or lighter; this mixing will also alter both the color's value and hue. The only dark or light pigments available that would change the value *without* altering the hue are black, white, or a gray. (For example, red mixed with white will become the color *pink*, but the hue will remain *red*.)

7.9 This three-dimensional model illustrates the three main characteristics of color. The center wheel could also be slightly tilted to indicate that yellow (at maximum intensity) is lighter in value than violet (at maximum intensity). See also figure 7.8. Photograph courtesy of Ronald Coleman.

7.10 The electromagnetic spectrum. The sun, being the most efficient source of light, sends radiation to the earth in a series of waves known as electromagnetic energy. This may be likened to throwing a pebble into the middle of a pond. Waves radiate from that point and can be measured from the crest of one ripple to the crest of the next ripple. Similarly, waves from the sun range from mere atmospheric ripples—gamma rays, which measure no more than six quadrillionths of an inch (0.000000000000006 in.) —to the long, rolling radio waves, which stretch 18½ miles from crest to crest. The wavelengths visible to the human eye are found in only a narrow range within this electromagnetic spectrum; their unit of measure is the nanometer (nm), which measures one-billionth of a meter from crest to crest. The shortest wavelength visible to mankind measures 400 nm—a light violet. The sensations of yellow, orange, and red are apparent as the waves lengthen to between 600 and 700 nm. Contained in a ray of light but invisible to the human eye are infrareds ("below reds") and ultraviolets ("above violets"). See figure 7.1.

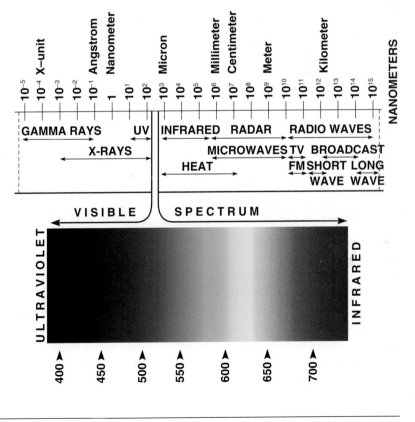

To use colors effectively, you should know the normal value of each of them. This normal value can be most easily seen when the colors of the wheel are placed next to a scale of neutral values from black to white, where the colors can be matched with their equivalent achromatic values (fig. 7.11). All colors that are above middle gray are called **high-key colors.** All colors that are below middle gray are referred to as **low-key colors.**

Whether a color remains low or high key is up to the artist. As noted, a low-key violet may be lightened with white. That adjustment will raise violet's value level, which can be increased until it corresponds to the value level for any color along the neutral scale; violet could even be made equal in value to yellow-orange on the gray scale. Similarly, a high-key color such as yellow may be adjusted with enough black that it becomes a low-key color (fig. 7.12).

Regardless of how the value level is obtained, *color* can be used to create a **value pattern** in the organization of a work. A wise artist once said, "Color gets all the glory . . . but value does all the work!" While many artists work intuitively using only color and its brilliance, the most insightful also understand and employ color's value as a compositional tool (see figs. 2.55 and 5.25).

Intensity

The third property of color, *intensity* (also sometimes called brightness, saturation, or **chroma**), refers to the quality of light in a color. Intensity distinguishes a brighter appearance from a duller one of the same hue; that is, it differentiates a color that has a high degree of saturation or strength from one that is grayed (neutralized) or less intense. The saturation point, or the purist color, can be found in the wavelengths produced when a beam of light passes through a prism. The artist's pigment that comes

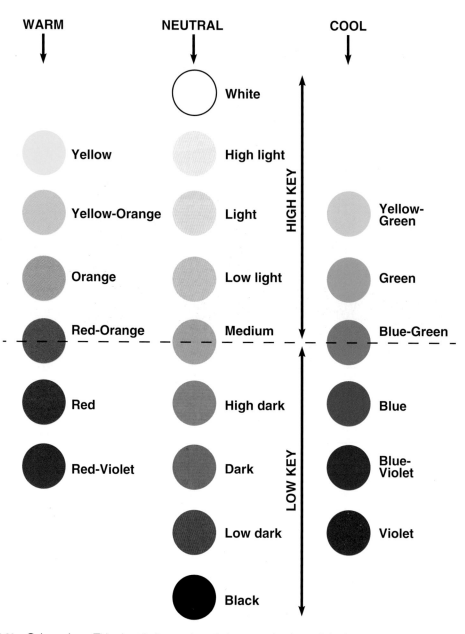

7.11 Color values. This chart indicates the relative normal values of the hues at their maximum intensity (purity or brilliance). The broken line identifies those colors and neutrals at the middle (50 percent) gray position. All neutrals and colors above this line are high key; those below it are low key. Warm colors are found on the yellow and red side, and cool colors are found with the greens and blues.

closest to resembling this color is said to be at maximum intensity.

The purity of the light waves reflected from a pigment produces the brightness or dullness of the color. For example, a pigment that reflects only the red rays of light is an intense red, but if any of the complementary green rays

are also reflected, the red's brightness is dulled or neutralized. If the green and red rays are *equally* absorbed by the surface, the resulting effect is a neutral gray. Consequently, as a color loses its intensity, it tends to approach gray.

There are several ways to alter the intensity of a color. One common

A **B**

7.12 **Color value chart.** Chart A shows how colors that are high key or low key at maximum intensity can be adjusted until they cover a wide range of values; chart B shows those colors at their equivalent achromatic gray levels. The use of chromatic value is an important component in creating effective color and value patterns.

approach is through placement; by placing a color next to its complement, the extreme contrast makes the intensity of both colors appear to increase. (This will be discussed more thoroughly in the section "Simultaneous Contrast.") Other methods usually involve the mixing of pigments—a physical blending of two or more colors—which will automatically decrease the intensity of the color.

Figure 7.13 shows the alteration of a hue (pigment) by adding neutrals (black, white, or gray). When white is added to any hue, the color loses its brightness or intensity as it becomes lighter in value. In the same way, when black is added to a hue, the intensity diminishes as the value darkens. We cannot change value without lowering intensity, although these two properties are not the same. We can, however,

lower the intensity without altering the value. By mixing the hue (pigment) with a neutral gray of the same value (as illustrated in the middle of fig. 7.13), the resulting mixture is a variation in intensity *without* a change in value. The color becomes less bright as more of that same gray is added, but it will not become lighter or darker in value.

The most efficient way to decrease the intensity of any hue is to add the complementary hue (fig. 7.14). Mixing two hues that occur exactly opposite each other on the color wheel (such as red and green, blue and orange, or yellow and violet) actually results in the intermixing of all three primaries. In theory, the two complements would cancel each other out and a black would be created, which would absorb all wavelengths and not allow any colors to be reflected. However, because of

impurities and an inability of surfaces to absorb all the wavelengths, a neutral gray is actually produced. In the studio, the combination of some complements—blue with orange, for example—may produce "better" grays than others. Note: the gray ink in these diagrams may appear darker and characterless when compared to your experiments.

When complements are mixed together, the three primaries are combined, and a *tertiary color* is produced. If the mixture has uneven proportions, the dominating hue creates the resulting color character, or **tonality.** Although the hue and intensity are neutralized to varying degrees relative to the amount of complement used, the resulting color will have a certain liveliness of character not present when a hue is neutralized with a *gray* pigment. Hundreds of tertiary colors

7.16 Pictured here are nine variations of a composition, each containing a different color scheme: (A) monochromatic, (B) analogous, (C) primary triad, (D) secondary triad, (E) tetrad, (F) complements, (G) split-complements, (H) warm, (I) cool. The scales beneath each block display some of the hues, values, and intensities available for use within each color scheme.

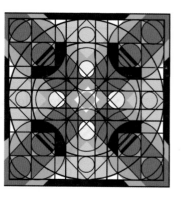

A

B

C

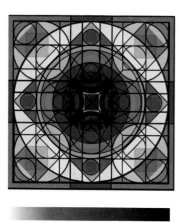

D

E

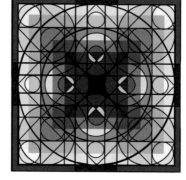

F

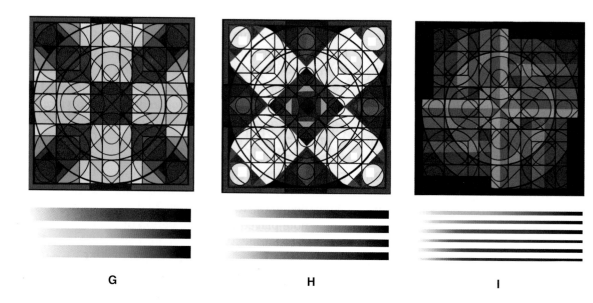

G

H

I

and its complement are placed in close proximity, a unique and vibrant relationship results from the contrast. Each color tends to increase the apparent intensity of the other color, and when used in equal amounts, they are difficult to look at for any length of time (see the section "Simultaneous Contrast"). This is overcome by reducing the amount of one of the colors or by introducing changes in the intensity or value level of one or both colors (see figs. 7.15 and 7.16F).

A subtle variation with slightly less contrast would be the **split-complement** system, which incorporates a color and the two colors on either side of its complement (see figs. 7.16G and 7.17). This color scheme provides a more complex palette than the straight complementary system, especially when incorporating changes of intensity or value. The color bars below the illustration 7.16G show the range of values and colors available for use in that split-complement composition. Color schemes in which the colors are fairly close to spectrum intensity are relatively easy to identify, but, as the colors become altered by neutralization or change of value (as indicated on the color bars), color schemes become more difficult to categorize. For example, the colors in figure 7.18 have all been adjusted in value or intensity. As a result, the image would probably not be readily identified as a split-complement composition, but its general tonality is based on the relationship of yellow-orange, red-orange, and blue, as shown in the color bars.

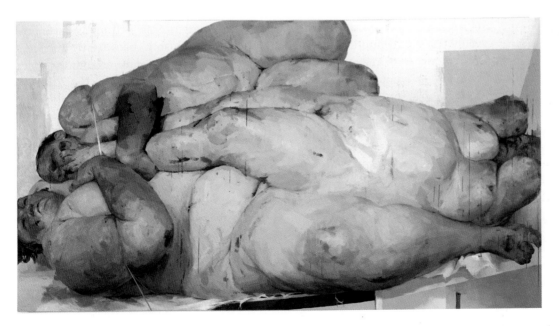

7.17 **Complementary colors.** In this diagram, complementary colors are connected by solid lines. They are of extreme contrast. An example of split-complementary colors (yellow, red-violet, and blue-violet) is shown by dotted lines. Though yellow is the example used here, the idea may be applied to any color and would include the color on either side of the hue's complement. Split-complements are not as extreme in contrast as complements.

7.18 Jenny Saville, *Fulcrum*, 1999. Oil on canvas, 103 × 192 in. (261.6 cm × 487.7 cm). While developing a very painterly surface, Saville confronts our traditional view of beauty regarding the female body. The color scheme, though not easily recognizable, makes use of hues altered in value or intensity. It seems to be based on a split-complementary organization of blue, yellow-orange, and red-orange. The color bars show the range of color available with such a color scheme.
© Jenny Saville. Courtesy Gagosian Gallery.

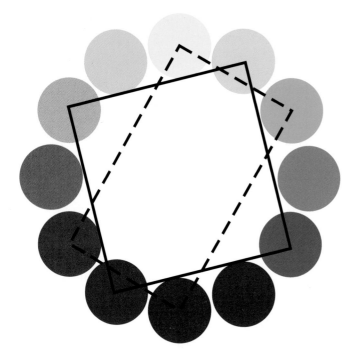

7.19 Color tetrad intervals (squares and rectangles). The color tetrad is composed of four colors equally spaced to form a square. A more casual relationship would have a rectangle formed out of two complements and their split-complements. The rectangle or square may be rotated to any position on the color wheel to reveal other tetrad color intervals.

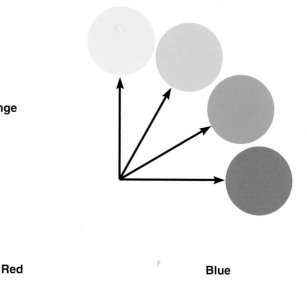

Orange

Red   Blue

Violet

7.20 Analogous colors (close relationships).

Triads

A triadic color organization is formed by an equilateral triangle on the color wheel. *Color triads* can be used in many combinations. A *primary triad,* using only primary colors, creates striking contrasts (see figs. 7.5 and 7.16C). With the *secondary triad,* composed of orange, green, and violet, the interval between hues is the same, but the contrast is softer (see figs. 7.5 and 7.16D). This effect occurs because any two hues of the triad share a common color: orange and green both contain yellow; both orange and violet contain red; and green and violet both contain blue. Intermediate color schemes may be organized into two *intermediate triads* (see fig. 7.6). Here, too, as we move farther away from the purity of the primaries, the contrast between the two triads is softer.

Tetrads

Another color relationship is based on a square rather than an equilateral triangle. Known as a **color tetrad,** this system is formed when four colors are used in the organization. They are equally spaced around the color wheel and contain a primary, its complement, and a complementary pair of intermediates (fig. 7.19; see also fig. 7.16E). A tetrad has also come to mean, in a less strict sense, any organization of color forming a "rectangular structure" that could include a double split-complement. This system of color harmony is potentially more varied than the triad because of the additional colors present, depending on which colors are selected for use and in what proportions. Avoiding the temptation to use all the colors in equal volumes will add interest to a work.

Analogous and Monochromatic Colors

Analogous colors are those that appear next to each other on the color wheel. They have the shortest interval and therefore an extremely harmonious relationship, because neighboring hues always contain a common color that dominates the group (fig. 7.20, see also fig. 7.16 B). Analogous colors can be found in all rings of the color wheel, from the spectrum intensity levels (the outermost ring of the color wheel) to the inner rings made by color neutralization (intensity changes) and value changes (fig. 7.21).

On the other hand, **monochromatic** color schemes use only one hue but explore the complete range of tints (value levels to white) and shades (value levels to black) for that hue (see figs. 7.33 and 7.16A). Even with thousands

7.21 Benjamin Butler, *In the Forest,* 2005. Oil on canvas, 48 × 72 in. In this work, Benjamin Butler has created a composition using analogous colors, featuring yellow-greens, greens, and blue-greens. For greater variety, he has added complementary colors in the form of browns (low-key oranges), pinks, and red-violets. Courtesy of the artist.

of variations of tints and shades, a monochromatic scheme has the potential to be monotonous. Sometimes, however, a monochromatic scheme is just the right color treatment for a particular subject.

Warm and Cool Colors

Color "temperature" is another way to organize color schemes. All of the colors can be classified into one of two groups: "warm" colors or "cool" colors. Red, orange, and yellow are associated with the sun or fire and thus are considered warm (see fig. 7.16H). Any colors containing blue (such as green, violet, and blue-green) are associated with air, sky, plants, and water; these are considered cool (see fig. 7.16I). This quality of warmth or coolness in a color can be affected by the hues around or near it. For example, the coolness of blue, like its intensity, may be heightened by placing a touch of its complement, orange, nearby (see fig. 7.4B).

Tertiary colors can also have a sense of color temperature based on their tonality. Brown, earthy tones generally feel warm, while olives are cool. In addition, artists working with neutral grays can introduce a hint of warmth or coolness to the grays to extend the palette; the gray changes from achromatic to chromatic, creating a subtle increase in variety and interest (see fig. 5.4).

Plastic Colors

Colors may also be organized according to their ability to create compositional depth. Artists are able to create the illusion of an object's volume or flatten an area using color. This ability to model a shape comes from the advancing and receding characteristics of certain colors. For example, a spot of red on a gray surface seems to be in front of that surface; a spot of blue, similarly placed, seems to sink back into the surface. In general, warm colors advance, and cool colors recede (fig. 7.22). The character of

such effects, however, can be altered by differences in the value and/or intensity of the color.

These spatial characteristics of color were fully developed by the French artist Paul Cézanne in the late nineteenth century. He admired the sparkling, brilliant color of the Impressionist artists of the period but thought their work had lost the solidity of earlier painting. Consequently, he began to experiment with expressing the bulk and weight of forms by modeling with color.

Before Cézanne's experiments, the traditional **academic** artist had modeled form using a technique known as *grisaille,* or *dead painting.* With this technique, the object was first painted in differing neutral values and later overglazed with a thin layer of the object's local (natural) color. Cézanne, however, discovered that a change of hue on a form could serve the purpose of a change of value, while imparting new possibilities of expression. He modeled the form by placing warm colors on the

blue background. The most striking effect occurs when complementary hues are juxtaposed: blue is brightest when seen next to orange, and green is brightest when seen next to red. When a warm color is seen in simultaneous contrast with a cool color, the warm hue appears warmer and the cool color cooler. A color always tends to bring out its complement in a neighboring color. If a green rug is placed against a white wall, the eye may make the white take on a very light red or warm cast. A touch of green in the white may be necessary to counteract this. When a neutral gray made of two complementary colors is placed next to a strong intense color, it tends to take on a hue that is opposite the intense color. When a person wears a certain color of clothing, the complementary color in that person's complexion is emphasized.

Parts of this phenomenon may be explained by the theory that the eye (and mind) seeks a state of balance with the three light primaries. More than a psychological factor, this seems to be a physiological function of the eyes' receptors and their ability to receive the three light primaries—some combination of all three is involved in most mixed colors. As our eyes flash unceasingly about our field of vision, all the light primaries are experienced, and the corresponding receptors are repeatedly activated. The mind seems to function with less stress when all three receptor systems are involved concurrently (although not necessarily in equal proportions). If one or more primaries are continually missing, the eye tries to replace the missing color or colors because of receptor fatigue. For example, if we stare at a spot of intense red for several seconds and then shift our eyes to a white area, we see an afterimage of the same spot in green, red's complement. The phenomenon can be noted with any pair of complementary colors (fig. 7.26).

7.25 Mark Rothko, *Number 10*, 1950. Oil on canvas, 7 ft. 6⅜ in. × 4 ft. 9⅛ in. (2.30 × 1.45 m). Using apparently simple masses of color on a large scale, the artist is able to evoke emotional sensations in the observer. Rothko was one of the American artists who worked in the pure abstract idiom. © 1998 Kate Rothko Prizel & Christopher Rothko/Artists Rights Society (ARS), New York. The Museum of Modern Art, New York, NY. Gift of Philip Johnson. Digital image © The Museum of Modern Art/Licensed by SCALA/Art Resource, NY.

Although we seem to desire the three primaries visually, our optic function may get overstimulated under certain conditions. Large amounts of clashing full-intensity complements can make us uneasy (see fig. T.77). Museum guards at an Op Art show were said to have asked for reassignment, complaining of visual problems ranging from headaches to blurred focus.

Balanced stimulation of the color receptors is much easier to experience when the three primaries are physically mixed together. The colors produced are less saturated or intense and seem easier to experience physically. This would explain why tertiary colors—neutralized sometimes nearly to the loss of hue—are thought of as being more relaxing. Hues such as blues and greens seem to be easier on the eye and mind when lightened with white; white adds more wavelengths to the reflected light (the colors) and thus stimulates additional combinations of receptors. Hues that have

7.26 Jasper Johns, *Flags*, 1965. Oil on canvas with raised canvas, 6 × 4 ft. (1.83 × 1.22 m). With this painting, Johns wanted the viewer to experience an afterimage. This occurs when the retina's receptors are overstimulated and are unable to accept additional signals. They then project the wavelengths of the complementary colors. Stare at the white dot on the upper flag for forty seconds. Then shift your focus to the dark dot on the lower flag, and you will see an afterimage in red, white, and blue. © Jasper Johns/Licensed by VAGA, New York, NY.

been muted, neutralized, or lightened in value will appear to recede compared to their most saturated or intense states. Intense blue walls will make a room appear smaller than a very light tint of the same blue.

Try some experiments to see the principles of simultaneous contrast in practice. See if the same color placed in the center of two related colors can be made to appear as two different hues, however subtle or different. Further, try making two subtly different colors appear to be the same by changing their surrounding colors. Notice the difficulty in finding edges when adjoining shapes or areas are closely related in value level or intensity. There may be a "pulsating" effect that occurs when the eye has the greatest struggle for edge definition—when complements are placed together. Black lines will give greater clarity to the image but may also tend to flatten the areas. Greater contrast in value or intensity levels will also help with the visual problem of edge resolution or image separation.

All these changes in appearance make us realize that no one color can be experienced in isolation, but each must be considered in relation to any other colors present. For this reason, many artists find it easier to develop a color composition globally rather than try to finish one area completely before going on to another.

Color and Emotion

Color may also be used according to its ability to create mood, symbolize ideas, and express emotions. Color, as found in art, can express a mood or feeling in its own right, even though it may not be descriptive of any specific object. Reds are often thought of as being cheerful and exciting, whereas blues can impart dignity, sadness, or serenity. Also, different values and intensities in a color can affect emotional impact. A wide value range (strongly contrasting light or dark hues) gives vitality and directness to a color scheme; closely related values and low intensities create feelings of subtlety, calmness, and repose (fig. 7.27).

Colors can evoke emotions that are personal and reinforced by everyday experiences. For example, some yellows look acidic and bitter, almost forcing a pucker, as would a sour lemon. Other colors carry with them cultural associations. Our speech is full of phrases that associate abstract qualities like virtue, loyalty, and evil with color: "true blue," "dirty yellow coward," "red with rage," "seeing red," "virgin white," "green with envy," and "gray gloom." In some cases, these feelings seem to be universal because they are based on shared experiences. Every culture understands the danger of fire (reds) and the great vastness, mystery, and consistency of the heavens and the seas (blues). Blues can imply reliability, fidelity, loyalty, and honesty, while reds suggest danger, bravery, sin, passion, or violent death. However, not all color has the same meaning in every culture. On pre-Columbian artifacts, priest-kings are shown in self-bloodletting rituals, and victims are sacrificed to the sun, with red symbolizing the renewal and rebirth of the sun. For other cultures, green rather than red is the sign of regeneration, hope, and life. Numerous color associations can be traced back historically. For example, purple has signified royalty since the ancient Greek and Roman civilizations, because only the royalty could afford the expense of extracting a purple dye from 10,000 tiny shellfish—which is what was required to produce a gram of color (fig. 7.28). However, even when dye became more affordable, the tradition (and the significance) remained. In China, ancient potters created very unusual glazes for their wares. Among the glazes was a very deep copper red that was so beautiful

7.27 Claude Monet, *Waterloo Bridge, Grey Weather,* 1900. Oil on canvas, 65.4 × 92.4 cm. The Impressionist Monet painted almost 100 views of the Waterloo Bridge during three trips to London. Painting the view from his room in the Savoy Hotel, he studied the characteristics of light at different times of the day and in differing weather conditions. As a result, the hues, values, and intensities are markedly affected. Gift of Mrs. Mortimer B. Harris, 1984.1173, The Art Institute of Chicago. Photography © The Art Institute of Chicago.

7.28 *Mosaic of Justinian I,* 548 A.D. This sixth-century mosaic portrays Emperor Justinian the Great clad in a purple robe, which emphasizes his wealth and royal status. The original color of the robe was Tyrian Purple, a rare hue made from tiny sea snails. © Christel Gerstenberg/Corbis.

that the very best ware in every kiln-load was immediately carried away to the emperor himself.

Psychological Application of Color

Research has shown that light, bright colors make us feel joyful and uplifted; warm colors are generally stimulating; cool colors are calming; and cool, dark, or somber colors are generally depressing. Medical facilities, trauma centers, and state correctional facilities are often painted in light blues or "institutional greens" because of these colors' calming effect. Winter skiing lodges are adorned in warm yellows, knotty pine, oranges, and browns to welcome those coming in from freezing temperatures. Stories abound of the use of motivating color in sports programs. One visiting team refused to use the assigned locker room, furious because the powder-puff pink walls implied they were sissies. In another incident, the home team's locker room was painted bright red to keep the players keyed up and on edge during halftime, while light blue surroundings in the visitors' locker room encouraged the opponents to let down and relax. It has been shown in some work situations that bright, intense colors encourage worker productivity, whereas neutralized or lighter hues slow down the workforce.

We are continually exposed to the application of color's emotive power. In a supermarket, the meat section is sparkling white to assure us of its cleanliness and purity. To encourage us to purchase the products, the best steaks are garnished with parsley or green plastic trim to make them appear redder and more irresistible. Color is extremely important in branding efforts: bright yellow and orange cereal boxes use contrasting lettering (often complementary) to scream for our attention. Extremely small spaces

7.29 Shepard Fairey, *Obama Poster*, 2008. Fairey created this poster in the style called "social realism," which often uses color for psychological purposes. The image, colored in red, white, and blue, provided a patriotic symbol for Obama supporters. © Shepard Fairey.

are rarely painted in dark or bright warm colors, which would make them feel even smaller. Instead, the space is made to appear larger by light cool colors. In 2008, Shepard Fairey made use of a triadic color scheme to create an iconic poster of then candidate Barack Obama (fig. 7.29). Psychologically, his choice of colors communicates patriotic sentiments and conveys bold intent.

An artist's emotional state—affected by an angry exchange, a love letter, a near miss in traffic—may subconsciously influence a choice of color. The power of color to symbolize ideas becomes a tool. It enriches the metaphor and makes the work stronger in content and meaning. Many artists have evolved a personal color style that comes primarily from

their feelings about their subjects rather than being purely descriptive. John Marin's color is essentially suggestive, with little concern for naturalistic form or solidity (see fig. 8.44). Frequently delicate and light in tone, his colors are in keeping with the medium in which he worked (watercolor). The color in the paintings of Vincent van Gogh is often vivid, hot, intense, and applied in snakelike ribbons of pigment. His uses of texture and color express the intensely personal style of his work (see figs. 1.15 and 1.19). In the work of Mark Rothko, color becomes a conduit for a spiritual or transcendent viewing experience (see fig. 7.25). Using various techniques, Rothko achieved a luminosity, an "inner light," to his works that made the colors

7.30 Wolf Kahn, *Web of Trees*, 2003. Oil on canvas, 64 × 78 in. (162.6 × 198.1 cm). Wolf Kahn is one contemporary painter who uses his subject—landscape—to express a personal joy found in color. The vibrant, even risky use of color structure is a hallmark of his later work, making it instantly recognizable. Art © Wolf Kahn/Licensed by VAGA, New York, NY.

7.31 Frida Kahlo, *Still Life with Parrot*, 1951. Oil on masonite, 9½ × 10¼ in. (24.1 × 26 cm). This still life is painted in local color—color that simulates the hues of the objects in nature. Art Collection, Harry Ransom Humanities Research Center, University of Texas at Austin. Reproduction authorized by National Institute of Fine Art and Literature of México and Banco de México. © 2011 Banco de México Diego Rivera & Frida Kahlo Museums Trust. Av. Cinco de Mayo No. 2, Col. Centro, Del. Cuauhtémoc 06059, México, D.F./Artists Rights Society (ARS), New York.

swirl and glow softly on the canvas. An emotional approach to color appealed particularly to the Expressionist painters, who used it to create entirely subjective treatments having nothing to do with objective reality (see fig. T.56). Contemporary artists like Wolf Kahn continue to interpret their environment in terms of personal color selection (fig. 7.30).

Filmmakers, too, recognize the power of color and use it to change the feel and impact of their work; movies are dramatically affected by using specific color schemes or altering the color tonality of the scenes. For example, in the film *O Brother, Where Art Thou?* (released in 2000), the colors were digitally altered—some more neutralized than others—so that sepia tones transmit the feeling of the Dust Bowl era. In *Pitch Black* (2000), many scenes consist only of shades of blue to indicate the

overexposure of sunlight on an alien planet. In the film *300* (2006), the majority of colors are neutralized, but a select few—like the scarlet robes or yellow embers—are made more intense for dramatic effect. We can see from these numerous examples that the emotional effects of color are unavoidable. Color impacts our senses directly as a psychological and physiological function of sight itself.

THE ROLE OF COLOR IN COMPOSITION

When painting was seen as a purely illustrative art, the description of appearances was considered color's most important function. Thus, for a long period in the history of Western art, color was seen as arising from the

object being represented. In painting, color used to indicate the natural appearance of an object is known as **local (objective) color** (fig. 7.31; see also fig. 6.1). Yet a much different (if not more) expressive quality is achieved when the artist depicts objects in colors other than their local color. When an entirely **subjective color** treatment is substituted for local color, the colors used and their relationships are invented by the artists for purposes other than mere representation (fig. 7.32; see also figs. 7.30 and 7.41). This style of treatment may even deny color as an objective reality; that is, we may have blue cows, green faces, or purple trees. When colors are subjectively applied, as in much contemporary art, an understanding of their use becomes critical to an understanding of their meaning.

7.32 Gilles Marrey, *1997*, 1998. Oil on canvas, 55 × 56 in. (140 × 142 cm). The subjective colors in this painting may not be as obviously invented as a "blue horse," but they effectively set up the mood and mystery within this painting. Courtesy of artist.

Regardless of whether color is used objectively or subjectively, it serves several purposes in artistic composition. These purposes are not separate and distinct but instead are interrelated. As we have discussed throughout this chapter, color can be used in the following ways:

1. To give spatial quality to the pictorial field.
   a. Color can supplement, or even substitute for, value differences to give plastic quality.
   b. Color can create interest through the counterbalance of backward and forward movement in pictorial space.
2. To create mood and symbolize ideas.
3. To serve as a vehicle for expressing personal emotions and feelings.
4. To attract and direct attention as a means of giving organization to a composition.

5. To accomplish aesthetic appeal by a system of well-ordered color relationships.
6. To identify objects by describing the superficial facts of their appearance.

Color Balance

Whether an artist chooses to work with color combinations that are extremely bold (even offensive) or chooses colors that are subtler and more psychologically soothing, all effective color combinations have at their root the consideration of similarity and contrast. The unity of the composition relies on harmonious relationships between the various colors, but these relationships must also be made alive and interesting through variety. This basic problem is the same one encountered in all aspects of form organization: finding an appropriate sense of equilibrium between similarity and contrast.

Color combinations are brought into a harmonious relationship when they have properties in common, including hue, intensity, and value; the more they share, the more harmonious the relationships become. However, any attempt to harmonize the interaction of colors must be balanced by the need to keep the relationships interesting—at times, even exciting. This is accomplished through *variety* in hue, value, or intensity and the resulting contrasts those variations create. Therefore, successful interaction of color is a matter of balancing the need for harmony with the natural desire for variety. Of course, the color relationships used in a composition must be determined primarily by the concept being explored.

Color schemes that contain hues in close proximity on the color wheel (and therefore, closely related in wavelength frequency) tend to create harmonious compositions, while colors that are farther apart have stronger contrasts and create a color scheme with more variety. As a general rule, a monochromatic

7.33 Georgia O'Keeffe, *Canna Red and Orange*, 1922. Oil on canvas, 10 × 16 in. (50.8 × 40.6 cm). Inspired by light, this Precisionist artist stripped away most features of reality to create her colorful, semiabstract images. Georgia O'Keeffe Museum, Santa Fe/Art Resource, NY. © 2011 The Georgia O'Keeffe Foundation/Artists Rights Society (ARS), New York.

color scheme is the most harmonious, followed by analogous colors, tetrads, triads, split-complements, and finally, complementary colors, which offer the most variety and are least harmonious (see fig. 7.16).

However, any attempt to base the aesthetic appeal of color patterns purely on fixed theoretical color harmonies will probably not be very successful. Effective color combinations depend as much on how we *distribute* our colors

as on the relationships among the hues themselves. The *amounts* or *proportions* of the colors used, as well as their location in the composition, affect the overall impact of the color choices.

Color and Harmony

Let us look first at how to harmonize a composition through its color relationships. The harmonious quality of a color pattern frequently depends on the amount or proportion of color used, and in general, compositions in which one color or one kind of color predominates are more easily harmonized than color arrangements with equal amounts of different colors. A simple way to create harmony is to repeat a color in differing values and intensities while controlling its placement in different parts of the composition (fig. 7.33). These areas will collectively contribute to an increase in frequency of that hue and to the general harmonic tonality for the image.

Even when many varied colors are used in a composition, a single hue can be a harmonizing factor if a little of it is physically mixed with every color used in the composition (see fig. 7.15). This tends to lower the intensity of all the colors involved and give them a hint of the shared hue. A similar

7.35 Romare Bearden, *Empress of the Blues,* 1974. Paper collage, 36 × 48 in. Bearden has created figures that are very active in their complexity of shape and visual detail and made them readable by contrasting them against a very uncomplicated and decorative background of slightly neutralized color. Photo © Smithsonian American Art Museum, Washington, DC/Art Resource, NY © Romare Bearden Foundation/Licensed by VAGA, New York, NY.

effect can be created by glazing over a varicolored pattern with a single transparent color, which becomes the harmonizing hue.

Unified patterns may also be created by adjusting color temperature—so that all the colors of a composition are made to share a hint of warmth or coolness. However, there are often times when it is desirable to encourage color relatedness without sacrificing the range of hue. In these situations, diverse colors may be harmonized by bringing them all to a similar value level or making their intensity levels correspond (see figs. 5.4 and 7.30). As we can see in figure 7.34, Ellen Phelan applies this concept by adding a dark neutral to all the colors involved, which lowers their intensity and value. Not only does this tie all the areas together, but it creates a low-key composition that adds to the hazy and amorphous nature of the image. Sharing a high or low key or sharing a similar loss of brilliance can make even unusual combinations have some degree of harmony relative to the amount of change involved. Even complementary colors, which of course vie for our attention through simultaneous contrast, can be made more unified if one of them is softened or neutralized.

When color predominance is not enough to pull an organization together, the image can be made more harmonious by changing the character of the surrounding areas. In such cases, an image that is hard to visually understand or distinguish may become more readable, in addition to becoming more unified. In figure 7.35, Romare Bearden makes a whole series of diverse images easier to recognize by using a very simple and flat background.

Another commonly used method of relating colors of extreme contrasts is to separate all or part of the colors by a neutral line or area. Absolute black or white lines are the most effective neutrals for this purpose because they are so positive in character (have a strong presence) themselves. They not only tie together the contrasting hues but also enhance their color character because of value contrast (see fig. 7.15). Georges

Rouault often found a black line effective in separating highly contrasting colors (fig. 7.36). Stained-glass windows are another great example of this technique: the neutral black leading between the brilliant colors unifies the entire window. A similar unifying effect can be brought about by using a large area of neutral light gray or other neutralized color as a background to clashing contrasts of color (fig. 7.37).

7.37 Joan Mitchell, *Untitled,* 1992. Oil on canvas, 110¼ × 78¾ in. (280 × 200 cm). Characterized by aggressive brushwork, Joan Mitchell's painting has a variety of highly contrasting colors and values: large areas of dark are balanced by even larger areas of light value; blues are countered by smaller oranges, green by pink, and yellowish white by touches of violet. © Estate of Joan Mitchell.

Color and Variety

In any color scheme, the basic problem is to create unified color relationships without destroying the general strength and intensity of expression found in their contrasts. There is often the danger that the composition may become too harmonious during the attempt to unify color—resulting in a level of visual monotony. In those situations, more variety can be introduced back into the work through greater contrasts in hue, value, or intensity. Sometimes this is a matter of reversing or softening some of the techniques that made the colors harmonize. In other words, if colors were related (in close proximity on the color wheel), then creating a wider separation of interval would introduce more vari-

ety and greater interest into the color organization (e.g., a scheme of red and red-violet could be changed to red and violet). In addition, colors related by lowered intensity or value levels could benefit from stronger contrasts of either or both. Selecting the widest array of hue, value, and intensity will imbue the relationships with even greater variety and interest.

Where the basic unity of a color pattern has already been established, strong contrasts of color hue, value, or intensity can be used as accents, providing variety but maintaining the basic unity of the color theme. Small amounts of complementary color or neutrals of contrasting value can add subtle variety to the color pattern

(fig. 7.38; see also fig. 4.14). Low-key or high-key compositions benefit greatly from such contrasting accents, which add interest to what might otherwise be a monotonous composition (see figs. 4.20 and 4.29).

With the right amount of contrasting color, an area can have more focus (fig. 7.39; see also fig. 7.23). A small, dark spot of color, through its lower value, can draw more attention than a larger lighter area surrounding it. Likewise, a spot of intense color, though small, can often balance a large area of gray or other neutralized color (see fig. 7.40). In addition, a small amount of warm color usually dominates a larger amount of cool color, even though both may be of the same

7.38 Jackson Pollock, *Full Fathom Five*, 1947. Oil on canvas with nails, tacks, buttons, key, coins, cigarettes, matches, etc. 50⅞ × 30⅛ in. Having established a color pattern of black, white, and green, Pollock uses small accents of contrasting color to provide interest and a feeling of spontaneity. Gift of Peggy Guggenheim, The Museum of Modern Art, New York, NY. Digital Image © The Museum of Modern Art/Licensed by SCALA/Art Resource, NY. Art © 2011 The Pollock-Krasner Foundation/Artists Rights Society (ARS), New York.

intensity (see figs. 7.22 and 7.24). If all the areas in a composition were made equally important, however, it would be difficult to find a spot on which to fix our attention; this would probably create a rather chaotic viewing experience.

Finally, we should remember that artists frequently produce color combinations that defy these guiding principles but are still satisfying to the eye. Artists use color as they do the other elements of art structure—to give highly personalized meaning to their work.

We must realize that there can be brutal color combinations as well as refined ones. The more extreme or turbulent combinations are appropriate if they accomplish the artist's intention to excite rather than calm. Some of the German Expressionist painters have proven that

7.49 Deborah Butterfield, *Not Yet Titled (#2891.1)*, 2005. Unique cast bronze with patinated surface, 37 × 48 × 13 in. This piece appears to be made of wood, but it is actually bronze that has been chemically colored (patinated) to resemble weathered wood. The three-dimensional artist has access to an unlimited range of color, which may be used to create this kind of trompe l'oeil effect or present textures and patterns that are completely invented. Courtesy of the artist.

7.50 Gabriel Dawe, *Plexus no. 3*, 2010. Gütermann thread, wood, and nails, 12 × 6 × 16 ft. Site-specific installation at Guerillaarts. Working with ordinary colored sewing thread, Dawe creates a sensual and ethereal viewing experience. Inspired by the vibrancy of his native Mexican culture, the artist uses bold and intense hues, showcasing the full color spectrum.
© Gabriel Dawe, Dallas, TX.

Obviously, color cannot be considered in isolation. The elements of value and color are so interwoven in sculpture that artists often use the two terms interchangeably. Thus, an artist may refer to value contrasts in terms of color, actually thinking of both simultaneously. This approach subordinates color to the structure of the piece. On the other hand, in certain historical periods (for example, early Greek art) the application of bright color was commonplace. Some revival of this technique is evident in contemporary works. In every case, the basic criterion for the use of color is whether it helps to express the artist's intentions.

Space

CHAPTER EIGHT

Gus Heinze, *Espresso Cafe*, 2003, Acrylic on gessoed panel, 32 × 35½ in.
Courtesy of the artist and Bernarducci.Meisel.Gallery, NY.

THE VOCABULARY OF
SPACE

Space — The interval, or measurable distance, between points or images; can be actual or illusionary.

atmospheric perspective
The illusion of deep space produced in graphic works by lightening values, softening details and textures, reducing value contrasts, and neutralizing colors in objects as they recede (see **perspective.**)

decorative (space)
Ornamenting or enriching but, more importantly in art, stressing the two-dimensional nature of an artwork or any of its elements. Decorative art (space) emphasizes the essential flatness of a surface.

four-dimensional space
An imaginative treatment of forms that gives a sense of intervals of time or motion.

fractional representation
A pictorial device (used notably by the Egyptians) in which several spatial aspects of the same subject are combined in the same image.

infinite space
A concept in which the picture frame acts as a window through which objects can be seen receding endlessly.

installations
Interior or exterior settings of media created by artists to heighten the viewers' awareness of the environmental space.

interpenetration
The positioning of planes, objects, or shapes so that they appear to pass through each other, which locks them together within a specific area of space.

intuitive space
The illusion of space that the artist creates by instinctively manipulating certain space-producing devices, including overlapping, transparency, interpenetration, inclined planes, disproportionate scale, fractional representation, and the inherent spatial properties of the art elements.

isometric projection
A technical drawing system in which a three-dimensional object is presented two-dimensionally; starting with the nearest vertical edge, the horizontal edges of the object are drawn at a 30-degree angle, and all verticals are projected perpendicularly from a horizontal base.

linear perspective
A system used to depict three-dimensional images on a two-dimensional surface; it develops the optical phenomenon of diminishing size by treating edges as converging parallel lines that extend to a vanishing point or points on the horizon (eye level) and recede from the viewer. (See also **perspective.**)

oblique projection
A technical drawing system in which a three-dimensional object is presented two-dimensionally; the front and back sides of the object are parallel to the horizontal base, and the other planes are drawn as parallels coming off the front plane at a 45-degree angle.

orthographic drawing
Graphic representation of two-dimensional views of an object, showing a plan, vertical elevations, and/or a section.

perspective
Any graphic system—including atmospheric perspective and linear perspective—used in creating the illusion of three-dimensional images and/or spatial relationships in which the objects or their parts appear to diminish as they recede into the distance.

plastic (space)
1. The use of the elements to create the illusion of the third dimension on a two-dimensional surface. 2. Three-dimensional art forms, such as architecture, sculpture, and ceramics.

relief sculpture
An artwork, graphic in concept but sculptural in application, that utilizes relatively shallow depth to establish images. The space development may range from very limited projection, known as "low relief," to more exaggerated space development, known as "high relief." Relief sculpture is meant to be viewed frontally, not in the round.

reverse perspective
A graphic system for depicting three-dimensional images, commonly seen in traditional East Asian art, in which the "parallel" lines of objects or their parts seem to converge toward the viewer, rather than away into the distance. (See **perspective.**)

shallow space
The illusion of limited depth. With shallow space, the imagery appears to move only a slight distance back from the picture plane.

space
The interval, or measurable distance, between points or images; can be actual or illusionary.

structured ambiguity
A condition in which the positive figure and the negative background seem to reverse roles, fluctuating back and forth between the two functions to create an ambiguous sense of space. Structured ambiguity is often employed as a transition between contrasting values or colors and is a valuable tool for creating optical illusions, denying space, and blending an image into its background.

three-dimensional
Possesses the dimensions of (or illusions of) height, width, and depth. In the graphic arts, the feeling of depth is an illusion, while in the plastic arts, the work has actual depth.

transparency
A visual quality in which a distant image or element can be seen through a nearer one.

two-dimensional
Possesses the dimensions of height and width, especially when considering the flat surface, or picture plane.

void
1. An area lacking positive substance and consisting of negative space. 2. A spatial area within an object that penetrates and passes through it.

INTRODUCTION TO SPACE

Today, the mention of **space** makes us think of spaceships, space stations, the solar system, and the infinite cosmos beyond. Artists, too, have been interested in exploring deep space, but one that can be found right here on earth. As we will learn in this chapter, artists use a variety of techniques that can give the illusion of infinite space. On the other hand, artists may choose to limit the degree of space we see. Space can be shrunk almost to the level of the picture plane, but not quite, because any element in an image creates some sense of space. All of this is, of course, pure illusion in two-dimensional art, but it is a very real aspect of three-dimensional art, in which depth is a fundamental consideration. One way or another, space concerns all artists, and they must find ways of dealing with it in a consistent manner.

The understanding and use of space has greatly evolved over the years. The earliest images, from the caves of southern Europe, reveal a minimal concern for the illusion of space, with many images superimposed randomly over each other. In the ancient Near East, however, a flat and hierarchical order became important and significant events or individuals were emphasized through size variations. Over the centuries, the desire to present images in a more realistic spatial context led to discoveries such as mechanical perspective, photography, and the use of film to capture moving objects; images were usually created with a singular point of view and were presented in a **two-dimensional** format. Today, however, contemporary artists and designers can use computers and other digital media to create things unthinkable even thirty years ago. Artists now design environments that allow the viewer to interact with the image—to move about in the setting in real time. For an artist, the importance of space lies in its function. A basic understanding of its implications and use is essential.

Our discussion of space in this chapter will not be limited to the graphic arts—drawing, painting, printmaking, and so forth—because the basic concepts can also be applied to many other mediums, such as video, computer-generated images, sculpture, and installations. In pictorial art, space is an illusion and will be presented as a "product" of the elements. However, in the **three-dimensional** arts—such as sculpture, ceramics, jewelry, architecture, and much installation work—space actually exists and will be treated as an element.

SPATIAL PERCEPTION

Our conceptions of space are conditioned by our experience of the world. Vision is perceived through the eyes but experienced by the mind. Visual experience involves this whole process of nerve and brain response. As our eyes perceive the world around us, we continually shift our focus of attention. In the process, we use two different types of vision: stereoscopic and kinesthetic. Having two eyes set slightly apart from each other, we receive two slightly different views of our visual field at the same time. The term *stereoscopic* refers to our ability to mentally combine these two slightly different views into one image. This process enables us to experience vision three-dimensionally and to judge distances. With *kinesthetic* vision, we experience space through the movements of our eyes and bodies. We explore an object's surface(s) with our eyes in order to recognize it; our eyes travel as we attempt to organize its separate parts into a whole. Objects close to us require more ocular movement than those farther away, and this kinesthetic eye activity adds to the spatial perception of our visual experience.

MAJOR TYPES OF SPACE

Two types of space can be suggested by the artist: decorative space and plastic space.

Decorative Space

Decorative space involves height and width but very little depth. It results from a very flat surface treatment of images or elements, which appear confined to the flatness of the picture plane without any concern for a deep spatial environment. As these images are developed, they seem to remain flat, enriching and embellishing the picture plane without creating the illusion of depth. In fact, a truly decorative space is difficult to achieve; any art element, when used in conjunction with others, will seem to advance and recede. However, when those areas or objects remain basically flat and limited to the picture plane, the space is said to be decorative (fig. 8.1).

Plastic Space

The term **plastic** refers to that which has been modeled or made to have the illusion of three dimensions. In this context, plastic space pertains to the environment in which objects appear. Artists locate objects in plastic space according to their needs and feelings for each situation. An infinite range of space is available to the artist and may be categorized into the following general areas based on the depth of the space employed.

Shallow Space

Shallow space occurs when the artist wants to create some depth but, at the same time, limit the viewer's penetration into the pictorial space. Interior views, still-life images, and various nonobjective works are often presented in varying degrees of limited

8.1 James Little, *Sneak-Attack,* 2003. Oil, wax, canvas, 78 × 102 in. (198.1 × 259.1 cm). Although the colors and other line qualities may seem to advance or recede in this painting, the images appear relatively flat on the picture's surface as a decorative treatment rather than create an illusion of specific spatial depths. Courtesy of James Little and June Kelly Gallery NY.

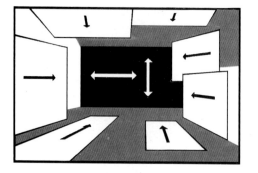

8.2 **Shallow space.** As a variation on the concept of shallow space, artists occasionally define the planes that make up the outer limits of a hollow boxlike space behind the picture plane. The diagram shows this concept, although in actual practice, a return to the picture plane would be made through objects occupying the space defined. The back plane acts as a curtain that prevents penetration into deep space.

8.3 Jacob Lawrence, *Cabinet Makers,* 1946. Gouache with pencil under-drawing on paper, 21¾ × 30 in. (55.2 × 76.2 cm). The use of shapes with solid colors and values, generally lacking in traditional shading, creates an overall feeling of flatness. In addition, a stagelike effect arises from the shallow space. © Hirshhorn Museum and Sculpture Garden, Smithsonian Institution, Washington, DC. Gift of Joseph H. Hirshhorn, 1966. Photograph by Lee Stalsworth. Art © 2011 The Estate of Gwendolyn Lawrence/Artists Rights Society (ARS), New York.

or shallow formats. Shallow space is comparable to the views of a stage. The space is limited by the placement of the sides and back wall. For consistency, any compositional objects or figures that might appear in such stagelike confines are usually narrowed in depth or flattened (fig. 8.2). In the painting *Cabinet Makers,* by Jacob Lawrence, the figures have been flattened and placed in a confined room (fig. 8.3).

Asian, Egyptian, and European medieval painters used comparatively shallow space in their art. Early Renaissance paintings were often based on the shallow sculptures that were popular then. Many modern artists also elected to use shallow space because it was more suited to their aesthetic purposes than deep space. For these artists, the use of shallow space allowed more control of the placement of decorative shapes as purely compositional elements. Gauguin, Matisse, Modigliani, and Beckmann were typical advocates of the concepts of limited space (see figs. 4.1 and 7.24).

Deep and Infinite Space

An artwork that emphasizes deep space starts with the picture plane and creates a spatial perception (feeling) that extends beyond and into that surface. The viewer's eye seems to move into the far distances of the picture field, as if looking through an open window over a landscape that rolls on and on into infinity. This infinite quality is produced by certain relationships of art form: size, position, overlapping images, sharp and diminishing details, converging parallels, and perspective are traditional methods of indicating deep spatial penetration (see fig. 6.17).

Concepts of **infinite space,** allied with **atmospheric perspective,** dominated Western art from the beginning of the Renaissance (about 1350) to the middle of the nineteenth century. During this period, generations of artists such as Botticelli, Ruisdael, Rembrandt, and Bierstadt, to name only a few, developed and perfected the deep-space illusion that seems to accord with visual reality (fig. 8.4).

Although there have been periods in the history of art when one spatial treatment or another seemed dominant, works of contemporary artists range from decorative space to profoundly infinite space without showing a prejudice toward any particular approach. Any space concept can be valid as long as its elements are consistent in relation to the spatial field chosen.

8.4 Albert Bierstadt, *King Lake, California,* early 1870s. Oil on canvas, 27¾ × 38½ in. (70.5 × 97.8 cm). Nineteenth-century American landscape painting, which aimed at the maximum illusion of visual reality, emphasized the concept of infinite space. The foreground areas move forward because of their greater textural contrasts and clarity, while the diminishing sizes of objects and hazy effects of atmospheric perspective give the viewer a sense of seeing far into the distance. Columbus Museum of Art, Ohio: Bequest of Rutherford H. Platt, 1929.003.

SPATIAL INDICATORS

Artistic methods of representing space are so interdependent that attempts to isolate and examine all of them here would be impractical and inconclusive. In addition, such attempts might leave the reader with the feeling that art is based on a formula. Instead, we will confine this discussion to basic spatial concepts.

Our comprehension of space, which comes to us through objective experiences, is enlarged, interpreted, and given meaning by the use of our intuitive faculties. Spatial order develops when the artist senses the right balance and the best placement, then selects vital forces to create completeness and unity. Ultimately, this process is not a purely intellectual one but rather a matter of instinct or subconscious response (see figs. 4.13A and B, 5.17, 8.37, and 8.38).

Because the subjective element plays so large a part in creating space, we can readily see that emphasis on formula here, as elsewhere, can inhibit the creative spirit. Art, as a product of human creativity, is uniquely dependent on individual perceptions and interpretations. Like the other elements of art, space is used according to the artist's subjective experience. It can be employed spontaneously or with premeditation. It can be created using strict formulas and methods or from a strictly intuitive approach. Therefore, the methods of creating space discussed in this chapter are merely approaches that have been frequently used and guarantee certain spatial effects.

Sharp and Diminishing Detail

Because we do not have the eyes of eagles, and because we view things through earth's hazy atmosphere, we are not able to see near and distant planes with equal clarity at the same time. A glance out the window confirms that close objects appear sharp and clear in detail, whereas those far away seem blurred and lack definition. Artists have long used this phenomenon in creating the illusion of space—presenting sharply defined images in the foreground but decreasing the clarity as the pictorial space recedes. In recent times, artists have used this method in abstract works, indicating that the illusion of space need not be limited to realistic scenarios. Sharp lines, clearly defined shapes and values, complex textures, and intense colors are associated with foreground, or near, positions. Hazy lines, indistinct shapes, grayed values, simple textures, and neutralized colors are identified with background, or distant, locations. These characteristics are often included in the definition of *atmospheric perspective* (see figs. 8.4 and 8.6).

8.5 Winslow Homer, *Returning Fishing Boats*, 1883. Watercolor and white gouache over graphite on off-white wove paper, 40.9 × 63.3 cm (16⅛ × 24¹⁵⁄₁₆ in.). The horizon line in this painting separates the space into a ground plane below and a sky plane above. The smaller size and higher position of the distant boats help achieve the spatial effect. *Harvard Art Museums/Fogg Museum, Anonymous Gift, 1939.233. Photo by Katya Kallsen © President and Fellows of Harvard College.*

Size

We usually interpret largeness of size as nearness. Conversely, a smaller size suggests distance. If two sailboats are several hundred feet apart, the nearer boat appears larger than the other. Ordinarily, we would interpret this difference in size not as one large and one small boat (although this could play a part in our perception) but as vessels of approximately the same size placed at varying distances from the viewer (fig. 8.5). Therefore, if we are considering depth, the size of an object or human figure corresponds to its distance from us, regardless of all other factors (fig. 8.6; see also fig. T.45). This concept of space has not always been prevalent. In some styles of art, largeness indicates importance, power, and strength rather than spatial location (see figs. 2.50 and 8.12).

Position

Artists and observers customarily assume that the horizon line, which provides a point of reference, is at eye level. Thus, the position of objects is judged in relation to that horizon line. The bottom of the picture plane is seen as the closest visual point, and the eye's rise up to the horizon line indicates the receding of space (see fig. 8.5). Evidence suggests that this manner of seeing is instinctive (resulting from continued exposure to the real world), for its influence persists even when viewing greatly abstracted and nonobjective work (fig. 8.7; see also figs. 2.17 and 3.7). The alternative, of course, is to see the picture plane as entirely devoid of spatial illusion and to register the distances between visual elements as simply what is actually measurable across the flat surface. It is difficult to perceive a picture in this way even when we discipline ourselves to do so, because it requires us to divorce ourselves entirely from all the intuitions about space we form through our experience.

Overlapping

Another way of suggesting space is by overlapping objects. If one object covers part of the visible surface of another, the first object is assumed to be nearer.

Overlapping is a powerful indicator of space, because it takes precedence over other spatial indicators. For instance, a ball placed in front of a larger ball appears closer than the larger ball, despite its smaller size (fig. 8.8). Color, value, and textural choices can then exaggerate or minimize the spatial effect of the overlapped shapes. If the colors, values, or textures are of minimal contrast, the overlapped areas tend to unite and create a shallow or ambiguous (equivocal) space (see fig. 2.18C). The Futurists often presented shallow or ambiguous space by overlapping multiple images of the same object in different positions (see fig. 9.9).

Transparency

The overlapped portion of an object is usually obscured from our view. If, however, that portion is visible through the overlapping plane or object, the effect of **transparency** is created. Transparency, which tends to produce a close spatial relationship, is clearly evident in the triangles in Leonardo Nierman's painting *Broken Star* (fig. 8.9). It is also found in the works of the Cubists

8.6 Jacques Callot, *The Great Fair at Imprunita*, 1620. Etching, 16¹⁵⁄₁₆ × 26 in. In Callot's print, note how the figures gradually get smaller and more blurry as they recede into the background areas. This, combined with the artist's use of linear perspective with the buildings, gives the viewer a strong sense of depth. The Metropolitan Museum of Art, Harris Brisbane Dick Fund, 1917 (17.3.2645). The Metropolitan Museum of Art/Art Resource, NY.

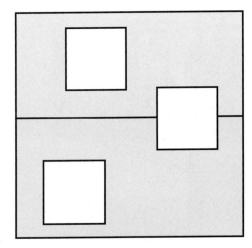

8.7 **Placement of squares.** A line across the picture plane reminds us of the horizon that divides ground plane from sky plane. Consequently, the lower shape seems close and the intermediate shape more distant, while the upper square is in a rather ambiguous position as it touches nothing and seems to float in the sky.

8.8 Larger objects usually advance more than smaller ones, but as an indicator of space, overlapping causes the object being covered to recede regardless of size.

and other artists who are interested in exploring shallow space (see figs. 4.2 and T.51).

Interpenetration

Interpenetration occurs when planes or objects appear to pass through each other, emerging on the other side. This generally provides a very clear statement of the spatial positioning of the planes and objects involved, and it can create the illusion of either shallow or deep space (figs. 8.10 and 8.11; also see fig. 2.21).

Fractional Representation

Fractional representation is a device in which several spatial aspects of a subject are combined in the same image. It can best be understood by studying the treatment of the human body by Egyptian mural artists. Here we can find, within one figure, the profile of the head with the frontal eye visible, the torso seen front-on, and a side view of the hips and legs—a combination of the most representative aspects of the different parts of the body (figs. 8.12 and 8.13). Fractional representation was revived in the nineteenth century by Cézanne, who used its principles in his still-life paintings (see the section "Multiple Viewpoints" in Chapter 9). It was also employed by many twentieth-century artists, most conspicuously Picasso. The effect is flattening in Egyptian work but plastic in the paintings by Cézanne because it is used to move us "around" the subjects (see fig. 9.5).

Converging Parallels

The space indicated by converging parallels can be illustrated using a rectangular plane such as a sheet of paper or a tabletop. By actual measurement, a rectangle possesses one set of short parallel edges and one set of long parallel edges (fig. 8.14). If the plane is

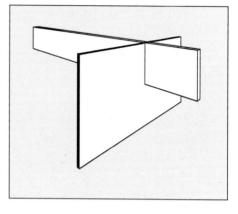

8.10 Interpenetrating planes. The passage of one plane or volume through another automatically gives depth to a picture.

8.9 Leonardo Nierman, *Broken Star*, 1991. Mixed media on masonite, 32 × 24 in. The precise, hard-edged geometric shapes in this work are a legacy of Cubism. Notice that the implied triangular shapes overlap, remain transparent, and create a shallow space that contrasts with the deeper space behind. Courtesy of the artist.

8.11 Gus Heinze, *Espresso Cafe*, 2003. Acrylic on gessoed panel, 32 × 35½ in. Object and reflection merge to create the illusion of interpenetrating planes and a sense of depth that goes beyond the building's structural beams and wall of glass. Courtesy of the artist and Bernarducci.Meisel.Gallery, NY.

8.12 Nebamun hunting birds, from the tomb of Nebamun, Thebes, Egypt, c. 1400 b.c.e., size unknown. This work illustrates the Egyptian concept of pictorial plasticity: various representative views of Nebamun are combined into one image (fractional representation) and are kept compatible with the flatness of the picture plane. The arbitrary positioning of the figures and their disproportionate scale add to this effect. Fragment of a fresco secco. Courtesy of the British Museum, London.

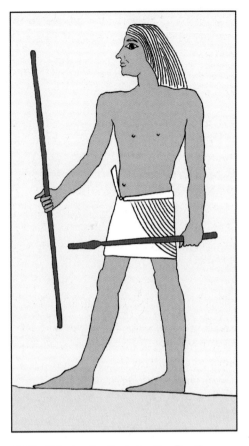

8.13 This drawing illustrates the Egyptian technique of fractional representation of the human figure. The head is in profile but the eye full-face. The upper body is frontal, gradually turning until the lower body, from the hips down, is seen from the side. This drawing combines views of parts of the body in their most characteristic or easily seen positions. In order to see all these views, one would have to move around the body.

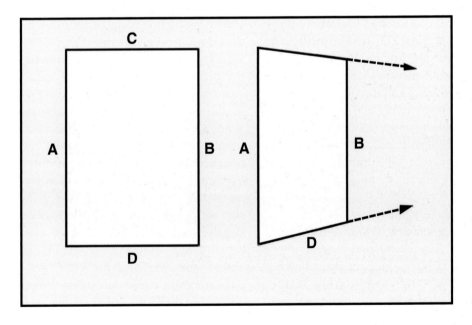

8.14 Converging parallels can make a shape appear to recede into the pictorial field.

8.15 Anselm Kiefer, *Osiris und Isis/Bruch und Einung,* 1985–87. Mixed media, 150 × 220½ in. (381 × 560 cm). Kiefer uses perspective to help him intensify the viewer's confrontation with scale in his enormous canvas. San Francisco Museum of Modern Art. Purchased through a gift of Jean Stein by exchange, the Mrs. Paul L. Wattis Fund, and the Doris and Donald Fisher Fund. © Anselm Kiefer. Courtesy of Gagosian Gallery.

arranged so that one of the long edges (A) is viewed head-on, its corresponding parallel edge (B) will appear to be much shorter. Because these edges appear to be of different lengths, the pair of parallel edges (C and D) that connect them must seem to converge as they move back into space. Either set of lines (A-B or C-D), even in the absence of the other set, would indicate space convincingly. This principle of converging parallels is found in many works of art that do not necessarily abide by the rules of **perspective.** The principle is closely related to perspective, but the degree of convergence is a matter of subjective or intuitive choice by the artist. It need not be governed by fixed vanishing points and other systematic rules governing the rate of convergence (fig. 8.15).

Linear Perspective

Linear perspective is a system for accurately representing sizes and distances of known objects in a unified visual space. This helps develop the illusion of three-dimensional images as they recede into the distance. Based on optical perception, it incorporates the artist's (and viewer's) judgments about concepts of scale, proportion, placement, and so on by using spatial indicators such as size, position, and converging parallels. Perspective underwent significant development in Renaissance Italy, during a revival of interest in ancient Greco-Roman literature, philosophy, and art. The Renaissance spirit swept Europe during the fourteenth and fifteenth centuries and brought this spatial system to a point of high refinement. Linear perspective focuses attention on one view—a selected portion of nature as seen from one position at a particular moment in time. The use of a horizon line, guidelines, and vanishing points gives this view mathematical exactitude (fig. 8.16A and B).

It is generally believed that perspective was developed by the Florentine architect Filippo Brunelleschi (1377–1446) and was quickly adapted to painting by his contemporary,

Masaccio (1401–1428; see fig. 8.16A). Employing their knowledge of geometry (an important subject in classical education), Renaissance artists conceived a method of depicting objects, both animate and inanimate, in a space more realistic than any other that had appeared in Western art since the Romans.

When artists use perspective in their works, the picture plane becomes a window through which a three-dimensional view is seen (fig. 8.17A). As seen in figure 8.17B, imaginary sightlines, called *guidelines,* are extended along the edges of the room's architectural planes to a point behind the angel's head. This point is on the viewer's eye level and is called the *vanishing point* (infinity). By convention, the eye level is synonymous with the *horizon line* (where the sky and ground meet), which is often clearly seen in landscapes (see figs. 8.4 and 8.5). While the horizon line reveals the height of the observer's/painter's eyes, it also demarcates upper and lower divisions called *ground plane*

A

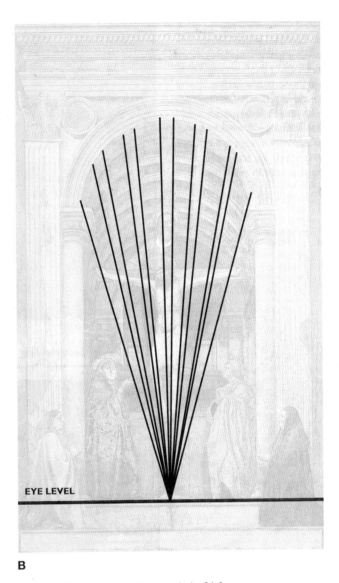

EYE LEVEL

B

8.16 Masaccio, *Trinity with the Virgin, St. John and Donors*, 1427. Fresco at Santa Maria Novella, Florence, Italy, 21 ft. 10 in. × 10 ft. 5 in. (6.65 × 3.18 m). According to some art history experts, Masaccio's fresco is the first painting created in correct geometric perspective. The single vanishing point lies at the foot of the cross, as indicated by the overlay (B).
Erich Lessing/Art Resource, NY.

(floor) and *sky plane* (ceiling). A vertical axis that passes through the vanishing point establishes the location of the artist or viewer. This is known as the *viewer's location point*. Changing this point will drastically alter the view of the room (fig. 8.18A and B).

Major Types of Linear Perspective

There are three major types of linear perspective: one-point, two-point, and three-point. Each system is related to the way the artist views the subject or scene. Perspective is based on the theoretical assumptions that the artist maintains a fixed position and views the subject with one eye. The Renaissance painter's approach was to imagine rays of light emanating from one fixed point (the artist's eye) to every point on the object being drawn. These rays passed through a grid or glass screen that was placed between the artist and the object, and the points where the lines passed through the grid were then transferred to the artist's canvas (see fig. 8.19 on page 236). This type of device helped the artist draw more accurate foreshortening and achieve the naturalistic view he wanted to re-create on the canvas. (This device is also similar in concept to the "camera obscura," which actually projects the image through a small hole onto a dark wall.)

In reality, most viewers casually move their eyes and heads as their focus travels from object to object within the image. While these movements increase the viewers' ability to understand the

8.25 Charles Sheeler, *Delmonico Building*, 1926. Lithograph, 9¾ × 6⅞ in. (24.7 × 17.4 cm). This painting makes use of three-point perspective—a "frog's-eye view." Harvard Art Museums/Fogg Museum, Gift of Paul J. Sachs, M3188. Photograph by Allan Macintyre. © President and Fellows of Harvard College.

8.26 Gene Bodio, *New City*, 1992. Computer graphic created using Autodesk 3D Studio–Release 2. This is a "bird's-eye view" generated by a computer. Though not strictly in three-point perspective, the picture is an unusual variation in the depiction of three-dimensional objects in space. Courtesy of the artist. San Rafael, CA.

sometimes referred to as a "frog's-eye view" (fig. 8.25) and a "bird's-eye view" (fig. 8.26), respectively.

The artist begins by locating the horizon line that indicates the location of the viewer's eyes—either relatively high or low in the picture—and fixing the left vanishing point (LVP) and the right vanishing point (RVP) at the appropriate locations (fig. 8.27). As with two-point perspective, the closer together the vanishing points are placed, the greater the exaggeration or distortion of the image. Next, the artist determines the viewer's location and extends an imaginary vertical line upward on the page, perpendicular to the horizon line. A third point, called the vertical vanishing point (VVP), is then located at an appropriate location on this vertical axis (see fig. 8.27). The location of the VVP helps control the distortion of the object; the farther away from the horizon line the third point is located, the less exaggerated the image will be.

Instead of starting with the nearest flat plane (as in one-point) or the nearest edge (as in two-point), three-point perspective begins with the nearest corner. In figure 8.27, the image (a rectangular solid that seems to be floating overhead) is started by establishing the nearest corner (a). From this point, guidelines are extended to the RVP and to the LVP. These locate the leading front edges of the bottom plane. The width of both edges should then be marked (b and c). From those points, new guidelines should be extended to the RVP and LVP. This completes the bottom plane and locates all four of its corners.

The "verticals" should now be drawn up and away from the three closest corners (marked a, b, and c); but because there are no true verticals in three-point perspective, these lines will have to converge to the VVP. Once the "verticals"

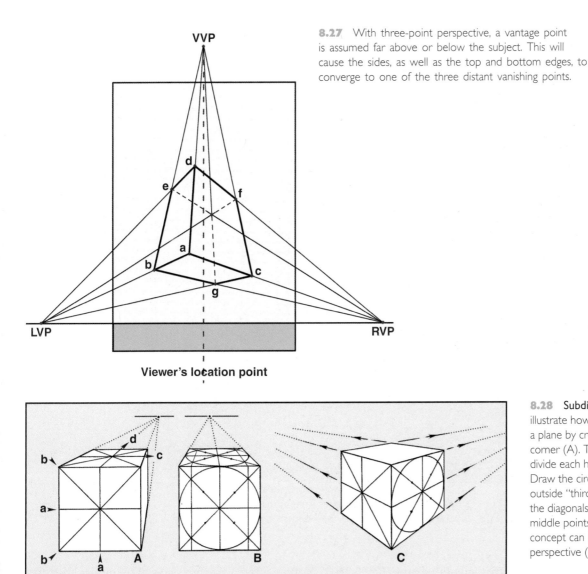

8.27 With three-point perspective, a vantage point is assumed far above or below the subject. This will cause the sides, as well as the top and bottom edges, to converge to one of the three distant vanishing points.

VVP

d
e
f
a
b
c
g

LVP   **RVP**

Viewer's location point

8.28 Subdividing a plane. These diagrams illustrate how to find the perspective center of a plane by crossing diagonals from corner to corner (A). To draw a circle on the same plane, divide each half of the diagonals into thirds. Draw the circle so that it passes through the outside "third" marks (closest to the corners) on the diagonals. The circle should also touch the middle points on the sides of the square. This concept can be applied to one- and two-point perspective (B and C).

b
d
c
a
b
a
A   **B**   **C**

are drawn, the height of the rectangular solid can be established on the center "vertical" edge. After marking this point (d), guidelines are extended from it to the RVP and to the LVP. This completes the drawing of the edges and fully defines the geometric solid as seen from below in three-point perspective. In certain cases, such as when the object walls are meant to be transparent, the hidden back edges (extended from the corners labeled e, f, and g) could also be added.

In three-point perspective, *all* lines recede to vanishing points. Guidelines are neither perpendicular nor parallel to one another but at oblique angles (see fig. 8.25).

Perspective Concepts Applied

Whether using one-, two-, or three-point perspective, the artist is working with a system that helps establish items of known size at various distances into the picture plane. Based on the angle and orientation of the receding plane, dimensions decrease at a predictable rate. But in order for the artist to depict the proper rate of recession, he or she must first be able to find the midpoints, or centers, of various planes.

As illustrated in figure 8.28A, a cube shown in one-point perspective has a frontal plane, a receding top, and a receding side plane. The center of any

frontal plane—square or rectangular—can be found by physically measuring the horizontal and vertical lengths and dividing them in half. Lines (a) drawn from those points parallel to the verticals and horizontals will divide the plane into quarters. However, this type of subdividing works *only* on flat frontal planes (which are found exclusively in one-point perspective—not two- or three-point perspective). It will *not* work on any plane with converging sides (regardless of whether one-, two-, or three-point) because the sides get smaller as they move away from the viewer, and their changing ratio is not measurable on a ruler.

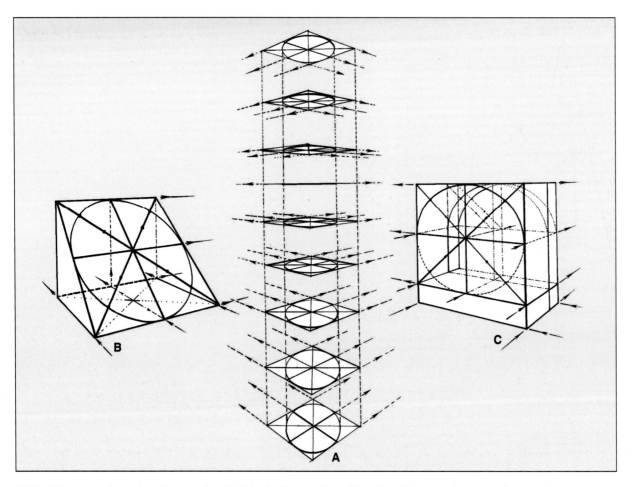

8.29 When seen from the side, a perfect circle looks like an ellipse. The ellipse flattens as it moves closer to the horizon line (A). It may be applied to an inclined plane (B) or used to create arches, tunnels, and so on (C).

Notice on the frontal plane, that the diagonals (b) drawn from corner to corner pass through the exact center found by measurement. The same type of diagonal lines drawn from corner to corner on a receding plane will pass through and reveal the *perspective center* of the receding plane. Lines drawn through this center point, parallel to the front edge (c) and to the vanishing point (d), then create an equal division of the four edges of the receding plane. This concept of corner-to-corner diagonals may be applied to cubes or rectangles in one-, two-, and three-point perspective to locate the perspective centers on *any receding plane*.

Using the center point of a cube's *front* square, a circle can be drawn with a compass to fit perfectly into

that frontal plane (fig. 8.28B). Notice that when the diagonals are divided in thirds between the center and each corner, the circle crosses the diagonal lines on approximately the outer third mark. When a *receding* plane is meant to contain a circle, the circle will actually appear as an ellipse and cannot be drawn using a compass. The appropriate ellipse can be drawn on the top receding plane when it passes through the third marks on the diagonals and touches the square on the center points of each side. This system may be applied to *any receding plane*—vertical or horizontal—in one-, two-, or three-point perspective (fig. 8.28C).

Occasionally, an artist must draw appropriate ellipses for the top and bottom of a cylindrical object. Figure 8.29A

shows how ellipses change as they rise and fall in relation to the horizon line. Notice that the ellipses flatten as they get closer to the horizon line but become more circular the farther they are away from the horizon line. Of course, ellipses do not always have to be horizontal or vertical—observe the ellipse drawn on a diagonal plane (fig. 8.29B). It is drawn using the same corner-to-corner diagonals used to find the center of the diagonal plane. The same concept can also be used to draw arches, bridges, and so on (fig. 8.29C). Although only the upper half of the ellipses are seen in an arch, it is necessary to know the basic cube or rectangle it is based on and the appropriate perspective centers.

Once a square or rectangle is created, it may be easily turned into a

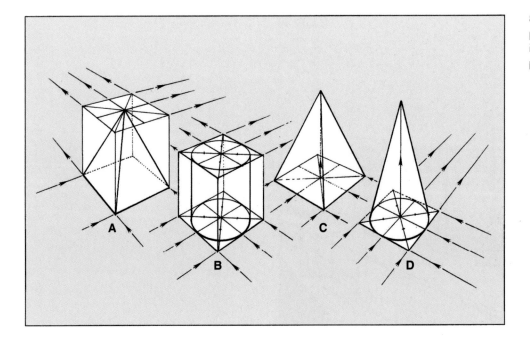

8.30 The concept of locating a plane's perspective center and the correct ellipse to indicate a circle can be extended to create pyramids, cylinders, and cones.

pyramid, cylinder, or cone by finding the perspective center for the top and bottom planes of the new shapes. For a pyramid (fig. 8.30A), simply draw lines from the top plane's perspective center to the four corners on the bottom plane. For the cylinder (fig. 8.30B), it will be necessary to first draw the proper ellipse on the top and bottom planes— as described earlier. Then draw vertical lines from the outermost limits of both ellipses. Also note that a second pyramid (fig. 8.30C) and cone (fig. 8.30D) can be drawn with only the establishment of the bottom plane. From the perspective center of the bottom plane, draw a vertical line at any desired length. Then from the end of this line, draw lines to the four corners (for a pyramid) or to the outer-edge points on an ellipse (for a cone).

The system for finding the perspective center of a receding plane can also be used to project known distances back or sideways into space at the proper diminishing rate or ratio. If a telephone company plants seven poles equally spaced down the road, how does an artist know exactly where they should be drawn on the picture plane? The answer to this lies in the ability to extend the diagonal guidelines from the perspective center. To illustrate, study figure 8.28A, covering up the top half of the illustration. Note that even though the diagonal lines (b) appear to stop at the center point, in fact they continue on toward the lower corners. Using the diagonal guidelines, you can project a known shape (in this case the upper half of the square) into a space on the opposite side of the center mark by extending the diagonals until they cross an extension of the bottom edge.

So, to draw equally spaced telephone poles in perspective, draw the first pole and extend guidelines from the top and bottom to the vanishing point (fig. 8.31). Draw the second pole touching the top and bottom guidelines at any distance from the first. The two poles should be parallel. Next, find the center of the second pole either by measuring or by finding the perspective center between poles (by intersecting diagonals) and running a guideline from that midpoint to the vanishing point—the guideline will run through the center of the second pole. Then draw a line from the top or bottom of the first pole through the midpoint found on the second pole, extending it until it touches the top and bottom guidelines. Where the extended line touches the guideline, draw another vertical; this will become the next pole at a perspective unit equal to the one just projected. Another single diagonal line can be drawn to project from the previous pole through the center point on the new pole to find the location of the next pole. This process may be repeated until the number of poles desired has been reached.

Spacing may be projected horizontally as well as vertically. You can see the same procedure at work with the horizontal guardrail shadows in the lower right corner of figure 8.31. In addition, linear projection may be applied to locate floor tiles, windows, or any architectural components with consistent spacing (fig. 8.32).

A perspective drawing may also have several vanishing points other than those located on the horizon line (fig. 8.33). Multiple vanishing points are often used when it is desirable to show multiple objects set at different angles, such as on a gable, a truss-roofed house, a door opening at an angle, or an open box lid. In such cases, the edges of the angular planes are extended to vanishing points separate from the LVP, RVP,

8.31 **Telephone poles showing vertical projection systems.** A given unit—the distance between two telephone poles—may be projected. Extending a diagonal guideline from a corner through the midpoint of the next pole to the appropriate top or bottom guideline reveals the location of the next pole. Units may be projected on a vertical or horizontal plane.

8.32 **A room interior.** Because horizontals and verticals in one-point perspective may be measured, all tile spacing was marked on the back edge of the floor. From the vanishing point, floor lines were extended through each of these points toward the viewer. After establishing the first row of tiles, a diagonal line was extended from corner to corner of one tile and beyond. Where the diagonal crossed each floor line, a horizontal line was drawn, thereby defining a new row of tiles. A second line, passing through the center of the edge of each tile, located points that were projected onto both walls to identify wallboard spacing and window widths.

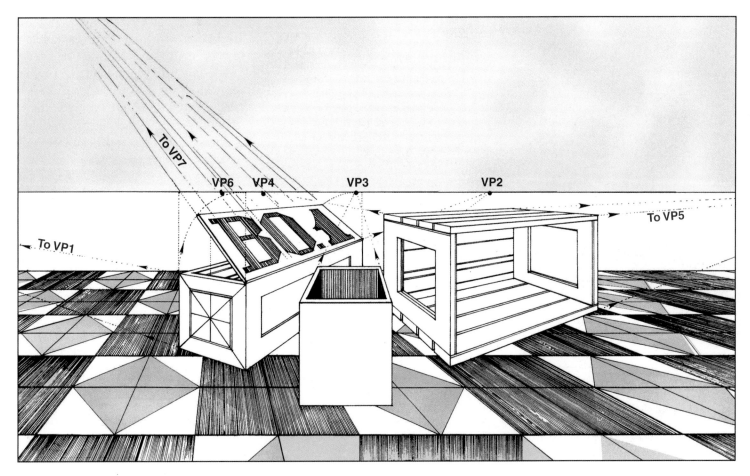

8.33 **Seven in one.** Seven vanishing points (VPs) were used to create this drawing. VPs 1 and 2 were used for the left box. VP 3 was used to create the center cube. VPs 4 and 5 were used for the open crate on the right. VP 6 was used for the floor tiles. VP 7 was used to define the inclined plane of the box lid and its lettering.

or VVP, and any additional images on those planes (like shingles or window panes) would be extended to those new points. A separate vanishing point may also be located to represent a source of light, with all cast shadows being indicated by guidelines projected from it to the ground plane. Furthermore, an artist may encounter situations where houses and other objects are not parallel to each other. As a result, one-, two-, and possibly three-point perspective systems may all be used in the same drawing.

The Disadvantages of Linear Perspective

Linear perspective has been a traditional drawing device used by artists for centuries. During that time, the system has evolved and undergone modifications in attempts to make it more flexible or more realistic in depicting natural appearances. Some of these include the use of multiple perspectives, with more than three vanishing points, and, at other times, the use of multiple eye levels. Linear perspective was most popular during periods of scientific inquiry and reached its culmination in the mid-nineteenth century. Despite the mathematical accuracy in which it depicts natural appearances, the method has certain disadvantages that, in the opinion of some artists, outweigh its usefulness. Briefly, the liabilities of linear perspective are as follows:

1. It can never depict a shape or mass as it is known to be.
2. It can portray appearances from only one position in space.
3. The necessary recession of parallel lines toward common points readily leads to monotonous effects.
4. The reduction of scale within a single object, resulting from the convergence of lines, is a type of distortion (see fig. 8.14; this diagram indicates that a rectangular shape depicted in perspective becomes a trapezoid and leaves spatial vacuums above C and below D).

These disadvantages are mentioned only to suggest that familiar modes of vision are not necessarily best in every work of art. At times, an intuitive use of perspective can be more expressive than systematic formulas for indicating pictorial depth (see fig. 8.38).

To a certain extent, artists can become prisoners of the system they use.

8.34 M. C. Escher, *Waterfall*, 1961. Lithograph, 15 × 11 in. (380 × 300 cm). From his early youth, Escher practiced the graphic technique of perspective and for many years strived to master that skill. Later, he found ideas he could communicate by extending his perspective technique, and he became fascinated with visually subverting our commonsense view of the three-dimensional world. In this print, Escher knew it was impossible to see multiple stories of the same building on one level. Yet, the water flows downhill from the first floor to the third. © 2011 The M. C. Escher Company-Holland. All rights reserved. www.mcescher.com.

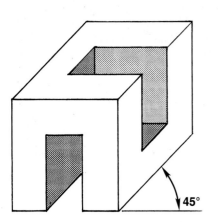

8.35A **Oblique projection.** This system for showing spatial relationships makes use of a flat frontal shape with nonconverging side planes drawn at a 45-degree angle from the front plane.

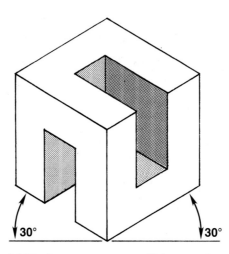

8.35B **Isometric projection.** This system for showing spatial relationships features a vertical front edge and nonconverging side planes, which are drawn at a 30-degree angle to the left and right.

Because of its inflexible rules, perspective emphasizes accuracy of representation—an emphasis that tends to make the presentation more important than what is being represented. If, however, artists see perspective as an aid rather than an end in itself, as something to be used when and if the need arises in creating a picture, it can be very useful (see fig. 8.15). Many fine works of art ignore perspective or show "faults" in the use of the system.

In such cases, the type of spatial order created by traditional perspective is not compatible with the aims of the artists (fig. 8.34). However, like any tool, perspective should be learned by artists because it extends the range of conceptual expression.

Other Projection Systems

The spatial position of objects may also be depicted using other graphic systems such as oblique projection, isometric projection, orthographic projection, and reverse perspective. Most of these methods use nonconverging parallel projecting lines, and because they present a stable and consistently measurable image that does not diminish as it recedes, designers, architects, and technical engineers use them for ease of drawing. These systems do, however, tend to flatten out objects when compared to traditional perspective systems that use vanishing points.

Oblique projection looks, at first glance, to be related to one-point perspective, for both present a flat frontal view that is always parallel to the picture plane (fig. 8.35A). However, with oblique projection, all the left- or right-side edges are drawn parallel and come off the frontal plane at a 45-degree angle. (They would converge at a singular vanishing point, if drawn in one-point perspective.) For engineering and architectural applications, the frontal plane is always drawn at full scale. This use of nonconverging parallel edges on receding planes is common in traditional Asian art.

Isometric projection may be compared to two-point perspective in appearance. Both begin with a vertical front edge. However, in isometric projection there are not any converging receding edges (fig. 8.35B). All edges that intersect at the vertical move away at a 30-degree angle, both to the left and to the right. For ease of drawing, all three dimensions of the object use the same measurement system (scale); there is no diminishing ratio on the receding planes. Hence, this system is used for technical illustration and drafting to illustrate and convey accurate dimensions. Artists often prefer this system to oblique perspective because all three faces are visible at the same time with less apparent distortion. No side of the image is drawn parallel to the viewer (picture plane).

A

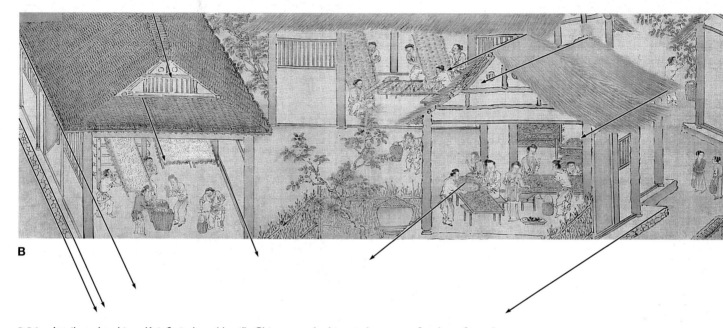

B

8.36 Attributed to Liang Kai, *Sericulture* (detail), Chinese, early thirteenth century, Southern Song dynasty. Handscroll, ink, and light color on paper, 26.5 × 98.5 cm. (A) This Chinese artist, following his own (Asian) concept of space as moving forward toward the observer, employs—from a Western point of view—a kind of reverse perspective. (B) A simple analysis of the *Sericulture* detail shows that if the lines defining the buildings are extended back toward the horizon line, they will never meet as they would in the linear perspective of Western artists. However, if they are extended forward, following the Asian concept of space, they seem to converge. As a result, the front of the buildings is narrower than the back—which is characteristic of East Asian perspective. © The Cleveland Museum of Art, John L. Severance Fund, 1977.5.

Orthographic drawing is perhaps less understood as a system for identifying objects in a spatial setting, but artists, engineers, industrial designers, and architects use it to present blueprints and schematic layouts (see fig. 9.6). With this system (which presents plan, elevation, and section views), all sides of the rectangular (geometric) object are drawn parallel or perpendicular to a base line, and the measurements are scaled to an exact ratio.

Reverse perspective, as seen in traditional East Asian art, is a dramatic contrast to the linear perspective of the West. Reverse perspective prescribes the convergence of "parallel" lines as they *approach* the viewer, rather than as they recede. This type of perspective closes the spatial depth so that the picture becomes a stage and the spectator becomes a participant in an active spatial panorama (fig. 8.36A and B). Works that use reverse perspective encompass the viewer, who feels surrounded by the content. Similar approaches have been employed in the West during various historical periods.

Ideas on perspective in art are formed by and, in turn, influence the prevailing intellectual climate of the society. In this sense, the very notion of space itself is a form of human expression.

Intuitive Space

The same planes and volumes that create illusions of space in linear perspective can also be used to produce **intuitive space**, which does not use strict rules and formulas. Intuitive space is based not on a system, but on the artist's instinct for manipulating certain space-producing devices. These devices include overlapping, transparency, interpenetration, inclined or receding planes (converging parallels), disproportionate scale, and fractional representation. In addition, the artist may exploit the inherent spatial properties of the art elements. The physical properties of the art elements can thrust forward or backward and, in doing so, can be used to define items spatially. By marshaling these spatial forces in any combination as needed, the artist can impart a sense of space to a work (fig. 8.37). The space derived from this method is intuitively sensed by the viewer. If judged by the standards of linear perspective, however, this type of space may seem strange, even distorted. Nevertheless, intuitive space has been the dominant procedure during most of the history of art; it rarely implies great depth, but it makes for tightly knit imagery within a relatively shallow spatial field (fig. 8.38).

THE SPATIAL PROPERTIES OF THE ELEMENTS

An artist must recognize and explore the spatial effects that arise from using the elements of art. Each of the elements possesses inherent spatial qualities, but the interrelationship between elements yields the greatest spatial feel-

8.37 Cory Arcangel, *Photoshop Gradient*, 2008. Digital art. Certain contemporary artists employ technology to create unusual spatial effects. In this work, Cory Arcangel uses the gradient tool in the popular software Photoshop to simulate one-point perspective. As a result, the colors seem to explode outward from a distant point. © Cory Arcangel.

ing. Many types of spatial experiences can be achieved by manipulating the elements—that is, by varying their position, number, direction, value, texture, size, and color. The resultant spatial variations are endless (see fig. 3.19).

Line and Space

Line, by its nature, implies continued direction of movement. Whether moving across the picture plane or deep into it, line helps indicate spatial presence. Because, by definition, a line must be greater in length than in width (or else it

would be indistinguishable from a dot or a shape), it tends to emphasize one direction. As a line extends into a certain direction, it creates continuity, moving the eye of the observer from one unit or general area to another. Line can be a transition that unifies the front, middle, and background areas.

In addition to direction, line contains other spatial properties. Long or short lines, thick or thin lines, straight, angular, or curved lines all take on different spatial positions in contrast with one another. The various methods of perspective that we have learned can be

8.38 Lyonel Feininger, *Hopfgarten*, 1920. Oil on canvas, 25 × 32¼ in. In this painting, the artist has used intuitive methods of space control, including overlapping planes and transparencies, as well as planes that interpenetrate one another and incline into space. Given in memory of Catharine Roberts Seybold by her friends and family. The Minneapolis Institute of the Arts.

combined with the physical properties of line. A long thick line, for instance, appears larger and hence closer to the viewer than a short thin line. Overlapping lines establish differing spatial positions, especially when they are set in opposite directions (e.g., vertical against horizontal). A diagonal line may be made to move from the picture plane into deep space, whereas a vertical or horizontal line generally appears comparatively static (fig. 8.39). In addition, the plastic qualities of overlapping lines can be increased by modulating their values. Lines can be lightened to the point that they disappear (become "lost") only to reappear (become "found") and

grow darker across the composition. This missing section, or *implied line*, in addition to controlling compositional direction and movement, invariably suggests change of position in space.

The spatial indication of line convergence that occurs in linear perspective is always in evidence wherever a complex of lines occurs. The spatial suggestions arising out of this principle are so infinitely varied that particular effects are usually the product of the artist's intuitive explorations. Wavy, spiral, serpentine, and zigzag line types adapt to all kinds of space through their unexpected deviations of direction and accent. They seem to move back and forth from one spatial plane to another.

Unattached single lines define their own space and may have plastic qualities within themselves. Lines also clarify the spatial dimensions of solid shapes (fig. 8.40).

Shape and Space

Shape may refer to planes, solids, or volumes, all of which occupy space and should therefore be discussed here. A planar shape, although physically two-dimensional, may create the illusion of three-dimensional space (see fig. 4.10). The space only appears two-dimensional when the plane seems to lie flat on the picture surface (see fig. 4.1). The space appears three-dimensional

8.39 Terry Winters, *Untitled (Indigo)*, 2003. Oil on linen, 77 × 59½ in. The physical characteristics and properties of each line contribute to the development of the space within this painting. Individual lines overlap, converge, and define their own space while collectively creating a relatively deep visual labyrinth. © Terry Winters, Courtesy Matthew Marks Gallery, New York.

8.40 Al Held, *B/WX*, 1968. Acrylic on canvas, 9 ft. 6 in. × 9 ft. 6 in. (2.90 × 2.90 m). Although the physical properties of the lines in this work are consistent throughout, their arrangement causes the enclosed shapes to be seen in different spatial positions. This is somewhat similar to the program of Op Art. Albright-Knox Art Gallery, Buffalo, NY. Gift of Seymour H. Knox, 1969. Art Resource, NY. Art © Al Held/Licensed by VAGA, New York, NY.

8.41 Planes and solids in space. The relationship of planes in this diagram describes an effect of solids or volumes that in turn seem to occupy space. The size, overlapping, and placement of these volumes further increase the effect of solidity. The horizontal shaded lines indicate an imaginary position for the picture plane, causing the near volume to project into the observer's space, or in front of the picture plane.

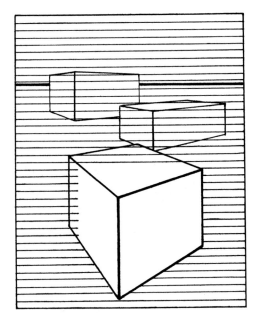

8.42 René Magritte, *The Unmasked Universe*, 1932. Oil on canvas, 29.5 × 35.8 in. (75 × 91 cm). On close inspection, one can see that this work is deliberately inconsistent in its use of space. As a Surrealist, Magritte often created ambiguous and unexpected effects to titillate our senses. Art © 2011 C. Herscovici, London/Artists Rights Society (ARS), NY. © Photo Herscovici/Art Resource, NY.

8.43 Tony King, *Map: Spirit of '76*, 1976. Acrylic and newspaper on canvas, 7 × 8 ft. (2.13 × 2.44 m). The format, with its papier collé surface, is perfectly flat, but the use of light and dark values creates a strongly three-dimensional illusion. Courtesy of Owens Corning Collection, Toledo, OH.

when its edges seem to converge at a point toward the front or the back of the picture plane (see figs. 2.21 and 8.23).

Solids, volumes, and masses automatically suggest three dimensions. Such shapes express the space in which they exist and become an actual part of it (figs. 8.41 and 8.42). The spatial position of planes, solids, and volumes can be made distant by diminishing their size in comparison to others in the foreground and by neutralizing their value, color, intensity, and detail (see fig. 8.38). This treatment relates back to the indications of space outlined earlier in this chapter.

Value and Space

Value is also an important way to control pictorial space. When a light source is assumed to be in front of a work, the objects in the foreground appear light. The middle and background objects become progressively darker as they move away from the picture plane (see fig. T.27). When the light source is located at the back of the work, the order of values is reversed (see fig. 6.17). The order of value change is consistent in gradation from light to dark or dark to light.

In the natural world, foreground objects are seen with clarity and great contrast, while distant objects are ill defined and gray. Therefore, neutral grays, when juxtaposed with blacks or whites, generally take a distant position (see fig. 8.4).

Cast shadows are sometimes helpful in describing plastic shape (see figs. 5.10A and 5.15), but they may be spatially confusing and even injurious to the design if not handled judiciously (see fig. 5.9). Shapes that are defined by multiple light sources, however, may appear flattened and decorative (see fig. 5.10B).

Value-modeling can be abstract in the sense that it need not follow the objective natural order of light and dark. Many artists totally ignore this natural order, using instead the inherent spatial position that results from the contrast of dark and light (fig. 8.43).

Texture and Space

Because of the surface enrichment that texture produces, it is tempting to think of this element purely in terms of decorative usefulness. However, texture can also have the plastic function of describing the spatial depth of surfaces. Sharp, clear, and bold textures generally advance, and fuzzy, dull, and minuscule textures generally recede (see fig. 6.17). When modified through varied use of value, color, and line, texture significantly contributes to a work's sense of space.

Texture is an important element used to produce the flat, decorative surface so valued in contemporary art. The physical character of texture is related to allover patterned design and therefore operates effectively on decorative surfaces. When patterned surfaces are repeated and distributed over the entire pictorial area, the flatness of the picture plane becomes vitally important. Many works by Pablo Picasso utilize surface textures to preserve the flatness of the picture plane (see fig. 6.16).

Color and Space

One of the outstanding contributions of modern artists has been their reevaluation of the plastic potentials of color. Color is now used specifically and purposefully to model the various spatial planes of surface areas (see the "Plastic Colors" section in Chapter 7). Since the time of Cézanne, a new awareness of the spatial characteristics of color has arisen in art. Prior to that, space was considered to be derived from the picture plane and the view that receded into or behind it. Later, John Marin and others dealt with the spaces on or in front of the picture plane chiefly through the use of color (fig. 8.44). Hans Hofmann, the abstractionist, often used colors to advance

8.44 John Marin, *Sun Spots,* 1920. Watercolor and charcoal on off-white wove paper, 16½ × 19¾ in. (41.9 × 50.2 cm). Marin used the watercolor medium to exhibit a free, loose style of painting. His play of color—sea against sunspots—helps create tremendous spatial interaction. The Metropolitan Museum of Art, Alfred Stieglitz Collection, 1949 (49.70.121). Photograph © The Metropolitan Museum of Art /Art Resource, NY.

8.45 Hans Hofmann, *The Gate,* 1959–60. Oil on canvas, 6 ft. 3⅛ in. × 4 ft. ½ in. (1.9 × 1.23 m). The large receding areas of cool greens and blues in this painting unify the color scheme. The smaller areas of warm yellows and reds contrast with the background colors and seem to float in space, creating a unique illusion of depth. Solomon R. Guggenheim Museum, New York, NY. 62.1620. Photograph by David Heald. © Estate of Hans Hofmann/Licensed by VAGA, New York, NY.

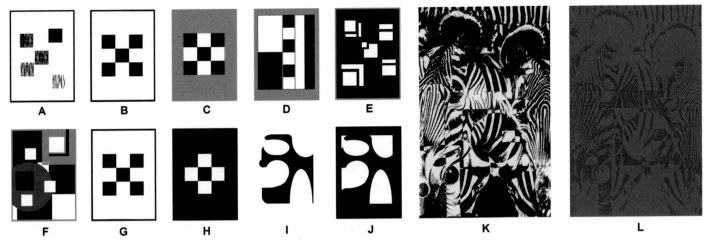

8.46 Structured ambiguity versus stable figure/ground relationships.

shapes seemingly beyond the picture plane. He controlled the degree to which they advanced or receded by contrasts of value, intensity, and hue (fig. 8.45).

Analogous colors, because they are closely related, create limited spatial movement; contrasting colors enlarge the space and provide varied accents or focal points of interest. Changes in value and intensity can also be used to explore the limitless dimensions of space.

STRUCTURED AMBIGUITY

We have learned about the development of three-dimensional space in the graphic arts, looking at the common spatial indicators like size, position, overlapping, clarity of detail, and so forth. In the process, we have seen that pictorial space often depends on the viewer's ability to recognize a line, a group of marks, or a shape. Once identified, the line, marks, or shape become the positive figure(s) within a spatial reference relative to the surrounding area or ground.

Now, however, we should consider for a moment a different type of space—albeit an ambiguous or uncertain space—called **structured ambiguity.** This space occurs when a mark, a group of marks, or a shape seems vague or unreadable—appearing to be positive (figure) at one moment but negative (background) at the next. It may even fluctuate back and forth between the two states. This is a situation that denies a clear shape identity and thus prevents a clear sense of space.

As a spatial condition, even though uncertain, structured ambiguity can be a very important tool in the development of optical illusions and softening spatial effects; it also can work to transition between areas of contrasting values or opposing colors, which makes for interesting value patterns (see figs. 2.19 and 3.14C). For these reasons alone, it is important to understand how structured ambiguities can be created. However, it's also important to know when to avoid them. Images will likely be more readable without ambiguous spatial references and confusing figure/ground identity. So, if structured

ambiguity is introduced where needed and avoided where inappropriate, the resulting images will have the best of both worlds: smooth transitions between opposing grounds, recognizable shapes, interesting value patterns, and convincing sense of space.

How, then, is a structured ambiguity created, and what conditions cause it to occur? When an artist's pen, pencil, or brush touches the white picture plane, two things happen. First, the resulting mark defines a location and divides, to some extent, the picture plane. Generally, the mark is seen as a positive image, while the remaining area is perceived as negative. Second, the mark may seem to take a position in front of or at some distance behind the picture plane. Each of these qualities will continue to be important as the work develops.

As marks accumulate and become shapes, the artist begins to design these shapes into an organized pattern. In figure 8.46A, the shapes are seen as black positive figures on a white negative ground. When the shapes are drawn close together, as in figure 8.46B, the black pattern still reads as positive and the white as the negative ground. But, when the areas of black and white are relatively equal in volume—neither surrounding the other—or when they are surrounded by a third value or color (fig. 8.46C), the figure/ground relationship between the black and white areas is much less obvious, even impossible to distinguish. One moment the black shapes are perceived as positive, making a pattern on a white ground, and the next moment the reverse seems to be true. The spatial relationship between the black areas and the white areas has been lost.

The primary cause of this ambiguity is a state of *equivalency*. Equal amounts of any or all of the following elements may cause the unstable figure/ground condition:

- The size of the positive and negative areas involved
- The volume of black and white or opposing color used to define the shapes
- The size of the marks made and the spaces between them
- The character of the marks and the character of the negative areas (including direction, width, and length)
- The shape type
- The application or general quality of any of the elements used to define the positive and negative areas (texture, color, value, intensity, and so forth).

Ambiguous space also occurs when one shape or color is not allowed to surround another (fig. 8.46D, see also fig. 2.8) or when all shapes run off the edges of the composition (see fig. 1.37). In both of these situations, the viewer cannot tell where the shapes begin or end, which adds instability to the spatial condition. Because the shapes in figure 8.46A, B, and E are surrounded, they have a greater probability of functioning as figures, or positive areas; the surrounding color becomes an area of

background because of the *difference* in the amount of black and white as well as the variation in size of those shapes.

It is interesting to note that there are times when a positive area can act as a negative *without* necessarily creating a sense of ambiguous space. This can be seen in figure 8.46F, where a large red circle (seen as a positive against the black) can also function as a background for smaller black and white squares (see also fig. 2.24). The smaller shapes remain positive while the red circle fluctuates between positive and negative, depending upon where we focus our attention.

Beginning artists are often advised not to mat with black mats, because doing so can destroy the pattern of the original figure/ground relationship. For example, in figure 8.46G, positive black shapes create a design on a white background. But when closely cropped with a black mat, as in figure 8.46H, the planned pattern of the black shapes becomes part of the background and the white background becomes the positive pattern—this unplanned shift could greatly alter the effectiveness of the original design. This may occur even with multisided shapes, as in figures 8.46I and 8.46J. The same concept applies to any colored mats used on works with similarly colored shapes.

Although simplified geometric shapes were used for the sake of clarity in these illustrations, the same principles apply to more complicated studio work. In figures 8.46K and 8.46L, structured ambiguity allows the zebras to be more difficult to discover, as if camouflaged within the elements of the composition. Shapes run off the edges of the composition. Implied edges create additional floating shapes that seem both positive and negative. Because it is unclear where the shapes truly begin or end, entire areas of the work fluctuate between figure and ground. The image is also filled with similar shape type, direction, length, width, texture, color,

and intensity. All of these factors contribute to the viewer's inability to find the animals.

To fully understand the variable ground conditions inherent in a structured ambiguity, it must be experienced firsthand. There is an exercise to help an artist discern the moment when developing forms reverse their ground relationships or become ambiguous. It requires a source of interesting typeface and a pair of cropper bars. The objective will be to slide the cropper bars around until shapes lose the identity of the typeface and create uncertainty about whether they function as figure or background. The exercise is illustrated in figure 8.47 A through L.

In figure 8.47A, the letters definitely read as yellow figure on a black background. As you slide the cropper bars around, reducing the amount of background, there will be a moment when the identity of the letters is destroyed and the relationship between what is positive and what is negative is lost (fig. 8.47B and C). When that moment occurs, try to discern the equivalency in the volume of both colors. Figure 8.47D illustrates the same solution but with multiple colors.

With letters that have distinct shapes, it may be more difficult to lose the letter's identity, as demonstrated in figure 8.47F through I. In order to create structured ambiguity in those cases, it may help to change the angle or work upside down; seeing the shape in a new context will probably help it lose its old identity (in fig. 8.47, compare H to I and C to E).

If you continue to crop in closer after reaching a state of structured ambiguity, you will see the figure/ground relationship reverse. In figure 8.47J, the green letter has been cropped so close that it has become the background—and the red background has now become the positive figure.

In figure 8.47K, this exercise is applied to a woodcut print that uses

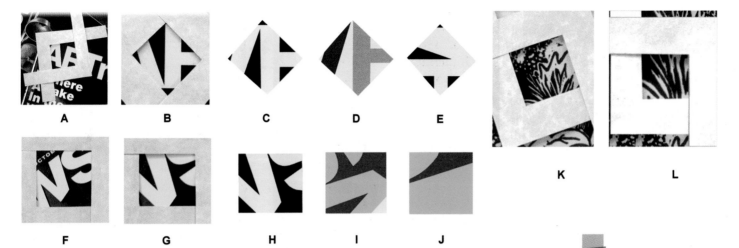

8.47 A structured ambiguity exercise.

Gotham

A

8.48 (A) Jonathan Hoefler and Tobias Frere-Jones, *Gotham typeface,* 2000; (B) Andy Rogerson, *Typography Is Graphic Design,* 2011. The typography example on the left (A) can be read easily because the relationship between positive and negative space is clear. In the example on the right (B), the designer blurred the relationship between background and foreground by overlapping the letters and using progressively darker shades of grey. The result is an ambiguous rendering of the word "typography."(A) © Hoefler & Frere-Jones, Inc.; (B) © Andy Rogerson.

B

black lines on white and white lines on black. By cropping in, you can see an area where the marks do not have a stable figure/ground relationship (fig 8.47L). This is an area of structured ambiguity that functions as a transition between the two ground systems.

When an artist understands what creates structured ambiguity, he or she can choose to incorporate it or avoid it. Images can be made to read clearly with the subtlest of adjustments to the relationship between the positive or negative areas; whether this is beneficial depends on the work and the artist's intention. Since the positive area gets the most attention by its very function, it is even more important to grow sensitive to how the negative areas are being planned and how they affect the compositions. Creating structured ambiguities will help establish optical illusions, create compositions in which you wish to deny a sense of space, transition between areas of contrast, or make an area or image softly blend into its surrounding area. Both structured ambiguity and stable figure/ground relationships are useful in the right setting, and both, when grasped, are valuable tools at the disposal of the artist.

THREE-DIMENSIONAL APPLICATIONS OF SPACE

In pictorial art, space is an illusion and has been presented as a *product* of the elements. However, in the three-dimensional arts—such as sculpture, ceramics, jewelry, architecture, and much installation work—space actually exists and must be treated as an element. For artists working in three-dimensional mediums, space is a boundless extension of area in all directions. Insofar as pure space has no visual qualities, a medium is necessary to define and limit the space that is to be used.

When artists use space, they tend to limit its vastness. They may mark

Time and Motion

CHAPTER NINE

Production still from *The Matrix*, 1999. Directed by Andy Wachowski and Lana Wachowski.

THE VOCABULARY OF
TIME AND MOTION

Time — A system or way of measuring the interval between events or experiences.
Motion — The process of moving, or changing place or position in space.

actual motion
The movement found in art forms like kinetic art, where bodies physically change their location during a period of time.

animation
The rapid succession of a sequence of drawings, computer-generated images, or pictures of objects such as clay figures that create the illusion of a moving image.

cell (or single cell)
One image from a series of related images that presents an idea. Cells are commonly found in comic strips, graphic novels, or storyboard presentations, which tend to isolate the images from each other by an outline in the shape of a rectangle. Cells also refer to the individual frames of animated cartoons.

close-up
A cinematic technique in which the subject fills the camera frame; used to focus the viewer's attention on specific imagery or detail.

crosscutting
A cinematic technique that abruptly shifts from one event or character to another and is often used to allow the viewer to move between characters and change points of view as the dialogue or action evolves.

dissolve
An aesthetic technique, used as a film or video transition between images or scenes, in which one shot disappears as another slowly appears.

duration
The length of time in which an activity takes place.

fade
An aesthetic technique, used as a film or video transition between scenes, in which the image slowly darkens to black.

flashback
A cinematic technique of jumping to a sequence of events in the story that are meant to have taken place in the past.

flash-forward
A cinematic technique of jumping to a sequence of events in the story that are meant to take place in the future.

four-dimensional space
An imaginative treatment of forms that gives a sense of intervals of time or motion.

frame
A single static image as applied to cartoons, storyboards, animation, films, videos, or computer-generated graphics.

Futurism
An early-twentieth-century movement that sought to express the fourth dimension through the speed, power, and motion of the Industrial Age.

implied motion
The sense or illusion of movement given to a static object.

installations
Interior or exterior settings of media created by artists to heighten the viewer's awareness of the environmental space.

kinetic
Derived from the Greek word *kinesis*, meaning "motion." Kinetic art includes the element of actual motion.

long shot
A cinematic technique in which the filmmaker provides a distant view with a broader perspective of image; often used to imply a larger conceptual context.

medium shot
A cinematic technique in which the filmmaker provides a view that seems to lie somewhere between a close-up and a long shot.

mobile
A three-dimensional moving sculpture.

motion
The process of moving, or changing place or position in space.

motion picture
The illusion of a moving image created by showing a series of still pictures in rapid sequence.

multimedia
The combination of many different groups of media such as text, still and moving graphics, and spoken and instrumental sounds; also often integrated with communication technologies involving television, video, telephones, and computers.

multiple exposures
A photographic technique that shows a figure in motion by displaying a rapid series of exposures within the same image.

slow motion
1. A cinematic technique that slows down the movement and time in a film; created by shooting a high number of frames per second and showing them at a much slower speed. 2. The sense that time and movement are progressing more slowly than normal.

still frame
One frame (or full-screen image) from a series of frames normally seen in a film or video presentation that when viewed in sequence present the illusion of a moving picture. Related to **cell.**

superimposing, superimposed images
A technique in which various views of the same subject are placed on top of each other in the same image.

time
A system or way of measuring the interval between events or experiences.

video
A recording of visual images that are stored in an electronic format (digital or videotape) and viewed on a television, computer monitor, or projection screen. The sensation of motion is an illusion created by the rapid sequence of images.

THE SEARCH FOR A NEW SPATIAL DIMENSION

Every great period in the history of art has espoused a particular concept of space. These spatial preferences reflect basic conditions and attitudes of the society that produced them. Whenever a new approach to space is introduced, it is at first resisted by the public. Soon, however, it becomes accepted and integrated into the artistic vocabulary. Eventually, it becomes the standard filter through which people view things and a jumping-off point for new explorations.

Artists of the Renaissance, for example, conditioned by the ideas of the period, sought to accomplish the optical, scientific mastery of nature by reducing it part-by-part to a static geometric system. By restricting their attention to one point of view, artists were able to develop perspective and represent illusory distortions of actual shapes as seen by the human eye. Modern artists, however, equipped with new materials and technology, have continued the search into spatial perception begun during the Renaissance. The acceleration of change prompted by the cataclysmic revelations of modern science has produced new concepts that are without precedent. Nature's inner and outer structures have been probed with microscope, camera, and telescope. Automobiles, airplanes, and spacecraft have given us the opportunity to see more of the world than our early predecessors even knew existed. The radically changed environment of the artist has brought about a new awareness of space. It has become increasingly evident that space cannot always be described from one point of view, and artists continue to explore the possibilities of space for expressive purposes.

The fast-paced modern world exhibits an intense and constant sense of **motion**, which increasingly has become a motivating factor in contemporary artistic expression. Motion and the resulting passage of **time** have both become a way of considering space, and artists represent them in ways that reflect the speed and pace of today's world. This new approach to spatial conception adds a new dimension—the *fourth dimension:* time. Whether the goal is to represent moving images or to create real-time interactive artwork, the power and energy of **four-dimensional space** continues to captivate. And as our methods of personal communication and entertainment change to incorporate the wonder of technological advancements, there is no doubt that artistic expressions of space, time, and motion will also continue to evolve.

PICTORIAL REPRESENTATIONS OF MOVEMENT IN TIME

Writers and musicians have some control over the amount of time their audiences must devote, from beginning to end, to a written or musical piece. By contrast, the work of graphic artists has nearly always been immediate and comprehendible at just a glance. In an effort to capture their audience for longer amounts of time, many graphic artists have explored ways of slowing the viewing experience by manipulating the sense of space and movement within the work.

As discussed in Chapter 2, various treatments and combinations of the elements will alter the viewer's eye movement across and through the composition. Although this entices the viewer to spend time looking at the work, it does not really express the ideas of movement and time as concepts themselves. In fact, visual artists have always struggled with the problem of depicting movement and the passage of time within the boundaries of the two-dimensional picture plane. How does one represent the movement of the subject, or the movement of the viewer? The search is not just about how to direct the amount of time spent looking at the image but also how to capture the sense of time through the appearance of physical motion, the expectation of motion, and/or the sensation of being moved.

Implied Motion through Line Direction or Shape Position

From time immemorial, artists have grappled with the problem of representing movement on a stationary surface. In the works of prehistoric and primitive cultures, the efforts were not organized but instead were isolated attempts to show observed activity (such as moving animals or ritualistic kills; see fig. 1.1). Then, as now, when the subject seems paused in the midst of action, and relatively imbalanced, the threat of gravity creates an almost tangible sense of impending movement (see fig. 2.6).

The subject's motion can also be implied through the general direction and repetition of lines and shapes (see figs. 1.19, 2.10, and 2.56). This applies even more so to nonobjective images, which do not have the power of suggestion so inherent in recognizable shapes (see figs. 2.8 and 3.19); movement is created by the direction of shapes, edge quality, and color placement. The feeling of motion is further enhanced when the elements create an optical illusion—contrasting colors and shapes can make the image pop out toward the viewer or create an undulating spatial movement (see fig. 9.1; see also fig. T.77). In figurative work, gestural line is often used to capture the excitement and activity of the characters that are portrayed (see figs. 3.23, 3.24, and 3.25); although, in the nonobjective works of artists like

9.1 Bridget Riley, *Drift No. 2*, 1966. Acrylic on canvas, 7 ft. 7½ in. × 7 ft. 5½ in. (2.32 × 2.27 m). Op artists generally use geometric shapes, organizing them into patterns that produce fluctuating, ambiguous, and tantalizing visual effects very similar to those observed in moire patterns, such as in door or window screens. Albright-Knox Art Gallery, Buffalo, NY. Gift of Seymour H. Knox, Jr., 1967. Albright-Knox Art Gallery/Art Resource, NY. Courtesy Karsten Schubert, London. © Bridget Riley 2011. All rights reserved.

Jackson Pollock, the gestural lines capture the very movement and energy of the artist himself (see fig. 7.38).

Sequenced Images

The artists of the medieval and early-Renaissance periods illustrated biblical stories by repeating a series of still pictures. The representation of the different phases of the narrative (either in a sequence of several pictures or a sequence within a single work) created a visual synopsis of the subject's movement within a designated space and over a given period of time (fig. 9.2). These pictures are antecedents of the modern comic strip and graphic novel (fig. 9.3). They are also the forebears of **animation,** in which individual **frames** are presented in rapid sequence to make the image appear to move on the screen (see fig. 9.14).

Some contemporary artists, such as Lanna Pendleton Hall, instill the sense of time's passage by creating subtly changing **cells** within a single image. Together, these segments seem to capture a fuller experience of the time spent lingering at that scene (fig. 9.4).

Multiple Viewpoints

In the nineteenth century, Paul Cézanne, a Post-Impressionist painter, tried another approach to introduce the concepts of movement, time, and space—and in turn, extended the viewer's involvement with a painting. His aim was to render objects in a manner more "true to nature." This nature, it should be pointed out, was not the Renaissance world of optical appearances; instead, it was a world of forms in space, conceived in terms of a plastic image. His images emphasized the mass and volume of forms by presenting them in a way that included many vantage points rather than a single one, as had been the traditional approach. In addition, he also often saw objects abstracted to their basic cone, cube, or square shape.

In his still-life paintings, Cézanne frequently shifted the viewpoint within the same work from the right side to the left side and from the top to the bottom, creating the illusion of looking around an object. He changed the eye levels, split the individual object planes, and combined all of these views in the same painting, creating a composite view of the group (fig. 9.5). It was almost as if the viewer had been invited to bring in a ladder and view part of the material from a low position and then climb far up the ladder to see other sections before moving the ladder and continuing to search for new views of the objects. This presentation of multiple views essentially reflects our typical experience of the volume and mass of actual objects—we move around them or turn them in front of us.

When table edges failed to align across the picture, tops of bottles and baskets seemed to tilt at different angles, or the bottoms of chairs seemed to set

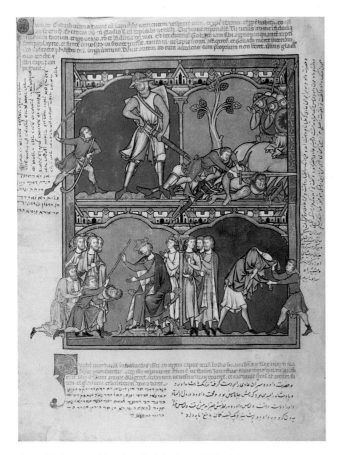

9.2 Unknown, *David and Goliath*, c. 1250. Manuscript, 15⅜ × 11¾ in. (39 × 30 cm). The element of time passing is present here but in a conventional episodic manner. The order of events proceeds in a style similar to that of a comic strip.
Pierpont Morgan Library, New York, M.638 f.28v./Art Resource, New York.

9.3 Bryan Lee O'Malley, *Scott Pilgrim vs. the World, Volume II*, 2005. O'Malley's popular comic, *Scott Pilgrim*, uses sequenced images to present the story. Here, the panels are used to evolve the narrative and show a budding romance.
© Bryan Lee O'Malley, Courtesy of OniPress.

9.4 Lanna Pendleton Hall, *Spectacular Sunrise*, 2006. Oil on linen, 24 × 72 in. (61 × 182.9 cm). This contemporary painting uses a sequence of images to create the sense of passing time. The subtle changes between segments capture the various lighting and atmospheric conditions found during the progression of a sunrise. Courtesy of the artist.

9.5 Paul Cézanne, *Still Life with Basket of Fruit (The Kitchen Table)*, c. 1888–90. Oil on canvas, 25⅝ × 31⅞ in. (65.1 × 81 cm). Cézanne was concerned with the plastic reality of objects as well as with their organization into a unified design. Although the pitcher and sugar bowl are viewed from a direct frontal position, the rounded jar behind them is painted as if it were being seen from a higher location. The handle of the basket is shown as centered at the front, but it seems to become skewed into a right-sided view as it proceeds to the rear. The left and right front table edges do not line up and are thus viewed from different vantage points. Cézanne combined these multiple viewpoints in one painting in order to present each object with a more profound sense of three-dimensional reality. Musée d'Orsay, Paris, France. Photo © Erich Lessing/Art Resource, New York.

on floor planes that couldn't exist under normal circumstances, early viewers thought of Cézanne as a bad draftsman. Many failed to understand that he was trying to establish a new visual vocabulary—one that represented objects and their space through multiple views.

In the early twentieth century, the Cubists working in a style known as "analytic" Cubism adopted many of the pictorial devices used by Cézanne.

They, too, usually showed an object from many views, except the subject matter was first broken down into faceted planes for each of the views. Objects were rendered in a type of orthographic drawing, divided into essential views that could be drawn in two dimensions, not unlike the Egyptian technique cited in Chapter 8 (see figs. 8.12 and 8.13). The basic view (the top view) is called a *plan*.

With the plan as a basis, the *elevations* (or *profiles*) were taken from the front and back, and the *sections* were taken from the right and left sides (fig. 9.6). The superimposing and juxtaposition of all this information showed much more of the object than would actually be visible at one time. Although this technique is a distortion of space, everything is present that we would normally expect to see.

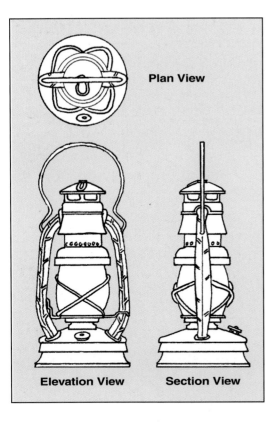

Plan View

Elevation View   **Section View**

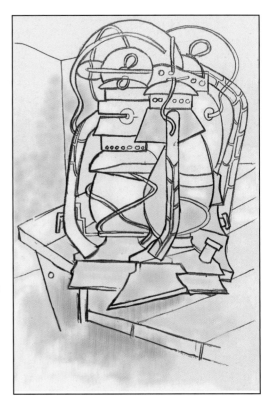

In fact, it is precisely these multiple viewpoints that create an implied movement around the objects within the context of a two-dimensional image (fig. 9.7).

In the works of the Cubists, we find that a picture can have a life of its own and that the creation of space is not essentially a matter of portrayal or rendering. The Cubists worked step-by-step to illustrate that the more a painted object departed from straightforward optical resemblance, the more systematically the full three-dimensional nature of the object could be explored. Eventually, they developed the concept of the "synthetically" designed picture. Instead of analyzing a subject into planes and shapes, they began by developing large, simple geometric shapes that were not based on a real-world model. Subject matter suggested by the shapes was then imposed, or synthesized, into this spatial system (see fig. 4.2).

Contemporary artists like David Hockney have revived the interest in the Cubists' sense of multiple viewpoints and viewer movement. Working from a different approach, Hockney has made composite images from multiple photographs, each taken at a slightly different angle. In this manner, the small jumps in position and misalignments between prints make the viewer continually adjust his or her viewpoint. These small segments must then be joined in the mind to form a single portrait (fig. 9.8).

Superimposed and Blurred Images

Another representational means to suggest the movement of an image involves **superimposing** (overlapping) a series of altered positions of the same figure or its parts within a single pictorial arrangement; as a result, the image may seem blurred or have indistinct

contours. This technique, in essence, catalogs a moving body's sequence of positions and indicates the visible changes.

Twentieth-century artists explored the possibility of fusing these changing figure positions by filling out the pathway of their movement. As a result, figures are not seen in fixed positions but as abstract moving paths of action (figs. 9.9 and 9.10). The subject in Marcel Duchamp's *Nude Descending a Staircase* is not the human body but the energy the human body emits as it passes through space. This painting signified important progress in the pictorialization of motion, in which the plastic forces are functionally integrated with the composition. The energy of motion was also captured and explored with the use of photography, which created superimposed images through **multiple exposures** of the film (fig. 9.11).

The **Futurists,** motivated by the power and speed of the Industrial Age,

9.8 David Hockney, *Mother I, Yorkshire Moors, August 1985 #1*, 1985. Photographic collage, 18½ × 13 in. (47 × 33 cm). By layering multiple photos of an image, each taken at a slightly different angle, the viewer is forced to continually adjust his or her viewpoint to see a complete image. This provides a potentially more rounded and realistic understanding of the subject. Photographic composites like this also allow for the creation of an image that has more width and depth than the view normally seen with a camera lens. © David Hockney

9.9 Marcel Duchamp, *Nude Descending a Staircase, No. 2*, 1912. Oil on canvas, 58 × 35 in. (147.3 × 88.9 cm). The subject of Duchamp's painting is not the human body but rather the type and degree of energy a body emits as it passes through space. Philadelphia Museum of Art, PA. Louise and Walter Arensberg Collection. Photograph by Corbis Media. © 2011 Artists Rights Society (ARS), New York/ADAGP, Paris/Succession of Marcel Duchamp.

9.10 Giacomo Balla, *Dynamism of a Dog on a Leash*, 1912. Oil on canvas, 35⅜ × 43¼ in. (89.9 × 109.9 cm). To suggest motion as it is involved in time and space, Balla invented the technique of repeated contours. This device was soon imitated in newspaper comic strips, thereby becoming a mere convention. Albright-Knox Art Gallery, Buffalo, NY. Bequest of A. Conger Goodyear and Gift of George F. Goodyear, 1964. © 2011 Artists Rights Society (ARS), New York/SIAE, Rome.

9.11 Alvin Langdon Coburn, *Portrait of Ezra Pound*, 1916. Photograph, size unknown. Strongly influenced by Cubism, the diversely talented photographer Coburn produced this multiple image of the poet Ezra Pound. Courtesy George Eastman House, International Museum of Photography and Film.

9.12 Gino Severini, *Dynamic Hieroglyphic of the Bal Tabarin*, 1912. Oil on canvas with sequins, 63⅝ × 61½ in. (161.6 × 156.2 cm). The works of the Futurists were devoted to motion for its own sake. They included not only the shapes of figures and objects and their pathways of movement but also their backgrounds. These features were combined in a pattern of kinetic energy.
The Museum of Modern Art, New York, NY. Acquired through the Lillie P. Bliss Bequest. Digital image © The Museum of Modern Art/Licensed by SCALA/Art Resource, NY. © 2011 Artists Rights Society (ARS), New York/ADAGP, Paris.

machines, flight, and warfare, were devoted to motion for its own sake. Their works included not only the shapes of figures and objects and their pathways of movement but also their backgrounds. These features were combined in a pattern of kinetic energy. Although this form of expression was not entirely new, it provided a new type of artistic adventure—simultaneity of figure, object, and environment (fig. 9.12; see also fig. T.59). Contemporary artists continue to experiment with the concept of superimposed images (fig. 9.13).

MOTION PICTURES: FILM AND VIDEO

Modern scientific study of the optics of an object in motion began around 1824 (with the Thaumatrope, a toy that alternated two different images to create the illusion of a moving object) and paralleled the discovery and development of photography. Among the pioneers to link photography with the study of motion were Coleman Sellers and Eadweard Muybridge. Sellers was an engineer who, in 1861, patented the Kinematoscope—a device that contained photographs mounted on a turning paddle wheel, which flashed the pictures in sequence so rapidly that the images appeared animated. Eadweard Muybridge was a photographer who was known for his photographs of animals and people in motion, as well as experiments using multiple cameras to capture the first series of split-second movements (fig. 9.14). In the late 1870s, Muybridge presented his individual images in sequence inside a Zoetrope (known as the "wheel of life"), which was basically a cylinder with regularly spaced vertical slots. As the images were viewed through the slots of the spinning Zoetrope, the animals appeared to come alive, running and jumping (fig. 9.15). By 1879, Muybridge was presenting his moving images using a Zoetrope that had been modified for projection. Muybridge, a leader in the study of objects in motion, drew worldwide acclaim from his extensive public lectures and book publications.

From this point onward, scientists and artists in many countries seemed to be in a desperate race to alter still photography into an art form that could depict motion in a new way. Rather quickly, glass-plate images were replaced by materials that could bend and flex, and by 1887 Thomas Alva Edison commissioned W. K. L. Dickson to invent a **motion-picture** camera. In 1891, Edison presented his first motion picture and patented a Kinetoscope (often called a "peep show"), in which a film loop, run on spools, passed between an incandescent lamp and a shutter to present moving images for individual viewing. By 1895 short

9.14 Eadweard Muybridge, *A Horse's Motion Scientifically Considered*, c. 1875. Engravings after photographs, size unknown. An American rancher friend and supporter of Muybridge encouraged his studies of horses in motion, which proved that at some point in midgallop all four hooves leave the ground (note the top row, numbers 2, 3, and 4). The photographer took the series with some of the earliest fast-action cameras and went on to influence Manet, Degas, and later artistic students of motion. Hulton Deutsch Collection/Corbis.

9.15 The Zoetrope. Also known as the "wheel of life," the Zoetrope was invented in 1834 in England by William Horner. As shown here, a strip of paper displaying a sequence of images was placed in the center of the cylinder. When the viewer looked through the vertical slots to the inside, the images appeared to move as the wheel was spun. © NMPFT/ SSPL/The Image Works.

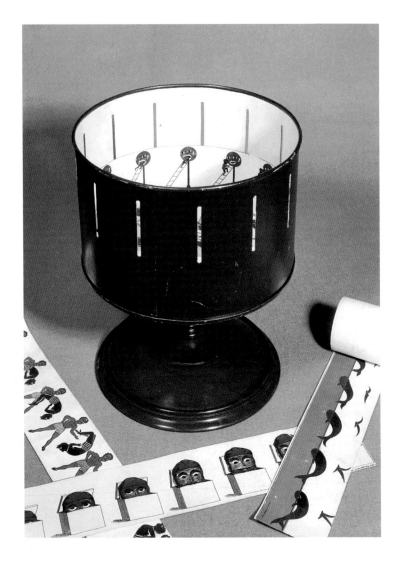

documentary films were being made in the United States, Germany, France, and the Netherlands; by 1900 film production had expanded to include Czechoslovakia, Italy, Japan, Russia, and Scandinavia. Projection systems began appearing, which made screenings for larger audiences possible. Soon film theaters appeared, like the Nickelodeon in Pittsburgh. Though the theaters were often set up in storefronts, the realism of the narrative and the excitement of the action of the new movie medium led the industry through many phases—from the silent-film era to the "talkies"—including melodramas, westerns, slapstick comedies, serialized episodes, fully animated

feature films, and epics like David O. Selznick's *Gone With the Wind* (1939) and MGM's *The Wizard of Oz* (1939).

Although the film industry in general was preoccupied with filling the public's appetite for action, color, and sound, the early work by film artists like D. W. Griffith had systematized many aesthetic techniques, creating a language of cinema that is still used today. In a film, the sense of space, movement, and time can all be controlled by altering the closeness of images, their sequencing, and the transitions in between. **Close-ups** draw attention to the character and their delivery. When combined with **medium** and **long shots,** the viewer can

see a character's facial expressions and body language, as well as their placement in a setting or environment (fig. 9.16). **Crosscutting** allows the viewer to move back and forth from one character to another as the dialogue evolves. In addition to its uses in portraying a conversation, crosscutting can function to simultaneously tell parallel and often diverse storylines. To aid in the change from one scene to another, certain transitions were also devised that have become standard. **Fades** allow a scene or image to softly blur and fade away; **dissolves** allow the image to disappear while another slowly appears—keeping the images or concepts from being completely isolated.

9.16 Movie stills from (top left) *The Lord of the Rings: The Two Towers*, 2002; (top right and bottom) *The Lord of the Rings: The Fellowship of the Ring*, 2001. Directed by Peter Jackson. These still frames illustrate some of the cinematic techniques that help tell a story even without dialogue or sound: long shot, medium shot, and close-up. New Line Cinema/Photofest.

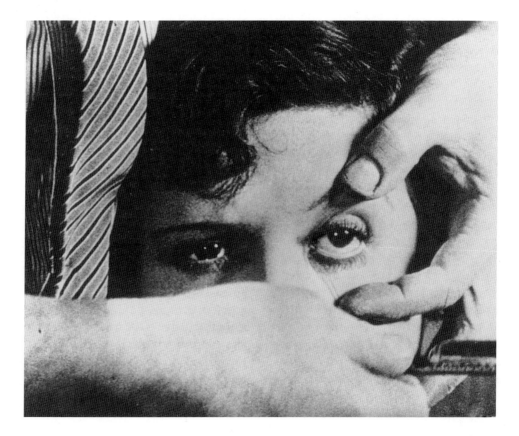

9.17 Salvador Dalí and Luis Buñuel (Director), *An Andalusian Dog*, 1929. Black-and-white silent film, sixteen minutes. This still frame from the film shows the moment just before a woman's eye is cut open, which is one of a series of events meant to shock the audience. © The Everett Collection. © 2011 Salvador Dali, Gala-Salvador Dali Foundation/Artists Rights Society (ARS), New York.

With a camera's ability to change viewpoints, not only is the image moving but the viewer is effectively changing position as well. The emergence of film, for the first time, allowed artists to use time as a significant element in two-dimensional works. In fact, the use of time was something that could now be manipulated—shifting slowly from face to face or flashing between cars or horses in a chase.

The ways in which filmmakers can manipulate the sense of time is various. In a film, a viewer can experience the time of a scene as expanding, contracting, or jumping around. While the **duration** of a scene happens in real time, a filmmaker can alter a work's *internal* time drastically. By decreasing or increasing the amount of frames shot per second, a filmmaker can make time seem to speed up or slow down. For example, time can be sped up by photographing at 1 frame per second, instead of the standard 24 frames per second (the speed of a film projector); if the subjects are captured in the middle of fast motion, this technique emphasizes the speed of their action. Similarly, time-lapse photography can present in a few minutes what might have evolved over several days, such as the blooming of a flower. Conversely, increasing the number of frames photographed per second (for example, 100 frames per second) will create a sense of **slow motion;** a particular action that in reality would only take seconds can be expanded into several minutes. Using this technique, a viewer can see a cowboy express several types of emotion as he flies off a horse before hitting the ground—an action that would be a blur in real time. Expanding the sense of time like this allows for more detail to be captured, providing greater emphasis to a scene. Further manipulation of time can be done through **flashbacks** and **flashforwards,** which can be inserted at any point in a film to present a viewer with a past episode, provide a glimpse into the future, or develop a parallel storyline.

While the exploration of these techniques and other practices like controlled lighting, sound, color, etc., all hinted at the possibilities of the new medium for individual self-expression, the scale of studio projects and the necessary equipment created financial obstacles. Smaller-scale work, however, often shown in art houses, allowed for more flexibility and individual self-expression. *An Andalusian Dog* (1929), for example, created by the painter Salvador Dalí and director Luis Buñuel, was a personal and emotional accomplishment that explored dreams and the subconscious mind. Disjointed in chronology, the sixteen-minute black-and-white silent film portrayed a nightmare using random sequences of images: the night sky, a wispy cloud, the full moon, an eye being sliced by a razor, ants in the

9.19 Nam June Paik, *Hamlet Robot*, 1996. Two radios, twenty-four TVs, transformer, two laser disc players, laser discs, crown, scepter, sword, and skull, 144 × 88 × 32 in. Nam June Paik's portrait of Hamlet is a video sculpture programmed with a kaleidoscopic mix of contemporary audio and visual technology. Courtesy Carl Solway Gallery, Cincinnati, OH, from the collection of The Chrysler Museum of Art, Norfolk, VA. Photograph by Chris Gomien.

well-financed studios. The sequences of scenes and camera shots can be altered with relative ease; sounds can be changed or lined up with different scenes; and the viewer's experience of time can be generally manipulated. Special effects can also be added (like snow patterns, lighting changes, or altered colors) and computer-generated images (CGI) can be seamlessly inserted onto shots of real objects and people—all of which may add emotional emphasis or place focus on a particular idea.

The motion-picture or **video** camera in the hands of a creative person can lead to fantastic developments. In *The Matrix* (1999), directors Larry and Andy Wachowski used an updated version of Muybridge's approach (see fig. 9.14) by setting up dozens of still cameras to capture a unique slow-motion, rotating action shot (fig. 9.18). Artists like Andy Warhol, working with traditional fixed-camera positions, have used motion pictures to study reality in a new way by presenting everyday activities such as sleeping. Brian Fridge even challenges our understanding of four minutes in a freezer (see fig. 6.11). Movies like *Avatar* (2009) have managed to fuse CGI characters with real ones in a seamless blend of fantasy and reality. James Cameron, the director of *Avatar*, has also revolutionized filmmaking by using new 3-D equipment, offering a startling and captivating visual experience.

Clearly, filmmaking has given individual artists a practical means for offering the direct action of human thoughts and movements, and when distributed through the Internet, TV, theaters, and portable devices, it provides a powerful new medium for artists to explore. Art museums and galleries have featured **installations** that incorporate TVs, LCD and plasma monitors, and projectors, glowing with artistic images of every imaginable human expression or action. This viewing equipment can be positioned

palm of a hand, a severed hand in the street. As illustrated by the **still frame** in figure 9.17, these images were meant to provoke, shock, and horrify, keeping with the spirit of the Surrealists' revolution.

As the cost of filmmaking equipment came down, the potential for film as a personal art medium was greatly enhanced. In the 1960s, Eastman Kodak introduced 8-mm film, and portable cameras that used 8-mm film were soon available. More recently, the introduction of high-definition digital cameras, projectors, and other equipment has provided an affordable means by which artists, designers, teachers,

students, home users, and professionals could view, produce, and create films.

With the development of the computer, new technology has engendered a transformation of the entire film industry. Today, a film can be produced digitally from start to finish. Compact cameras can record both still and moving images as digital information on a memory chip. When the images are transported to a computer, they may be easily altered and saved in many formats. Computers also provide access to editing programs that allow the creation of quality images that were previously available only to

9.20 Nam June Paik, *Megatron/Matrix*, 1995. Two hundred and fifteen monitors, eight-channel color video, and two-channel sound, 12 × 33 × 2 ft. overall. This giant video/sound installation displays an intricate matrix of changing animation and video. Laser-disc images, controlled by computer, scroll across the screens and constantly change sequence to reflect the "microtime" of TV: commercials, sound bites, and news briefs. © Smithsonian American Art Museum, Washington, DC/Art Resource, NY.

9.21 Bill Viola, *Going Forth by Day*, detail, installation view of "The Path" and "The Deluge," 2002. Video and sound installation with seven projectors, ten speakers, subwoofer, seven amps, six equalizers, cables, speakers, projector mount, and two servers; dimensions vary with installation. *Going Forth by Day* is a video installation inspired by the Egyptian Book of the Dead and the great fresco paintings of the Italian Renaissance. It comprises five panels that examine cycles of birth, death, and rebirth. The "panels"—actually state-of-the-art high-definition video projections seen directly on the walls of a space—are approximately thirty-five minutes long and play simultaneously on continuous loops. The suite of works is an epic about nature's cycles and the flow of time. Commissioned by the Deutsche Bank in consultation with the Solomon R. Guggenheim Foundation for the Deutsche Guggenheim Berlin, 2004, 2004.59. Photograph by David Heald © The Solomon R. Guggenheim Foundation, New York.

in various ways—in some installations, screens appear as if they were paintings, drawings, prints, or sculptures. Their size and scale can range from very tiny to massive.

The Korean-born artist Nam June Paik is considered to be the first video artist. He often synchronized video images and music with a live performance. Paik also assembled video screens, radios, and TVs into sculptured forms that were as much works of art as the videos (fig. 9.19). He produced numerous performance works, along with rewired TVs and multimonitor sculptures in almost every possible arrangement—even giant walls of television sets: *Information Wall* in 1992 featured 429 monitors; *Megatron* in 1995 included 215 monitors with eight-channel color video and two-channel color video and two-channel sound (fig. 9.20); and a blinking, flashing light show used laser beams, TV sets, and a waterfall at the Guggenheim in 2000.

Early contact with Paik and other sound and video artists encouraged another artist, Bill Viola, to further explore the medium, creating video artworks and installations since the 1970s. Viola has become a pioneer in the use of video and the exploration of the moving image in artworks that reflect art history, spirituality, and conceptual issues. The work illustrated in figure 9.21, commissioned by a museum in Berlin, is an example of these subjects. Viewers enter the space and encounter five image-sequences playing simultaneously on every wall of a large gallery. Once inside, they stand at the center of an image-sound world. Each panel tells a story that is part of a larger narrative cycle. Viewers are free to move around and watch each panel individually or to experience the piece as a whole.

COMPUTERS AND MULTIMEDIA

Viola's work is a good example of the degree to which the computer has become a tool in the field of art today. In his case, the computer undoubtedly aided during the planning phase, the scriptwriting, the editing of audiovisuals, and the control of the presentation. But we do not call it "computer art" as such.

Computer art can be traced back to 1962, when Ivan Sutherland introduced Sketchpad, a computer-based drawing program utilizing a light pen and a mainframe computer. During the course of the 1960s, other computer scientists—engineers and mathematicians—demonstrated various properties of computer programming by creating drawings using the computer in conjunction with ink plotters and other printing devices. George Nees's 1965 show in Stuttgart of his computer-generated drawings is often credited with being the first exhibition of "computer art." A 1968 exhibition in London titled "Cybernetic Serendipity" is considered to be the first to draw widespread international attention to the potentials of computer-based applications in art.

After the introduction of the personal computer around 1979, the focus of computer art shifted from printed output to the animation of graphics onscreen. In order to represent 3-D perspective realistically in films, hardware and software developers had to find ways to achieve high resolution and

9.22 Screenshot from *World of Warcraft*. *World of Warcraft* is an online, imaginary world that allows a player to explore and interact with fellow players in detailed 3-D landscapes. Courtesy of Blizzard, Inc.

the realistic lighting of moving scenes. What resulted are now common effects seen in films and advertisements, such as the penetration, melting away, or shape changing (morphing) of objects. This development and improvement of computer graphics during the past generation rivals or even exceeds in scope the transformation of painting during the Italian Renaissance.

In its early stages, computer art was looked down on as the hobby of technicians. But the boundaries of science, technology, entertainment, and art are blurring, and now more artists are engaging in computer art. Video games are a great example of this cross-disciplinary approach. Although video games are meant to be entertainment, a great deal of artistic input is necessary to create the highly complex and realistic worlds that serve as a game's setting.

Artists and designers are employed to dream up new, alien worlds and execute them using the latest computer software programs. One such game, *World of Warcraft*, makes its world available through the Internet, so anybody who can go online can enter the environment. The designers of these worlds need to have a total grasp of the elements of art to create believable and aesthetically beautiful landscapes (fig. 9.22).

Indeed, computers have opened a new era of **multimedia** for communications, information gathering, processing, education, and entertainment—and they are changing the world like nothing before them. Not only do computers provide users access to an unlimited supply of information and entertainment, they function as tools for creative artistic development.

Computers allow extremely complex multimedia works to be created and executed. First, as its name suggests, multimedia combines many different groups of media—such as text, still and moving graphics (animation), and spoken and instrumental sounds—into a single unifying force. Second, multimedia may be integrated with the communication technologies of television, cell phones, tablet devices, Internet, film, and video. Because computers have become powerful enough to process almost any type of data, there seems to be no limit to their uses; endless groups of software programs exist, many of which are quite user friendly and available for ready use by artists and designers. Some of the most frequently used software programs include paint programs (drawing and painting), image manipulation, 3-D modeling, animation, audio editing and authoring, and digital video (motion sequences). Many artists create their own software so that they can control the most implicit specialized areas. Some programs are even made to accept feedback from the spectator, which then alters the projection of sound and visual information to allow the viewer to directly interact with the artwork.

Multimedia, because it involves combinations of various art forms, naturally leads to collaboration between artists of different disciplines. For example, artist Bill Viola, theater director Peter Sellars, and conductor Esa-Pekka Salonen worked together to produce a video-enhanced production of Richard Wagner's opera *Tristan und Isolde.* Viola created images that projected throughout a staged four-hour performance, synchronizing the video to the music. Through their collaborative efforts, the work, called *The Tristan Project,* offered a new way of listening to and looking at the notion of eternal love (fig. 9.23).

For centuries, the work of artists was flat and restricted to a single

9.23 Esa-Pekka Salonen conducts his Los Angeles Philharmonic orchestra as soprano Christine Brewer performs *The Tristan Project,* under a projected video by artist Bill Viola, at Avery Fisher Hall in New York, May 2, 2007. *The Tristan Project* was a true collaboration between the arts, uniting music, video, and theater. The work focuses on the essential nature of myth, extending Richard Wagner's original intentions into a more abstract exploration of metaphysical concepts. The marriage of the artistic mediums sought to give the audience a transcendent experience beyond words. Richard Termine/Lincoln Center for the Performing Arts/AP Images.

point of view. Now, because of concepts made possible by the computer, artists are able to create images never possible before. Artists now have the capability to enter an image and control the exploration within that space—flying over, around, and through objects on command. Images can also be created in real time and real space. These concepts have become commercially viable, being adopted for training films and video games and for specific applications like medical diagnostic imaging and architectural design. Clients can take a virtual tour of a prospective new home; they can move freely about in the structure, to see it and all the furnishings from every possible angle—even rearrange the contents of the space. With this technology, artists can turn over to the audience the controls for experiencing a work of art.

Today, image manipulation and 3-D modeling are commonplace, and new ideas about Web space, real time, and virtual reality are starting to take hold. For artists around the world, the use of technology and the computer are well-embedded in artistic practice, and the digital workbench has become a key ingredient in how modern art is made.

THREE-DIMENSIONAL APPLICATIONS OF TIME AND MOTION

As we have seen, the contemplation of time and motion has been an important concept for two-dimensional artists. Artists have developed many methods to make a viewer feel the effects of time and motion, from creating areas of visual interest to using motion pictures. Nevertheless, in 2-D works, time and motion are only artificial constructs, approximating our experiences in real life. In contrast, three-dimensional artists must deal with time and motion in a very real way. In a plastic work, the viewer is enticed to move about the piece, constantly being drawn from one set of relationships to the next.

9.24 Umberto Boccioni, *Unique Forms of Continuity in Space*, 1913. Bronze (cast 1931), 43⅞ × 34⅞ × 15¾ in. (111.4 × 88.6 × 40 cm). Boccioni was a leading founder and member of the Futurist group. An accomplished painter and sculptor, he was preoccupied for much of his career with the dynamics of movement. Acquired through the Lillie P. Bliss Bequest. (231.1948) The Museum of Modern Art, New York, NY. U.S.A. Digital image © The Museum of Modern Art/Licensed by SCALA/Art Resource, NY.

9.25 Renato Bertelli, *Continuous Profile of Mussolini*, 1933 (later manufactured by Ditta Effeffe, Milan, with Mussolini's approval). Bronzed terra-cotta, 11¾ in. high × 9 in. in diameter (29.8 cm. high × 22.9 cm in diameter). Bertelli, following the influence of the Futurists, explored the concepts of simultaneity and continuous movement in portraiture. Mussolini recognized the appeal to "modernity" and organized the mass distribution of the sculpture. Courtesy of The Mitchell Wolfson Jr. Collection, The Wolfsonian–Florida International University, Miami Beach, Florida. Photograph by Bruce White.

9.26 Dan Collins, *Of More Than Two Minds*, 1994. Three-dimensional laser digitizing, cast hydrocal from CNC wax original, 3¾ × 3⅝ × 2½ in. Though inspired by timeless concepts of the body in motion, current technology has opened new means of exploration and expression. Courtesy of the artist.

Some sculptures also create the illusion of movement. In those cases we have **implied motion.** In an early attempt to add movement to otherwise static figures, Greek sculptors organized the lines in the draperies of their figures to accent a continuous flowing direction. By following these linear accents, the eye of the observer readily moves smoothly over the figure's surface. The stance or position of the subject can also produce an expectation of movement. For example, the viewer can feel Ernst Barlach's figure *The Avenger* charging through space, about to deliver a blow with the uplifted sword (see fig. 2.69). In *Unique Forms of Continuity in Space*, a sculptural

work by the Futurist artist Umberto Boccioni, movement is implied by the shape and directionality of the faceted planes that make up this abstracted figure (fig. 9.24). The sculptures shown in figures 9.25 and 9.26 are even able to capture the energy of blurred and superimposed images found in two-dimensional artwork.

While implied motion can be understood rather quickly, some three-dimensional works employ **actual motion** that is distinctive and requires a viewer to observe for a specific amount of time. In some works, the amount of time is very short, perhaps a few seconds; in others it can be very long, possibly even decades. In

the case of **kinetic** sculpture, the artwork itself, not the observer, moves. **Mobiles,** for example, present a constantly changing, almost infinite series of views (see figs. 2.7 and 2.70). Water, wind currents, motors, and vibrating or rotating pedestals can all provide a source of movement for work. With José de Rivera's *Construction 8*, the work rotates on its base, and time is a planned element. The viewer must wait for the piece to assume its original orientation in order to experience all the compositional aspects of the work (see fig. 3.31). In the work of Calder and de Rivera, there is a feeling of spontaneity and unpredictability, which is even further developed in

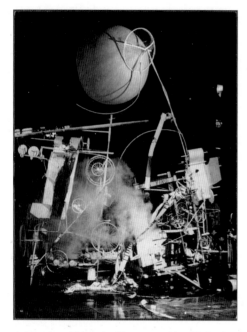

9.27 Jean Tinguely, *Homage to New York,* 1960. Scrap metal, bicycle parts (eighty bicycle, tricycle, and baby-carriage wheels), washing machine drum, bathtub, piano, several electric fans, old Addressograph, baby bassinet, bells, car horn, playing cards, American flag scraps, many bottles of chemical stinks, apparatus to make smoke, fire extinguishers, orange meteo-rological sounding balloon, radio, oil canister, hammer, and saw—all powered by fifteen engines—8 m high. Time and motion were definite composites in this piece. Constructed of wheels, pulleys, and motors, the work was de-signed to self-destruct over a period of twenty-seven minutes in homage to the energy of a city that keeps rebuilding itself. Courtesy of Museum Tinguely. Photo: David Gahr.

9.28 Arthur Ganson, *Machine with Chair* (time-lapse photograph of 1995 version), 1995. Steel (machine), fiberglass over foam (chair), motor, electronic switches and circuits, rubber; track 30 ft. long, machine 5 ft. high, chair at highest point 13 ft. from track. Like Jean Tinguely, Arthur Ganson has found the machine to be an instrument for the poet/artist. He produces some machine-driven sculptures that involve kinetic ironies, mechanical awareness, and a sense of time, space, and motion. Arthur Ganson is a sculptor at the Massachusetts Institute of Technology. Photograph by Henry Groskinsky.

the work of artists like Jean Tinguely (fig. 9.27), whose work was planned to be presented as it self-destructed—flying apart in all directions. In some cases, the memory of the event by those who were present is the only record of the work's existence. Other artists like Arthur Ganson use time-lapse photography to record the duration, path, and energy of the presentation (fig. 9.28).

Just as the boundaries between sculpture and painting are blurred by artists working with assemblages (see fig. 6.22), so too are the boundaries between sculpture-in-the round and multimedia presentations. As artists create installations that combine audio, computer-generated animation, and sculptural constructions in self-directed interactive experiences, the

9.29 Closing Ceremony of the Beijing 2008 Olympic Games at the National Stadium, August 24, 2008, Beijing, China. The closing ceremony for the 2008 Beijing Olympic Games was a performance created through the collaborative efforts of several artists. Combining music, light shows, dance choreography, and fireworks, the artists played with both time and motion in the event. The ephemeral nature of the ceremony created a sense of wonder among the spectators: this was a special moment in time. © Victor Fraile/Corbis.

viewer must spend a somewhat designated amount of time experiencing the work—listening, watching, exploring, interacting. In the process, the viewer may change position, and the work may physically move. In addition, the sense of time may be altered even though there is real-time interaction.

The exploration of space in terms of the four-dimensional space-time continuum is in its infancy. As technology advances and research reveals more of the mysteries of the natural world, artists will continue to absorb and interpret them according to their individual experiences. It is reasonable to assume that even more revolutionary concepts will emerge in time, producing great changes in art styles. The important point to remember is that distortions and unfamiliar forms of art expression do not occur in a vacuum; they usually represent earnest efforts to comprehend and interpret our world in terms of the latest frontiers of understanding (fig. 9.29).

Regardless of what technologies the future may present—be it rapid proto-typing, laser definition, or holographic imaging—artists must learn to use time as a tool in establishing appropriate levels of emphasis within the work, providing spatial harmonies among the compositional elements, and developing sufficient contrasts within the work to maintain visual interest. By these means, the human scene—in whatever way it may evolve in time, space, and action—will become an inspiration for study and creativity in many exciting forms.

NOTE: From here on, listed artists are painters unless otherwise indicted in parentheses.

1300

Proto-Renaissance Italy: Duccio, Giotto, Pisano (sculptor)

1400

Early Renaissance Italy: Donatello (sculptor), Masaccio, Francesca, Fra Angelico, Fra Filippo Lippi, Brunelleschi (architect), da Vinci

1503 Renaissance/1919 Dadaism

T.1 Leonardo da Vinci (1452–1519), *Mona Lisa,* 1503–06. Oil on panel, 30½ × 21 in. (76.2 × 52.5 cm).

T.2 Marcel Duchamp (1887–1968), *Replica of L. H. O. O. Q.,* 1919. Color reproduction of Mona Lisa altered with a pencil, 8 × 5 in. Photograph © Boltin Picture Library/ The Bridgeman Art Library International. Art © 2011 Succession Marcel Duchamp/Artists Rights Society (ARS), New York/ADAGP, Paris.

1505 Renaissance/1927 Surrealism

T.3 Leonardo da Vinci (1452–1519), *Virgin and Child with Saint Anne,* c. 1510. Oil on panel, 168.5 × 130 cm. Louvre, Paris, France/ Giraudon/The Bridgeman Art Library.

T.4 Max Ernst (1891–1976), *The Kiss (Le Baiser),* 1927. Oil on canvas, 50¾ × 63½ in. Photograph © The Art Archive/Peggy Guggenheim Collection Venice/Gianni Dagli Orti. Art © 2011 Artists Rights Society (ARS), New York/ADAGP, Paris.

TIMELINE

Early Northern Renaissance: Modified by vestiges of Medievalism
Netherlands: van Eyck, van der Goes, van der Weyden
France: Limbourg brothers, Fouquet
Germany: Dürer, Lochner, Moser, Witz, Pacher, Schongauer (printmaker)

1500

High Renaissance Italy: Giorgione, Titian, Raphael, Michelangelo (sculptor), Tintoretto

1505 Renaissance/1863 Realism

T.5   Giorgione (c. 1477–1511), *The Tempest*,
c. 1505. Oil on canvas, 32¼ × 28¾ in. (82 ×
73 cm). Galleria dell' Accademia, Venice, Italy/Bridgeman Art
Library, London/SuperStock.

T.6   Édouard Manet (1832–1883), *Le Déjeuner sur l'Herbe*, 1863. Oil on
canvas, 84¼ × 106¼ in. (214 × 269 cm). © Réunion des Musées Nationaux/Art
Resource, NY.

1509 Renaissance/1857 Pictorialism

T.8   Oscar Rejlander (1813–1875), *Two Ways of Life*, 1857.
Albumen silver print, 16 × 31 in. Courtesy of George Eastman House,
International Museum of Photography and Film.

T.7   Raphael (1483–1520), *The School of Athens*, 1509–11. Fresco, size
unknown. © Scala/Art Resource, NY.

TIMELINE

High Renaissance in Western Europe (affected by Italy)
Netherlands: Bosch, Breughel
Germany: Dürer (printmaker), Grünewald
France: Master of Moulins

1515 Renaissance/1982 Postmodernism

T.9 Matthias Grünewald (c. 1455–1528), *The Resurrection of Christ,* from the Isenheim altarpiece, c. 1515 (detail). Oil on wood, 105⅞ × 120⅞ in. © The Art Archive/Unterlinden Museum Colmar/Gianni Dagli Orti.

T.10 Jasper Johns (b. 1930), *Perilous Night,* 1982. Encaustic on canvas with objects, 67 × 96 × 5 in. Robert and Jane Meyerhoff Collection. Courtesy of the Board of Trustees, National Gallery of Art, Washington, 1982. Art © Jasper Johns/Licensed by VAGA, New York, NY.

1518 Renaissance/1989 Postmodernism

T.11 Raphael (1483–1520), *La Fornarina,* c. 1518. Oil on panel, 33 × 23 in. © Scala/Art Resource, NY.

T.12 Cindy Sherman (b. 1954), *Untitled #205,* 1989. Color photograph, 53½ × 40¼ in. Edition of six. Courtesy of the artist and Metro Pictures.

T.13 Titian (c. 1488–1576), *Allegory on the Theme of Prudence*, c. 1565–70. Oil on canvas, 76.2 × 68.6 cm. © Image Asset Management Ltd./SuperStock, Inc.

T.14 Ben Shahn (1898–1969), *After Titian*, 1959. Tempura on fiberboard, 53½ × 30½ in. Gift of the Sara Roby Foundation, Smithsonian American Art Museum, Washington, DC/Art Resource, NY. Art © Estate of Ben Shahn/Licensed by VAGA, New York, NY.

1520

Mannerism and Early Baroque Italy
Italy: Caravaggio, Bernini (sculptor), Borromini (architect)
Spain: El Greco

BAROQUE AND ROCOCO ART (c. 1600–1800)

1600

Baroque Art in Europe
Netherlands (Belgium, Holland): Rubens, Van Dyck, Hals
France: Poussin, Claude
Spain: Ribera, Velázquez

TIMELINE

T.15 El Greco (1541–1614), *Portrait of Jorge Manuel*, c. 1603. Oil on canvas, 81 × 56 cm. © Scala/Art Resource, NY.

T.16 Pablo Picasso (1881–1973), *Portrait of a Painter, after El Greco*, 1950. Oil on wood panel, 39⅝ × 31⅞ in. Peter Willi/SuperStock, Inc. Art © 2011 Estate of Pablo Picasso/Artists Rights Society (ARS), New York.

T.17 Rembrandt Harmenszoon van Rijn (1606–1669), *Susanna and the Elders*, 1647. Oil on mahogany panel, 30 × 36 in. Bildarchiv Preussischer Kulturbesitz/Art Resource, NY.

T.18 Bea Nettles (b. 1946), *Suzanna . . . Surprised*, 1970. Photo emulsion on muslin, photolinen, stitching, 28 × 35 in. Courtesy of the artist.

TIMELINE

T.19 Diego Velázquez (1599–1660), *Innocent X,* c. **1650.** Oil on canvas, 141 × 119 cm. © Alinari/Art Resource, NY.

T.20 Francis Bacon (1909–1992), *Study after Velázquez's Portrait of Pope Innocent X,* **1953.** Oil on canvas, 5 × 4 ft. Bridgeman-Giraudon/Art Resource. Art © 2011 The Estate of Francis Bacon/Artists Rights Society (ARS), New York/DACS, London.

T.21 Diego Velázquez (1599–1660), *Las Meninas,* **1656.** Oil on canvas, 10 ft. 5 in. × 9 ft. 1 in. © Erich Lessing/Art Resource, NY.

T.22 Salvador Dalí (1904–1989), *Portrait of Juan de Pareja, the Assistant to Velázquez,* **1960.** Oil on canvas, 29¼ × 34¾ in. (74.3 × 88.27 cm). Minneapolis Institute of Arts, gift of Mrs. John Sargent Pillsbury, Sr. © 2011 Salvador Dali, Gala-Salvador Dali Foundation/Artists Rights Society (ARS), New York.

TIMELINE

TIMELINE

T.23 Diego Velázquez (1599–1660), *Las Meninas,* 1656. Oil on canvas, 10 ft. 5 in. × 9 ft. 1 in. © Erich Lessing/Art Resource, NY.

T.24 David Hockney (b. 1937), *Self-Portrait with Charlie,* 2005. Oil on canvas, 72 × 36 in. Collection of the National Portrait Gallery, London. Photography by Richard Schmidt. © David Hockney.

1701 Baroque/1973 Neo-Figurative

T.25 Diego Velázquez (1599–1660), *Las Meninas,* 1656. Oil on canvas, 10 ft. 5 in. × 9 ft. 1 in. © Erich Lessing/Art Resource, NY.

T.26 Fernando Botero, *After Velázquez,* 1976. Oil on canvas, 76 × 62½ in. Photo © Marianne Haas/CORBIS. Art © Fernando Botero. Courtesy of The Marlborough Gallery.

Early Colonial Art in the Americas: Primarily limners (or primitive portraitists) in English colonies; church or cathedral art in Latin America

1700

Rococo Art: Primarily France but spreads to other European countries
France: Watteau, Boucher, Chardin, Fragonard
Italy: Canaletto, Guardi, Tiepolo
England: Gainsborough, Hogarth, Reynolds

Colonial Arts and Early Federal Art in the United States: Copley, Stuart, West

NINETEENTH-CENTURY ART (c. 1780–1900)

c. 1780

Neoclassicism
France: Ingres, David (see fig. T.27)

T.27 Jacques-Louis David, *The Oath of the Horatii,* 1786. Oil on canvas, approx. 14 × 11 ft. (4.27 × 3.35 m). The Louvre, Paris, France. SuperStock, Inc.
Italy: Canova (sculptor)

T.27

1814 Romanticism/1989 Feminist Postmodernism

T.28 Auguste-Dominique Ingres (1780–1867), *La Grande Odalisque,* 1814. Oil on canvas, 91 × 162 cm. SuperStock, Inc.

T.29 Guerrilla Girls, *Do women have to be naked to get into the Met. Museum?,* 1989. Poster, 11 × 28 in. © Guerrilla Girls, Inc., www.guerrillagirls.com.

c. 1820

Romanticism
France: Barye (sculptor), Delacroix, Géricault, Niépce (first permanent camera image), Daguerre (photographic process), Rejlander (painter and photographer)
Spain: Goya
England: Turner, Fox Talbot (photographic process)
United States: Ryder

1850

Realism and Naturalism
France: Daumier (see fig. 1.22), Courbet (see fig. 1.21), Rodin and Claudel (Romantic/Realist sculptors)
England: Constable
United States: Eakins, Homer, Brady, Gardner, Jackson and O'Sullivan (photographers)

TIMELINE

T.30   Sir John Everett Millais (1829–1896), *Ophelia*, 1851–52. Oil on canvas, 30 × 44 in. Tate Gallery, London/Art Resource, NY.

T.31   Victor Burgin (b. 1941), *The Bridge—Venus Perdica*, 1984. Gelatin silver print with text panel, 112.3 × 76.6 cm. Courtesy of George Eastman House, International Museum of Photography and Film and John Weber Gallery.

T.32   Utagawa Hiroshige (1797–1858), *Sudden Shower over Shin-Ohashi Bridge and Atake (Ohashi Atake no Yudachi)*, plate 58 from "One Hundred Famous Views of Edo." 1857. Woodcut print, size unknown. Brooklyn Museum of Art, New York/The Bridgeman Art Library.

T.33   Vincent van Gogh (1853–1890), *Japonaiserie: Bridge in the Rain (after Hiroshige)*, 1887. Oil on canvas, 73 × 54 cm. © Francis G. Mayer/Corbis.

Chronological Outline of Western Art

TIMELINE

T.35 Max Ernst (1891–1976), *Le Déjeuner sur l'Herbre (Luncheon on the Grass)*, 1944. Oil on canvas, 68 × 150 cm. Photograph © DACS/The Bridgeman Art Library International. Art © 2011 Artists Rights Society (ARS), New York/ADAGP, Paris.

T.34 Édouard Manet (1832–1883), *Le Déjeuner sur l'Herbe*, 1863. Oil on canvas, 84¼ × 106¼ in. (214 × 269 cm). © Réunion des Musées Nationaux/Art Resource, NY.

T.36 Édouard Manet (1832–1883), *Le Déjeuner sur l'Herbe*, 1863. Oil on canvas, 84¼ × 106¼ in. (214 × 269 cm). © Réunion des Musées Nationaux/Art Resource, NY.

T.37 Pablo Picasso (1881–1973), *Les Déjeuners II*, 1961. Oil on canvas, 60 × 73 cm. Photograph © DACS/The Bridgeman Art Library International. Art © 2011· Estate of Pablo Picasso/Artists Rights Society (ARS), New York.

TIMELINE

T.38 Timothy H. O'Sullivan (1840–1882), *"Pyramid," Pyramid Lake, Nevada,* 1868. Albumen print, 19.8 × 27.0 cm. Courtesy of George Eastman House, International Museum of Photography and Film.

T.39 Mark Klett (b. 1952), for the Rephotographic Survey Project, *Pyramid Isle, Pyramid Lake, NV,* 1979. Gelatin silver print, size unknown. Courtesy of Mark Klett.

1870

T.40

Impressionism

France: Monet (see fig. T.40), Pissarro, Renoir, Degas (some sculpture), Morisot
England: Sisley
United States: Cassatt, Hassam, Twachtman, Muybridge (Anglo-American photographer)
Italy: Medardo-Rosso (sculptor)

T.40 Claude Monet, *Haystack at Sunset,* 1880. Oil on canvas, 28⅞ × 36½ in. (73.3 × 92.6 cm.) The Museum of Fine Arts, Boston, MA. Juliana Cheney Edwards Collection/The Bridgeman Art Library.

T.41 Thomas Moran (1837–1926), *Grand Canyon of the Yellowstone,* 1872. Oil on canvas, 84 × 144 in. Lent by the Department of the Interior Museum. © Smithsonian American Art Museum, Washington, DC/Art Resource, NY.

T.42 Mark Klett, *Viewing Thomas Moran at the Source, Artist's Point, Yellowstone National Park, NP 8/1/00,* 2000. Pigmented ink-jet print, 24 × 30 in. Courtesy of Mark Klett.

T.43 August Rodin (1840–1917), *The Thinker,* 1879–87. Bronze, 27½ in. © The Gallery Collection/Corbis

T.44 Alvin Langdon Coburn (1882–1966), *Le Penseur,* 1906. Gum-platinum print, 28.7 × 22.9 cm. Gift of Alvin Langdon Coburn. Courtesy of George Eastman House, International Museum of Photography and Film.

1880

T.45

Post-Impressionism
France: Seurat (see fig. T.45), Cézanne (see figs. 7.23 and 9.5), Gauguin, Toulouse-Lautrec
Holland: Van Gogh (see fig. 1.19)
> **T.45** Georges Seurat, *Sunday Afternoon on the Island of La Grande Jatte,* 1884–86. Oil on canvas, 81¾ × 121¼ in. Erich Lessing/Art Resource, NY.

Symbolism
France: Bonnard

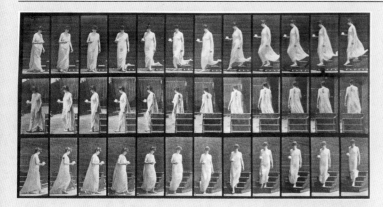

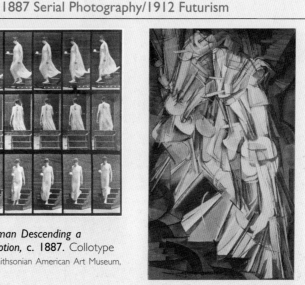

T.47 Marcel Duchamp (1887–1968), *Nude Descending a Staircase,* No. 2, 1912. Oil on canvas, 147.5 × 89 cm. Philadelphia Museum of Art, PA. Louise and Walter Arensberg Collection. Photograph by Corbis Media. © 2011 Artists Rights Society (ARS), New York/ADAGP, Paris/Estate of Marcel Duchamp.

T.46 Eadweard Muybridge (1830–1904), *Woman Descending a Stairway and Turning Around,* from *Animal Locomotion,* c. 1887. Collotype on paper, 7⅞ × 15¼ in. (20.1 × 38.6 cm). © Smithsonian American Art Museum, Washington, DC/Art Resource, NY.

TIMELINE

T.48   Eadweard Muybridge (1830–1904), *Two Men Wrestling*, plate 347 from *Animal Locomotion*, **c. 1887.** Collotype on paper, 7⅞ × 15¼ in. (20.1 × 38.6 cm). © Private Collection/The Stapleton Collection/ The Bridgeman Art Library.

T.49   Francis Bacon (1909–1992), *Three Studies of Figures on Beds,* 1972. Oil and pastel on canvas, triptych, each panel 6 ft. 6 in. × 4 ft. 10 in. Private Collection/The Bridgeman Art Library International. © 2011 Estate of Francis Bacon/Artists Rights Society (ARS), New York/DACS, London.

T.50   Paul Cézanne (1839–1906), *Portrait of Ambroise Vollard,* **1899.** Oil on canvas, 39½ × 32 in. © Réunion des Musées Nationaux/Art Resource, NY.

T.51   Pablo Picasso (1881–1973), *Portrait of Ambroise Vollard,* 1909. Oil on canvas, 36 × 26 in. SCALA/Art Resource, NY. Art © 2011 Estate of Pablo Picasso/Artists Rights Society (ARS), New York.

TIMELINE

NOTE: Artists often change styles and media, so some names appear under more than one category. Note Pablo Picasso in particular.

1900

Sculpture in the Early 1900s
France: Maillol
United States: Lachaise
Germany: Lehmbruck, Kolbe

1905–1908

Fauvism (Early Expressionism)
France: **Les Fauves (Wild Beasts)** Matisse (see fig. 4.1), Derain, Dufy, Vlaminck, Modigliani (**Italian**), Rouault, Utrillo, Picasso (**Spanish:** Blue, Rose, and Negro periods).

1903 Pictorialism/1930 Modernism

T.52 Alfred Stieglitz (1864–1946), *The "Flat-Iron,"* c. 1903. Photogravure, 6⅝ × 3¼ in. Réunion des Musées Nationaux/Art Resource, NY. © 2011 Georgia O'Keeffe Museum/Artists Rights Society (ARS), New York.

T.53 Berenice Abbott (1898–1991), *Flatiron Building, Manhattan,* c. 1930s. Gelatin silver print, 23¼ × 17⅝ in. Minneapolis Institute of Arts, Gift of the William R. Hibbs Family. © Berenice Abbott/Commerce Graphics Ltd., Inc.

TIMELINE

T.54 Pablo Picasso (1881–1973), *Les Demoiselles D'Avignon,* 1907. Oil on canvas, 8 ft. × 7 ft. 8 in. (243.9 × 233.7 cm). The Museum of Modern Art, New York, NY. Acquired through the Lille B. Bliss Bequest. Digital image © The Museum of Modern Art/Licensed by SCALA/Art Resource, NY. © 2011 Estate of Pablo Picasso/Artists Rights Society (ARS), New York.

T.55 Faith Ringgold (b. 1930), *Picasso's Studio,* 1991, French Collection #7. Acrylic on canvas with fabric border, 73 × 68 in. Wooster Museum of Art. © Faith Ringgold 1991.

1905–1913

German Expressionism

Die Brücke (The Bridge): Munch (**Norwegian**; fig. T.56) Kirchner, Nolde, Schmidt-Rottluff

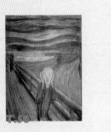

T.56 Edvard Munch, *The Scream,* or *The Cry,* 1893. Oil and tempera on board, 35¼ × 28 in. (89.5 × 73.7 cm). National Gallery, Oslo, Norway. Bridgeman Art Library, London/SuperStock, Inc. © 2011 The Munch Museum/The Munch-Ellingsen Group/Artists Rights Society (ARS), New York.

Der Blaue Reiter (The Blue Rider): Jawlensky (**Russian**), Kandinsky (**Russian**), Macke, Kuehn (photography)

1905–1917

Stieglitz and Steichen found 291 Gallery in New York City to advance acceptance of photography and avant-garde art

T.57 Henri Matisse (1869–1954), *Dance,* 1910. Oil on canvas, 8½ × 12 ft. Hermitage Museum, St. Petersburg/SuperStock, Inc. © 2011 Succession H. Matisse/Artists Rights Society (ARS), New York.

T.58 Roy Lichtenstein (1923–1997), *Artist's Studio: "Dancers,"* 1974. Oil and synthetic polymer (paint) on canvas, 8 ft. × 10 ft. 8 in. © Estate of Roy Lichtenstein. Gift of Mr. and Mrs. S. I. Newhouse, Jr. (362.1990) Photo © The Museum of Modern Art/Licensed by SCALA/Art Resource, NY.

TIMELINE

Cubism
France: Picasso (**Spanish** painter, sculptor, potter), Braque, Léger, Gris (**Spanish**; see fig. 4.2)

Futurism
Italy: Balla (see fig. T.59), Severini, Carra, Boccioni (painter and sculptor; see fig. 9.24), Bragaglia (photographer)
France: Duchamp (see fig. T.47)

T.59

T.59 Giacomo Balla, *Speeding Automobile*, 1912. Oil on wood, 21⅞ × 27⅛ in. (55.6 × 68.9 cm). © 2011 Artists Rights Society (ARS), New York/SIAE, Rome. The Museum of Modern Art, New York, NY. Digital image © The Museum of Modern Art/Licensed by SCALA/Art Resource, NY.

1910–1920

Abstract Art
Germany: Albers, Hofmann, Kandinsky (**Russian**; see fig. 1.23), Archipenko (**Russian** sculptor), Feininger (**American**)

1913–1922

Constructivism
Russia: Tatlin, Malevich, Larionov, Gabo and Pevsner (sculptors)
Holland: Mondrian (see fig. 1.8)
France: Delaunay, Brancusi (**Romanian** sculptor; see fig. T.60), Arp (sculptor)
England: Nicholson
United States: Dove, Marin, O'Keeffe, Sheeler, Davis, Stieglitz (photographer), Steichen (photographer), Strand (photographer), Coburn (**English** photographer)

T.60

T.60 Constantin Brancusi, *Bird in Space*, 1928. Bronze (unique cast), 54 × 8½ in. (137.2 × 21.6 × 16.5 cm). © 2011 Artists Rights Society (ARS), New York/ADAGP, Paris. The Museum of Modern Art, New York, NY. Digital image © The Museum of Modern Art/Licensed by SCALA/Art Resource, NY.

Fantasy in Art—Individual Fantasists
France: Chagall (**Russian**), Rousseau (primitive painter)
Italy: de Chirico
Germany: Schwitters, Klee (**Swiss**)

1913

Armory Show, New York: Helped introduce avant-garde art to the United States

1914

Dadaism
France: Arp, Duchamp (see fig. T.47), Picabia
Germany: Schwitters, Ernst
United States: Man Ray (photographer, painter)

c. 1918/19–1924

Die Neue Sachlichkeit (The New Objectivity)
Germany: Dix, Grosz, Heckel, Schlemmer, Sander (photographer)

Independent German Expressionists: Beckmann, Kokoschka (**Austrian**)

TIMELINE

T.61 Vladimir Tatlin (1855–1953), *Model for Monument to the Third International, 1919–20,* **replica 1968.** Wood, metal, and motor, 15 ft. high. © Jacques Faujour/Réunion des Musées Nationaux/Art Resource, NY.

T.62 Dan Flavin (1933–1996), *"Monument" for V. Tatlin,* **1969.** Fluorescent tubes and fixtures, 96 1/16 × 32 1/16 × 4 3/4 in. Collection Walker Art Center, Minneapolis, MN. Gift of Leo Castelli Gallery, 1981. © 2011 Stephen Flavin/Artists Rights Society (ARS), New York.

1919 Soviet International Style/1998 Postmodernism

T.64 Ilya and Emilia Kabakov (b. 1933), *The Palace Project,* 2000. Installation, exterior view, London, 24 × 54 × 77 ft. Photo by Dirk Powels. Organized by the Public Art Fund. © Ilya and Emilia Kabakov. Photography: Gil Amiaga. Courtesy Sean Kelly Gallery, New York.

T.63 Vladimir Tatlin (1855–1953), *Model for Monument to the Third International, 1919–20,* replica 1968. Wood, metal, and motor, 15 ft. high. © Jacques Faujour/Réunion des Musées Nationaux/Art Resource, NY.

TIMELINE

Later Expressionism
    France: Soutine, Buffet, Balthus, Dubuffet
    United States: Avery, Baskin, Broderson, Lawrence, Levine, Shahn, Weber
    Mexico: Kahlo, Orozco, Rivera, Siqueiros

1924

Surrealism
    France: Arp (sculptor), Cartier-Bresson (photographer), Delvaux (**Belgian**), Magritte (**Belgian**), Masson, Miró (**Spanish**), Picasso (**Spanish**), Tanguy, González (**Spanish** sculptor)
    Switzerland: Giacometti (sculptor, painter; see fig. T.65)
    England: Bacon
    Germany: Ernst
    United States: Dalí (**Spanish** painter; Surrealist cinemas with Luis Buñuel; see fig. T.66), Man Ray (photographer, painter)

T.65 Alberto Giacometti, *Three Walking Men,* 1948–49. 29½ in. (74.9 cm) high. Edward E. Ayer Endowment in memory of Charles L. Hutchinson, 1951.256, The Art Institute of Chicago. © 2011 Artists Rights Society (ARS), New York/ADAGP, FAAG, Paris.

T.66 Salvador Dalí, *Persistence of Memory,* 1931. Oil on canvas, 9½ × 13 in. (24.1 × 33 cm). © 2011 Salvador Dalí, Gala-Salvador Dalí Foundation/Artists Rights Society (ARS), New York. The Museum of Modern Art, New York, NY. Digital image © The Museum of Modern Art/ Licensed by SCALA/Art Resource, NY.

T.65

T.66

1936 Surrealism/1955 Postmodernism

T.67 Joan Miró (1893–1983), *Poetic Object,* 1936. Assemblage, 32 × 12 × 10 in. Gift of Mr. and Mrs. Pierre Matisse. © 2011 Successió Miró/Artists Rights Society (ARS), New York/ADAGP, Paris. Photo © The Museum of Modern Art/Licensed by SCALA/Art Resource, NY.

T.68 Robert Rauschenberg (b. 1925), *Odalisk,* 1955–58. Mixed media, 6 ft. 9 in. × 2 ft. 1 in. × 2 ft. 1 in. Photograph © Rheinisches Bildarchiv Köln. Art © Estate of Robert Rauschenberg/Licensed by VAGA, New York, NY.

T I M E L I N E

1930–1940

Realist Painting and Photography (Straight) in the United States: Wyeth, Wood, Benton, Burchfield

F-64 Group of photographers: Weston, Adams, Cunningham

1936 Farm Security Administration Photography/1981 Postmodernism

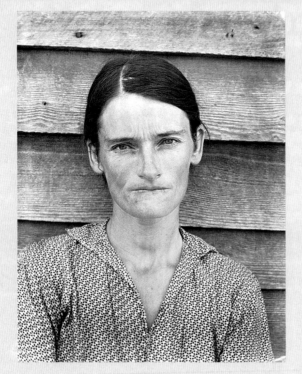

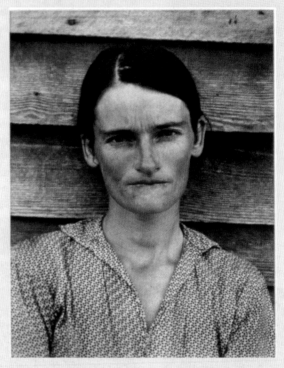

T.69 Walker Evans (1903–1975), *Allie Mae Burroughs, Wife of a Cotton Sharecropper, Hale County, Alabama,* **1936.** Gelatin silver print, 9½ × 7⁹⁄₁₆ in. Walker Evans Archive, The Metropolitan Museum of Art, New York, NY.
© The Metropolitan Museum of Art/Art Resource, NY.

T.70 Sherrie Levine (b. 1947), *After Walker Evans,* **1981.** Gelatin silver print, 6¼ × 5 in. (15.9 × 12.7 cm).
© S. Levine. Courtesy of the artist and the Paula Cooper Gallery, New York.

LATE-TWENTIETH-CENTURY INTO TWENTY-FIRST-CENTURY ART

1920s–1950s

Kinetics and Light Sculpture: (Early 1900s examples)
France: Duchamp (1920s)
United States: Calder (U.S. Wire Circus, c. 1928), Wilfred (Clavilux color organ, 1930–63)

c. 1951–1965

Abstract Expressionist Painting

Action or Gestural Group (predecessors from abroad)—Albers (**German**), de Kooning (**Dutch**), Gorky (**Armenian**), Hofmann (**German**), Matta (**Chilean**), Mondrian (**Dutch**), Tamayo (**Mexican**)

U.S. New York School—Frankenthaler (see fig. 4.26), Kline (see fig. 1.24), Louis, Mitchell, Pollock (see fig. T.71), White (photographer)

T.71 Jackson Pollock (1912–1956), *Autumn Rhythm (Number 30)*, 1950. Oil on canvas, 8 ft. 9 in. × 17 ft. 3 in. (2.67 × 5.26 m). The Museum of Modern Art, New York. George A. Hearn Fund, 1957 (57.92). Image © The Metropolitan Museum of Art/Art Resource, NY. Art © 2011 The Pollock-Krasner Foundation/Artists Rights Society (ARS), New York.

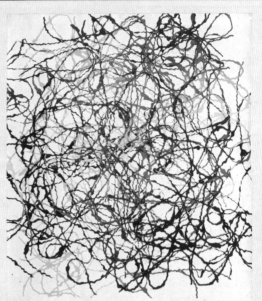

T.72 Andy Warhol (1928–1987), *Yarn*, 1983. Synthetic polymer paint and silkscreen on canvas, 101.6 × 101.6 cm. Art © 2011 The Andy Warhol Foundation for the Visual Arts, Inc./Artists Rights Society (ARS), New York. Art Resource, NY.

Color Field Painting Group (Hard-Edge)
United States: Diebenkorn, Callahan (photographer), Kelly, Newman (see fig. 2.59), Noland, Stella, Rothko (**Russian**; see fig. 7.25)

Painters elsewhere similar to Abstract Expressionism
France: Mathieu, Manessier, Soulages
Portugal: Vieira da Silva
Spain: Tapies

Surreal Abstract or Abstract Expressionist Sculptors
England: Moore (see fig. 4.36), Hepworth, Chadwick
France: Richier, Lipchitz (**Latvian**)
United States: Calder, Smith, Noguchi

c. 1958–1965

T.73

T.74

Pop Art and Assemblage Predecessors
England: Hamilton, Kitaj (**American**)
United States: Johns, Rauschenberg, Chamberlain (assembler), Dine, Frank (**Swiss** photographer), Friedlander (photographer), Hockney (**English**), Indiana, Kienholz (assembler), Lichtenstein, Marisol (**Venezuelan** sculptor, assembler), Nevelson (sculptor or assembler; see fig. T.73), Oldenburg (sculptor, assembler; see fig. 2.48), Samaras (**Greek** assembler), Segal (sculptor), Stankiewicz (assembler), Warhol (see fig. T.74), Wesselman, Winogrand (photographer).
T.73 Louise Nevelson, *American Dawn*, 1962. Painted wood, 18 × 14 × 19 ft (5.49 × 4.27 × 3.05 m) in situ. Grant J. Pick Purchase Fund, 1967.387, The Art Institute of Chicago. © 2011 Estate of Louise Nevelson/Artists Rights Society (ARS), New York.
T.74 Andy Warhol, *100 Cans*, 1962. Oil on canvas, 6 ft. × 4 ft. 4 in. (1.83 × 1.32 m). Gift of Seymour H. Knox Jr., 1963. Art © 2011 The Andy Warhol Foundation for the Visual Arts, Inc./Artists Rights Society (ARS), New York. Albright-Knox Art Gallery, Buffalo, New York, NY/Art Resource, NY.

TIMELINE

———. *Color Atlas.* New York: Barron's Educational Series, 1982.

LANE, R. *Images from the Floating World.* Secaucus, NJ: Cartwell Books, 1978.

LERNER, ABRAM, ET AL. *The Hirshhorn Museum and Sculpture Garden.* New York: Abrams, 1974.

LEWIS, R. L., and S. I. LEWIS. *The Power of Art.* Orlando, FL.: Harcourt Brace, 1994.

Life Library of Photography. New York: Time-Life, 1971.

LOCKER, J. L. *The World of M. C. Escher.* New York: Abrams, 1971.

LOTHROP, SAMUEL K. *Treasures of Ancient America: The Arts of the Pre-Colombian Civilizations from Mexico to Peru.* Cleveland, OH: Skira, 1964.

LOWE, SARAH M. *Frida Kahlo.* New York: Universe, 1991.

LUCIE-SMITH, EDWARD. *Late Modern: The Visual Arts since 1945.* New York: Praeger, 1969.

———. *The Thames and Hudson Dictionary of Art Terms.* New York: Thames and Hudson, 1984.

MACAULAY, DAVID. *The New Way Things Work.* Boston: Houghton Mifflin/ Lorraine Books, 1988.

MEISEL, L. K. *Photorealism since 1980.* New York: Abrams, 1993.

MENDELOWITZ, DANIEL M., and DUANE A. WAKEMAN. *A Guide to Drawing.* Orlando, FL: Harcourt Brace Jovanovich, 1993.

MYERS, JACK FREDRICK. *The Language of Visual Art.* Orlando, FL: Holt, Rinehart and Winston, 1989.

National Gallery of Art. *Johannes Vermeer.* Washington, DC: Author, 1995.

POIGNANT, R. *Oceanic Mythology.* London: Hamlyn, 1967.

Rendezvous: Masterpieces from the Centre Georges Pompidou and the Guggenheim Museums. Paris: Centre Georges Pompidou; New York: Guggenheim Museum, 1998.

RUBIN, W. *Primitivism in 20th Century "Art."* 2 vols. New York: Museum of Modern Art, 1984.

RUSSELL, STELLA PANDELL. *Art in the World.* Orlando, FL: Holt, Rinehart and Winston, 1978.

SAFF, DONALD, and DELI SACILOTTO. *Printmaking.* New York: Holt, Rinehart and Winston, 1978.

SMITH, BRADLEY. *Mexico: A History in Art.* New York: Doubleday, 1968.

SMITH, B., and W. WENG. *China: A History in Art.* New York: Harper and Row, 1972.

SPARKE, PENNY, FELICE HODGES, EMMA DENT, and ANNE STONE. *Design Source Book.* Secaucus, NJ: Chartwell, 1982.

STRUPPECK, JULES. *The Creation of Sculpture.* New York: Holt, 1952.

SUTTON, P. *Dreamings: The Art of Aboriginal Australia.* New York: Braziller, 1988.

TERUKAZU, AKIYAMA. *Japanese Painting.* New York: Rizzoli, 1977.

THORP, R. L. *Son of Heaven: Imperial Arts of China.* Seattle: Son of Heaven Press, 1988.

TOMASSONI, ITALO. *Mondrian.* London: Hamlyn, 1970.

TOWNSEN, CHRIS. *The Art of Bill Viola.* New York: Thames and Hudson, 2004.

TROYEN, CAROL, and ERICA E. HIRSHLER. *Charles Sheeler: Paintings and Drawings.* Boston: Little, Brown, 1987.

VERITY, ENID. *Color Observed.* New York: Van Nostrand Reinhold, 1980.

VINCENT, GILBERT T., SHERRY BRYDON, and RALPH T. COE, EDS. *Art of the North American Indians: The Thaw Collection.* Cooperstown: New York State Historical Association; Seattle: University of Washington Press, 2000.

WAX, CAROL. *The Mezzotint.* New York: Abrams, 1996.

WEISS, HILLARY. *The American Bandanna.* San Francisco, CA: Chronicle, 1990.

WESTERMANN, MARIT. *Rembrandt.* London: Phaidon, 2000.

WINGLER, M. HANS. *The Bauhaus.* Cambridge, MA: M. I. T. Press, 1986.

WONG, WUCIUS. *Principles of Color Design.* New York: Van Nostrand Reinhold, 1987.

———. *Principles of Form and Design.* New York: Van Nostrand Reinhold, 1993.

———. *Principles of Three-Dimensional Design.* New York: Van Nostrand Reinhold, 1977.

YENAWINE, PHILIP. *How to Look at Modern Art.* New York: Abrams, 1991.

ZEMEL, CAROL. *Van Gogh's Progress.* Berkeley: University of California Press, 1997.